CW00382625

Work-Life Integration

Also by Paul Blyton and Ali Dastmalchian

CHANGES IN WORKING TIME: An International Review

STATE, CAPITAL AND LABOUR: Changing Patterns of Power and Dependence (*With G. Ursell*)

TIME, WORK AND ORGANIZATION (*With J. Hassard, S. Hill & K. Starkey*)

THE CLIMATE OF WORKPLACE RELATIONS (*With A. Dastmalchian & R. Adamson*)

REASSESSING HUMAN RESOURCE MANAGEMENT (*With P. Turnbull*)

THE REALITIES OF WORK (*2nd edition with M. Noon*)

THE DYNAMICS OF EMPLOYEE RELATIONS (*3rd edition with P. Turnbull*)

Work-Life Integration

International Perspectives on the Balancing of Multiple Roles

Edited by

Paul Blyton, Betsy Blunsdon, Ken Reed and Ali Dastmalchian

First published 2006 by
PALGRAVE MACMILLAN
Houndmills, Basingstoke, Hampshire RG21 6XS and
175 Fifth Avenue, New York, N. Y. 10010
Companies and representatives throughout the world

PALGRAVE MACMILLAN is the global academic imprint of the Palgrave Macmillan division of St. Martin's Press, LLC and of Palgrave Macmillan Ltd. Macmillan® is a registered trademark in the United States, United Kingdom and other countries. Palgrave is a registered trademark in the European Union and other countries.

ISBN-13: 978–1–4039–4618–8   hardback
ISBN-10: 1–4039–4618–3   hardback

This book is printed on paper suitable for recycling and made from fully managed and sustained forest sources.

A catalogue record for this book is available from the British Library.

Library of Congress Cataloging-in-Publication Data
Work-life integration : international perspectives on the balancing of
    multiple roles / edited by Paul Blyton ... [et al.]
      p. cm.
    "The genesis for this volume was a colloquium held at Deakin University,
Australia, in December 2004"–Pref.
    Includes bibliographical references and index.
    ISBN 1–4039–4618–3 (hardback)
    1. Work and family. 2. Quality of work life. I. Blyton, Paul.

HD4904.25.W738 2005
306.3′6–dc22   2005053019

10   9   8   7   6   5   4   3   2   1
15   14   13   12   11   10   09   08   07   06

Printed and bound in Great Britain by
Antony Rowe Ltd, Chippenham and Eastbourne

Contents

v

List of Tables and Figures

List of Tables

List of Figures

Preface

The genesis for this volume was a colloquium held at Deakin University, Australia in December 2004. The colloquium brought together academics, research students and practitioners from parts of Europe, North America, Asia and Australia, to discuss their research and experience relating to the integration of different aspects of life, including work, family, leisure and civic participation. The approaches adopted by participants to their subject varied both in the types of data they discussed (ranging from large-scale national and cross-national survey data to material gathered from small-scale observation and interview programmes) and in the perspectives taken – both adult and child perspectives, for example, as well as those of trade unions, employers and state institutions.

The convenors of the colloquium, who also form the editorial team for this volume, would like to thank all those who participated, and extend a particular thanks to Judy Heath, Nicola McNeil and Bridget O'Brien for their valued organisational assistance and their subsequent help with several of the papers.

Paul Blyton
Betsy Blunsdon
Ken Reed
Ali Dastmalchian

Cardiff, Melbourne and Victoria,
July 2005

List of Contributors

Betsy Blunsdon is a Senior Lecturer in Management at Deakin University, Australia. Her main research interests include understanding the relationship between individuals' lives and the communities in which they live; workplace norms and trust relationships; and the impact of organisational change on work, family and community. Her publications include work on organisational flexibility, employee-management trust and confidence in Australian institutions. Her current projects include an Australian Research Council Linkage grant to create a knowledge base to better understand the interactions between individuals and their communities.

Paul Blyton is Professor of Industrial Relations and Industrial Sociology at Cardiff Business School, and a Research Associate in the ESRC Centre for Business Relationships, Accountability, Sustainability and Society (BRASS) at Cardiff University. His main research interests include workers' response to work organisation change, their experience of different work time schedules, and the implications of working time patterns for non-work life. He is currently preparing a new 3rd edition of *The Realities of Work* (with M. Noon, 2006) and co-editing (with N. Bacon, E. Heery and J. Fiorito) *The Handbook of Industrial Relations* (2007).

Brita Bungum is a Doctoral student in the Department of Sociology and Political Science at the Norwegian University of Science and Technology (NTNU), Trondheim. Her main research interests cover deregulation and new time cultures in work organisations, work and family balance issues, gender studies and children's perspectives. She has been a researcher at the Institute of Social Research in Industry (SINTEF IFIM), and is now engaged in her doctoral project at NTNU on how children experience and negotiate with the adult working life.

Ali Dastmalchian is Professor of Organisational Analysis and Dean of the Faculty of Business, University of Victoria, British Columbia, Canada. His main research interests include: organisational design, change and flexibility, organisational and industrial relations climates, cross-national leadership and organisational practices. Among his current research projects is a Canadian Health Services Research Foundation-funded project on organisational change in health care. He has published widely, with articles in such journals as *Academy of Management Executive, Applied Psychology: An International Review, Journal of Applied Behavioral Science* and *International Journal of Human Resource Management*.

Linda Duxbury is a Professor at Sprott School of Business at Carleton University, Canada. She has published widely in the areas of work-family conflict, supportive work environments, stress, telework, the use and impact of office technology, managing the new workforce and supportive management. Within the past decade she has completed studies on balancing work and family in the public, private and not-for-profit sectors; HR and work-family issues in the small business sector; and generational differences in work values. She has recently completed a major follow-up study on work-life balance in which 32,800 Canadian employees participated.

Carmel Goulding is a PhD student at Deakin University, Australia. Her main research interests include the role of values in lifestyle choice and alternative lifestyle patterns. She has a Masters in Business (Tourism Management) and has worked as a tourism economist and project manager with organisations in industry and government. Her experience covers projects in urban and regional economic development and land use planning; economic and social impact assessments; tourism strategies and projects; presentation of expert evidence at panels; and community consultation.

Edmund Heery is Professor of Employment Relations at Cardiff Business School. His main research interest is in the revitalisation strategies of trade unions and he has carried out work on union organising and union representation of workers with non-standard contracts. Recent and forthcoming publications include *The Future of Worker Representation* (co-edited with G. Healy, P. Taylor and W. Brown, 2004) and *The Handbook of Industrial Relations* (co-edited with N. Bacon, P. Blyton and J. Fiorito, 2007).

Christopher Higgins is a Professor at the Ivey School of Business, University of Western Ontario, Canada. His research focuses on the impact of technology on individuals, including such areas as computerised performance monitoring in the service sector; champions of technological innovation; office information systems; alternative work arrangements; and, most recently, work and family issues and their impact on individuals and organisations. He has published articles in many journals including *The Journal of Applied Psychology, Administrative Sciences Quarterly, Sloan Management Review, Information Systems Research,* and *Management Information Systems Quarterly.*

Heh Jason Huang received his PhD from Washington State University, USA. He is a Professor of Management and the Dean of International Affairs, National Sun Yat-sen University, Taiwan. In 2004, he became a member of the Founding Committee, Asia Pacific Association for International Education (APAIE). Dr. Huang's work has been published in journals including *Human Resource Management Journal, Canadian Journal of Administrative Sciences, Asia Pacific Journal of Human Resources, Research & Practice in Human Resource Management,* and *Journal of Southeast Asian Studies.*

Pauline Maybery is a Human Resources professional who has worked at both strategic and operational levels in HR. Since setting up as an independent HR Consultant, she has worked with more than 50 organisations in Wales, primarily SMEs. Her principal professional interests are in the fields of change management, equality and diversity, work-life balance, high performance working, competency frameworks and Best Practice benchmarking. She has worked on a number of funded projects, including the Wales Assembly Government's Work Life Challenge Initiative. She holds individual chartered status of the Chartered Institute of Personnel and Development.

Gill Musson is a Senior Lecturer in Organisational Behaviour/Human Resource Management at Sheffield University Management School, UK. Her research interests are all within the broad area of change and new organisational forms, but in a variety of contexts. Her methodological focus is on language and communication and the role these play in structuring organisational realities. She is presently involved in projects investigating how people manage the material and symbolic boundaries between work and home, when work actually takes place in the home environment. The current chapter is based on the ESRC grant which she holds with Susanne Tietze.

Nicola McNeil is a Lecturer in Management at LaTrobe University, Australia. She is currently completing her doctoral studies, which entails an investigation of the effect of organisations' histories on their strategies. Her broad area of research interest is in understanding the relationship between organisations and the environments in which they operate. Her main research interests are institutional theory, population ecology and contingency theory and understanding the impact of government policy on organisations.

Ken Reed is Associate Professor of Management Research and Associate Director of the Centre for Business Research, Deakin University, Australia. His main areas of research are in organisational theory and the sociology of work. He has published studies on workplace norms and trust, organisational flexibility, public confidence in Australian companies, measuring workplace morale, the relationship between organisations and their environments, and a typology of Australian workplaces. His main focus presently is a project to develop a national computer-assisted survey research facility through a network of centres in universities throughout Australia.

Tracy Scurry is currently a Research Fellow at Nottingham Trent University, England on an ESRC-funded study concerned with the use and experience of home-based working in four local authorities. She is particularly interested in researching issues surrounding the employment relationship, careers and identity of individuals employed in flexible working patterns. She is currently completing her doctoral thesis, which explores the notion of graduate underemployment and the consequences of the experience for the individual.

Claudia Steinke is a doctoral student at the University of Victoria, Canada, pursuing a PhD in Organisational Studies. Her main research and teaching interests are in the areas of organisational design, organisational climate, management of change, health services management, and human resource management. She has a degree in Nursing from the University of British Columbia and postgraduate Management degree from the University of Lethbridge. She continues to work as a registered nurse and clinical nurse educator while pursuing doctoral studies.

Susanne Tietze is a Senior Lecturer in Organisational Behaviour and Human Resource Management at Bradford University School of Management, England. Her interests lie in the area of organisational flexibility in general and the work-life balance discourse in particular. Currently, she leads a funded study on the introduction and management of home-working practices across different organisations. Recently publications have appeared in the *Journal of Management Studies, Language and Intercultural Communication, Organization Studies* and the *Journal of Organizational Change Management*.

Rainer Trinczek is Professor of Sociology at the Technische Universitaet in Munich, Germany. His main research interests include industrial relations, working time policies, management sociology and organisational studies. He has published and edited several books and many articles in these research areas. Currently, he is co-editing a reader on the regulation of employment relations in companies without works councils and is preparing a book on the structural change of the German system of industrial relations.

1
Introduction. Work, Life and the Work-Life Issue

Betsy Blunsdon, Paul Blyton, Ken Reed and Ali Dastmalchian

The issue of work-life balance and the difficulties of integrating multiple and sometimes conflicting roles, attracts considerable interest in the media, public policy discussions and academic research. The simultaneous presence of, and interrelationship between organisational, labour market and societal change has ensured that debates on questions of work-life integration or work-life balance show no signs of slackening. A central aim of the present collection is to seek to broaden the focus of these debates and to present recent research findings to stimulate further theoretical development and empirical study.

Much of the research work and comment informing this area of public and personal concern has been characterised by single-country perspectives, so in response this collection offers a more international gaze, drawing data and discussion from countries located in Europe, North America, Asia and Australasia. Further, much previous research has focused on the challenges faced by working mothers and dual-income parents, in achieving work-life balance. Given the significance of women's rising economic activity levels, this is an important focus; but it is insufficient in itself to capture the breadth of the work-life agenda. The research presented in this volume introduces several perspectives that have not been prominent in previous work in the field, such as the voice of children, those working from home and the challenges facing those simultaneously working and studying. Consistent with the search for a greater breadth of discussion, the roles of employers, trade unions and the state are also considered, how different occupational groups develop work-life balancing strategies, and more generally how some seek balance by opting out or 'downshifting'.

In this introduction, we consider first the question 'What is work-life balance?' Second, we discuss how time allocation works, as one of the key issues in achieving balance is how we allot time to different activities. Third, we consider the emergence of work-life balance as a problem, particularly related to a number of trends in modern life. Fourth, we review possible solutions to these issues, and finally, we sketch a brief outline of the contributions to give a sense of how each contributes to the volume's broader aims.

What is work-life balance?

Before the 1970s the domains of 'work' and 'family' were treated as largely separate arenas (Campbell Clark, 2000). Since then, a growing recognition has been given to the interdependence of work and family spheres (see for example, Kanter, 1977) and the difficulties of maintaining a balanced life when faced with competing demands from these two spheres. The notion of 'work-life balance' denotes that an individual can manage both work and other aspects of their life, such as the domestic or family sphere, without a conflict or without the opposition of one domain to the other. Work-life balance implies that managing one's time is like balancing a scale – the more time one puts on one side of the scale the less will be available on the other. It does not mean equal time spent in different domains but rather, depending on individual circumstances and context, balance points to the ability to fulfil roles in each arena.

Work-life balance means that individuals have 'successfully' segmented or integrated 'life' and work so as to achieve a satisfying quality of life, overall satisfaction and less strain or stress around juggling conflicting role demands. Nippert-Eng (1996a, 1996b) points out that people deal with differences between, for example, the employment sphere and the domain of family along a continuum of segregation and integration. Segregation implies complete separation between the two spheres while integration implies no distinction between spheres. Campbell Clark argues that 'happy productive individuals, as well as people who describe their lives as less than ideal, can be found on all ranges of the spectrum' (2000: 755). Put differently, work-life balance denotes fulfilment of multiple roles while maintaining a positive quality of life.

Two consequences of the difficulty of balancing work and family are 'work-family conflict', defined as the inability to fulfil family responsibilities because of work pressure, and 'family-work conflict', which reflects the inability to fulfil work obligations due to family pressures (Fox and Dwyer, 1999; Frone, Yardley and Market 1997; Greenhaus and Parasuraman, 1986). The main focus of both of these conflicts is a lack of fit resulting in a tension or imbalance between the domains of work and family (Fox and Dwyer, 1999). Related concepts include 'work-family opposition' and 'work-family incompatibility' (Edwards and Rothbard, 2000) where the main problem is seen to be one of inter-role conflict, making it difficult to fulfil demands and obligations in both domains (also known as 'role interference' see Higgins, Duxbury and Lee, 1994; Gutek, Searle and Kelpa, 1991).

Greenhaus and Beutell (1985) identify three main sources or manifestations of 'work-family' or 'family-work conflict': time-based conflict (time spent in one domain resulting in less time than needed in the other domain), strain-based conflict (strain in one domain making it difficult to fulfil obligations in the other) and behaviour-based conflict (role behaviours required in one domain being inappropriate for role behaviours needed in another). So, for example, 'time-based conflict' can result from pressures to spend long hours at work, creating problems for fulfilling obligations at home. This has been variously termed a 'time squeeze' (Schor, 1991), 'time bind' (Hochschild, 1997), or 'time famine' (Googins, 1997) and implies that there is more to do and more roles to fulfil than there is time available. An example of strain-based conflict on the other hand could be stress at home resulting from illness or personal problems, creating problems in attempting to fulfil work obligations. Behaviour-based conflict may occur when individuals exhibit work-related behaviours in the home that are inappropriate in a domestic setting, thereby causing conflict between actors in the household.

An important way of understanding the consequences of a particular aspect of life (such as work) on other aspects of life, is through the notion of role conflict, that is the conflict experienced 'when pressures experienced in one role are incompatible with pressures arising in another role' (Greenhaus and Beutell, 1985: 77). 'Work-family conflict' is one type of role conflict. However, the emphasis given to work-family conflict has tended to obscure the fact that people occupy multiple roles in addition to their roles as employee, parent and partner/spouse. Such recognition is important, as are the potential consequences of role conflict. Previous research has shown that role conflict in general, and work-life conflict in particular, can reduce satisfaction with life and with work (Kossek and Ozeki, 1998); increase life stress (Parasuraman et al, 1992); and can lead to 'overload', defined as a decreased ability to fulfil obligations required by the various roles (Frone et al, 1997; Glezer and Wolcott, 1999; Grzywacz et al, 2002; Probert et al, 2000; Russell and Bowman, 2000; Weston et al, 2002). For those combining work and study (the twin roles of 'student' and 'employee') role conflict has been found to be negatively related to class attendance, class preparation, and assignment work (Markel and Frone, 1998) as well as to lower satisfaction with the educational experience (Hammer et al, 1998).

The most conspicuous work-life conflict may be experienced when roles are rigidly bound as in the contrast between traditional work roles (for example, working a strict work day in a fixed location) and domestic and caring roles (for example, the need to be at home to care for young children, disabled or aged family members). Roles are rigid when they are spatially and temporally restricted and are highly inflexible; such role rigidity prevents the performance of one role while in the physical domain of another (Ashforth et al, 2000; Nippert-Eng, 1996a, 1996b). However, achieving 'work-life balance' may entail different configurations and different states of integration or segmentation of work and family for different groups (Campbell Clark, 2000). Further, Campbell and Charlesworth point out that, 'For many workers, work and family "balance" is to do with taking charge of aspects of their lives that seem to be eluding their control' (2004: A1-2). It is important to recognise, however, that individuals vary considerably in their power and ability to take charge and control their daily lives.

The occurrence of role conflict in general, and work-life conflict in particular, depends on a number of internal and external factors, as does the ability to deal with this conflict. The more roles one occupies, for example, the greater the potential for conflict between those roles. Individuals vary in their ability to control or alter their situation in order to fulfil the requirements of multiple roles, including time allocation and accessing resources and support. Indeed, how individuals allocate their time across activities, and the role of resources and power in time allocation choices, represent important issues in understanding debates about work and family.

How do people allocate time?

The way people spend time is a very concrete expression of their lifestyle. The time available to an individual is fixed and the same for everyone. Time functions in some ways like money: spending time on one activity reduces available time for other activities. Unlike money, however, there are only twenty four hours in a day, there are no credit facilities and time cannot be saved up to use at a later date. Planning and time management may increase one's discretion over time allocation (the potential to increase free time and decrease 'wasted time'). Yet, while people can organise their activities in more or less efficient ways, 'investing time' does not actually produce additional time in the future. It is for this reason that time allocation has been identified as a 'zero sum game' (Greenhaus and Beutell, 1985).

The ability to choose or determine time allocation depends on the extent to which people can either substitute some activities for others (leisure for work, for example) or use power, in its various forms, to increase discretionary time. For example, economic power provides the potential to purchase services in order to 'free up' time. To date, several studies have employed time use data to uncover the relationships between forms of power, especially gender, and the activities of daily life. For example, Bittman and Rice (2002) analyse the effects of gender, employment status and life-course stage on leisure time; Mattingly and Bianchi (2003) assess gender differences in free time; and Baxter (1997) compares gender differences in involvement in housework across five countries.

Time allocation is not wholly voluntary. First, it is a necessity to allocate time for some activities, such as sleep. The Australian Time Use Survey (1997) indicates that, on average, people older than 14 daily spend eight hours and twenty eight minutes sleeping, though with substantial differences by age (ranging from nine hours and twenty nine minutes for those aged 15 to 19 years, to eight hours and four minutes for those aged 45 to 49). Secondly, institutional pressures and social expectations (also termed 'normative constraints' by McRae, 2003) influence time allocation decisions: the requirement that children of a certain age attend school, for example, expectations that mothers should stay at home and care for their own young children; or values such as 'laziness is a vice' and 'diligence a virtue'. Belief systems, religious or otherwise, can underpin normative expectations and resulting role behaviours (see Reed and Blunsdon, in this volume). There are also various structural constraints on time allocation decisions, such as the availability of jobs and transport, the availability and cost of childcare, and organisational provisions around working conditions and leave provisions (McRae, 2003). Research has also shown that while power and privilege can increase discretionary time allocation, powerlessness will tend to reduce it (Gershuny and Robertson, 1994).

Time allocation therefore reflects a combination of personal preference, location in power structures, institutional and organisational arrangements and macro-level structural effects. Among other places, these influences have been identified through the debate between Hakim (2000), Crompton (2002) and others (see for example, McRae, 2003) concerning the extent to which the over-representation of mothers in part-time jobs reflects their preferences, or their powerlessness, in the face of normative and structural constraints. Understanding work-life balance or work-life conflict involves investigating time allocation across a range of activities within the context of individual lives and circumstances, taking into account normative and structural constraints. Warren (2004) for example, argues that identifying work-life balancing strategies requires an understanding of time allocation across activities such as paid employment, unpaid duties such as childcare and domestic work, social interactions, and leisure that take place within the context of an individual's economic and financial security.

Analysis of time allocation commonly draws on the concepts of 'necessary time', 'contracted time', 'committed time' and 'free or discretionary time' (Bittman and Rice, 2002; Golden, 1998; Robinson and Godbey, 1999). All individuals need to spend some time on necessary things, for example personal care, including sleeping. Contracted time comprises time in paid employment, while committed time includes time on unpaid domestic duties including childcare and voluntary activities. Free or discretionary time denotes time in which an individual has the potential to exercise choice over how time is spent. This potential is limited by the power and resources available to individuals and households. A number of contributions to this volume consider the nature and range of time allocated to particular activities, the extent to which individuals can exercise choice, and the importance of context – including structural and normative constraints – on work-life outcomes.

The emergence of work-life balance as a problem

It has been argued that the core of the problem of work-life conflict is the strain created for those trying to balance work and family responsibilities by employment systems that have evolved largely around the notion of a single 'breadwinner'. As Esping-Andersen (1999: 5) notes:

> Contemporary welfare states and labour market regulations have their origins in, and mirror, a society that no longer obtains: an economy dominated by industrial production with strong demand for low-skilled workers; a relatively homogenous and undifferentiated, predominantly male, labour force (the standard production worker); stable families with high fertility; and a female population primarily devoted to housewifery.

The origin of work-life balance as an area of research stems, for the most part, from the problems faced by the increasing number of working mothers responding to the demands of work and family (see Dex and Joshi, 1999; Gray and Stanton, 2002; Morehead, 2002). It also reflects a series of social and economic changes at the institutional, organisational, workplace and individual levels that began in the 1960s and accelerated through the 1970s and 80s. It has been argued that these changes reflect a fundamental or 'epochal' transformation of modern society (Beck, 2000; Esping-Andersen, 1999; Urry, 2000).

Changing workplaces

The choices that individuals make in time allocation must be understood in the context of labour market dynamics and, in particular, trends in working time (ACIRRT, 1999; Bittman and Pixley, 1997; Noon and Blyton, 2002). Since the 1950s there has been an erosion of the 'standard' working time model – the working time arrangement premised on an eight-hour day worked over a five-day work week during 11 months of the year over an approximately 45-year working life (Buchanan and Bearfield, 1997; Healy, 2000; Wooden, 2000). More generally, 'standard employment' has typically been construed in terms of continuous and full-time work, with regular employment arrangements, standard non-wage benefits and full employee status (Burgess and Mitchell, 2001).

An erosion in standard working arrangements has been evident in recent years, however, resulting from a variety of demand and supply factors, including organisational changes designed to secure greater labour flexibility and lower unit labour costs, which in turn have fuelled developments such as the growth in non-standard jobs (temporary contracts and use of agency staff, for example) and sub-contracting (see Blyton and Dastmalchian, in this volume). Extended opening and operating hours in various sectors of the economy have also occasioned a much wider range of working hours arrangements, most notably a variety of part-time work patterns. At the same time, many employees in various sectors of the economy have experienced an increase in overall working hours. This increase in hours reflects, for many, an increased workload, in turn related to structural changes in organisations (include downsizing and delayering), increased hours of operation, and greater demands for work-related travel and mobility (Rutherford, 2001; Simpson, 1998). Thus, one consequence of organisational and labour market change has been a bifurcation of working time – very long hours being worked by some, and very short part-time schedules by others.

Changing roles

Analysis of time use data consistently underlines the extent of gender differences in time use, particularly gender differences in time spent in domestic duties and childcare (Bittman, 1999; Wajcman, 1996). Despite the substantial and continuing increase in female participation in paid employment, women still spend significantly more time than men in unpaid domestic work and childcare. However, there is some evidence that cultural pressures for men to take on more domestic responsibility, especially in relation to fatherhood, is resulting – following a significant time-lag – in some narrowing of the gaps in time use between men and women. Consistent with this, Bittman and Pixley (1997) report that the majority of men and women in Australia say that they believe childcare and domestic duties should be equally shared. However, Bittman (1999) highlights that behavioural changes do not necessarily reflect this change in values. Time diary analyses, for example, reveal that differences between the sexes narrows amongst professionals (Bedeian, Burke and Moffett, 1988; Hakim, 1991). This does not necessarily mean, however, that men are spending more time on domestic duties (in fact the evidence does not support this) but rather that the explanation lies more in the outsourcing of domestic labour. As Wajcman found in her study of senior managers, 'male managers are still serviced by their wives, women managers are serviced by housewife substitutes in the form of other women's labour.' (1996: 626) Yet, this opportunity is only available to those in positions of occupational and economic power.

Changing values and aspirations

Normative and cultural pressures create both incentives and disincentives for individuals to spend more or less time at work and more or less time at home. For example, in a seminal study of domestic work Vanek (1974, 1978) showed that the time spent on household maintenance and cleaning remained constant between 1925 and the mid-1970s, despite an increase in domestic labour-saving devices and household appliances. She argues that while improvements in domestic technology reduced the labour required for any particular task, the number of tasks increased because of a growth in more stringent household standards including cleanliness.

Normative pressure also exerts influence on the time spent in paid employment. For example, 'presenteeism', where individuals stay at work after standard working hours to signal their commitment, arises partly because of work norms that give a positive value to long hours working (Perlow, 1999). Probert, Ewer and Whiting (2000) also argue that workers feel compelled to work longer hours without claiming entitlements because norms of what comprise 'normal hours' have gradually eroded over time.

Other social changes have also impacted on the values and expectations around time spent at work and in the home. Higher education levels for example, have been identified as an important influence on career expectations, particularly amongst women, and especially those pursuing professional and higher status occupations (Campbell Clark, 2000). This, coupled with economic changes such as the prevalence of dual-income households and greater pressure for increased consumption, have been linked to lower fertility rates and delaying the decision to have children.

Changing families and households

Families and households, like employing organisations, provide an important context to individual lives and decision-making. The type of household in which one lives has an impact on the roles that structure and constrain individual choice about time allocation. For many writers, maintaining work-life balance is a problem primarily for dual-income households with dependent children (Bittman and Rice, 2002). These households are in a stronger position to buffer labour market dynamics and organisational changes (such as pressures for greater flexibility) than sole income households but they may face greater challenges in managing conflicting roles. It is well documented that there has been a widespread increase in family instability, evidenced by an increase in the rates of divorce and separation (Crompton, 2002; Esping-Andersen, 1999). This has resulted in an increase in single-parent households (and single-person households), creating particular challenges for 'work-family' balance. In addition, increased variety in the timing of key life events include: age at marriage, age at first birth, age of dependents leaving the family home and age at entering a career (Bedeian, Burke and Moffett, 1988). All of these changes have increased the heterogeneity of family and household structures and increased variation in the types of work-family challenges that individuals face.

Changing support structures

Social and economic changes that have occurred since the 1950s have also resulted in an erosion of the traditional caring capacity for both dependent children and aged family members in households (Esping-Andersen, 1999).

Increased geographic mobility has lessened social support networks such as extended families, as has the decline in the influence of the church and other community support systems, by reducing the people available to assist with family roles. Putnam (1995, 2000) characterises this in terms of an erosion of 'social capital', including people's involvement in community and civic organisations and affairs. For Putnam, social capital refers to 'the features of social organization such as networks, norms, and social trust that facilitate coordination and cooperation for mutual benefit' (1995: 67). Social capital manifests itself as higher levels of civic participation, more time spent helping others and higher levels of trust. The identified decline in community support can create additional pressure on work-life balance, for individuals and households, as they deal with issues such as caring for sick children when parents need to work, aging parents, transport of dependents to appointments and before and after-school care of children.

Possible solutions

What solutions may be available to address the problems associated with work-life balance, including personal, collective and institutional solutions, remains an important social policy issue. Of the many levels where solutions may be sought, the personal level remains the primary focus for many. Thus, work-family conflict is often dealt with as a personal or household issue that requires individualised solutions. Hochschild (1997) for example, found that the 'time bind' she identified was most often dealt with as a purely personal problem. She cites, for example, the frequent attempts to free up time by outsourcing domestic and childcare responsibilities to professional services, relatives or neighbours. The negotiation of domestic responsibilities within households is also a common means to rectify issues, especially amongst dual-income parents. However, the equity between males and females in domestic work is improving more because women are spending less time in domestic duties than because men are spending more. Women are spending less time because they are spending more time in paid work (and as we noted earlier, time is a zero sum game). Thus, while work-life conflict is often dealt with either personally or in the household, these solutions have not substantially changed the social division of labour. There are no doubt many instances of innovative individual or household solutions but these have not been translated into major changes in society.

As discussed above, outsourcing domestic services might offer a solution to work-family conflict but is limited by the availability of such services and the ability to pay for the services. There is Australian evidence that the greatest growth in domestic outsourcing is in the care of children, whereas evidence of a rise in other types of domestic outsourcing is mixed (Bittman,

1999). Interestingly, Bittman also highlights that one area of non-childcare outsourcing that has increased is 'yard work' (gardening and related activities), a traditional masculine activity in the home; there is no evidence, however, that the outsourcing of 'cleaning' (a traditionally feminine household activity) has risen. Overall, however, despite little evidence to date that there has been a dramatic increase in the use of the market to solve work-life conflict, predictions continue that this will represent an increasingly popular solution in the future (Wheelock, 2001).

While some look for personal, short-term solutions to solve work-family issues, others look to longer-term solutions or lifestyle changes such as 'downshifting' or 'voluntary simplification' in one form or another. The fact that time stress is a major factor in work-life imbalance has created interest in the idea that voluntarily reducing working hours and other time stressors can help restore balance. 'Downshifting', the voluntary reduction of both working hours and income, is a longer-term lifestyle solution to work-life imbalance. Research in both the UK and Australia shows that between 20 and 25 per cent of adults have downshifted in one form or another over the last ten years (Hamilton and Mail, 2003a, 2003b). Goulding and Reed (in this volume) examine the role that normative constraints, by social networks and personal communities, play in lifestyle choice.

In terms of possible collective solutions to work-life balance problems, trade unions and other special interest groups attempt to address problems associated with work-life conflict by challenging organisations to effect policies and practices recognising more the presence of employees' non-work responsibilities (see Heery, in this volume). As Hochschild (1997: 245) argues, 'the truth of the matter is that many working parents lack time because the workplace has a prior claim on it'. If this is the case, solutions to problems associated with work-family balance relate to groups in society and therefore need to be addressed through collective as well as individual means. While a number of family-friendly issues have been taken up by trade unions, however, important broader issues such as excess workload, have yet to be given sufficient priority.

High levels of social capital can also assist in managing work-family conflict by constructing neighbourhood or community solutions to collective issues. Neighbourhood houses, community-based before and after-school programmes, community-based emergency care services and helping neighbours, are all examples of ways in which communities with high social capital can provide solutions to the problems associated with work-life conflict. This type of support could be especially helpful given the decline in the 'traditional' family unit. To date, however, not only the traditional family but also forms of social capital have been in decline, potentially heightening the extent of work-family pressures.

State policies are also important for providing an institutional framework and context for addressing the problems that arise from work-life conflict.

It has been argued that the social and economic disadvantage that women face, due to their unequal share of unpaid work, can be addressed in one of three ways: within households by renegotiating the division of labour; through the market; or through the state provision of key services (Bittman, 1999; Lewis, 1999; Walby, 2003). Esping-Andersen's (1999) typology of welfare states highlights the wide variation between states in the provision of services such as childcare, eldercare and statutory leave provisions. Overall, however, the state represents a vital vehicle for providing opportunities for individuals to exercise work-life choices and lifestyle preferences. Bittman's (1999) comparison of Finland and Australia suggests that public policy can make a significant difference in reducing the gender differences in time use.

'The Scandinavian experience shows that entitlements to generous parental leave, high quality childcare, and to family-friendly hours of paid work are all necessary components of an equitable solution to the difficulties of combining work and family in the twenty-first century' (Bittman, 1999: 40).

Much of the current discussion about public policy relates to what happens at work (the appropriate level of parental leave, or the right to request transferring to a part-time contract, for example) but an equally important policy area is what happens in households around domestic labour and childcare (see Blunsdon and McNeil, in this volume).

Outline of the collection

A number of the themes we have identified in this Introduction are examined in more detail in the remainder of this volume. In the first contribution, Blyton and Dastmalchian examine issues arising from the changing context of work, chronicling a series of labour market and organisational changes that have given work-life balance a higher profile within the media, public policy and academic debates.

Following this, and drawing on evidence from a variety of countries, a number of different stakeholder perspectives on work-life balance are considered, including those of employing organisations, trade unions and other advocacy groups, the state, particular occupational groups, household members (including parents and children) and those seeking to combine work and study. In the first of these, Maybery reviews work-life balance from an employer perspective and considers a number of issues including: the question of take-up of work-life balance policies; the role of managers in work-life balance; and the role of informal versus formal policies. Following this, Heery examines the development of UK trade union policy on work-life balance. Drawing on documentary, interview and survey data, Heery considers the nature and significance of attempts by trade unions in the UK to restore balance between paid employment and other spheres of social life. In their analysis of public policy, Blunsdon and McNeil then review the changing role of state policy in relation to issues of work-life balance – change evident both within and between different national contexts.

Work-family conflict and family-work conflict are considered by Duxbury and Higgins, who draw on survey data from two large-scale Canadian studies undertaken in 1991 and 2001. They analyse the extent to which work demands have increased for all employee groups in Canada, with many employees reporting an inability to complete their work tasks during regular hours of employment. In his contribution, Trinczek focuses on the question of the extent to which new flexible working hours initiatives can advance work-life balance in Germany, and the significance of working time cultures in mediating the impact of those initiatives.

Using data from a set of international surveys, the International Social Survey Programme (ISSP) 2002, Reed and Blunsdon examine whether religion is a normative influence on beliefs about gender roles. In particular, they investigate the impact religion has on beliefs about the appropriateness of mothers participating in the labour market, and the effect of such norms on the employment status of women.

With working parents (particularly mothers in paid employment) acting as the main focus of discussion in much of the debate, children constitute a neglected stakeholder in issues of work-life balance. In her discussion of the Norwegian context, Bungum introduces the child's perspective on adult working life, arguing the case for children as an independent voice that needs to be included in debates about work-life balance. In a similar way that the voice of children has been little heard in work-life balance discussions, another such group are students in general, and those seeking to combine employment and study, in particular. Huang's study focuses on the demands of working students in Taiwan. Taiwan has one of the longest working hours cultures in the world and those combining full-time work and studying face considerable challenges in attempting to achieve a balanced life. Huang's study shows how support systems, particularly the family, are central to alleviating pressure from conflicting time demands.

Just as work-life balance means different things to different groups in society, different organisational and societal groups face different opportunities and constraints in their attempts to balance work and non-work life. In their contribution, Tietze, Musson and Scurry introduce a stakeholder view of work-life balance. Their in-depth case study of homeworking reveals the extent to which more powerful individuals, such as managers and professionals, can be better placed to achieve personal and organisational objectives around work-life balance. They reveal how, in their study, less powerful individuals, although still affected by work-life issues, were less able to shape their organisational world to achieve personal aims. Organisational-level changes and initiatives impact on the work-life balance of individuals working within those organisations. Developments in organisational flexibility in the 1980s and 1990s, for example, substantially changed the terms and conditions of employment for many workers. Steinke's contribution examines the relationship between organisational practices and the lives of healthcare providers in Canada. This case demonstrates the impact that organisational-level changes and the changing nature of work can have on the lives and lifestyles of employees.

Finally, the issue of lifestyle is explored by Goulding and Reed, who outline a theoretical model for understanding lifestyle choices. They provide a framework in which to understand better the influence of work-life conflict on lifestyle choice. Among other issues, Goulding and Reed consider the role of social networks and personal communities in shaping the norms, values and beliefs that influence the lifestyle choices that individuals make. The authors also consider the question of why people choose to construct lives that are less than fully satisfying and what influences people to make major changes to their lives, such as the decision to 'downshift'.

References

Ashforth, B.E., Kreiner, G.E. and Fugate, M. (2000) 'All In A Day's Work: Boundaries And Micro Role Transitions', *Academy of Management Review*, 25: 472–91.

Australian Centre for Industrial Relations Research and Training (ACIRRT) (1999) *Australia at Work: Just Managing*, Sydney, Australia: Prentice-Hall.

Australian Time Use Survey (1997) *Confidentialised Unit Record File and Codebook*, Canberra, Australia: Australian Bureau of Statistics.

Baxter, J. (1997) 'Gender Equality and Participation in Household Work: A Cross National Experience', *Journal of Comparative Family Studies*, 28(3): 220–48.

Beck, U. (2000) 'The Cosmopolitan Perspective: Sociology in the Second Age of Modernity', *British Journal of Sociology*, 51(1): 79–105.

Bedeian, A.G., Burke, B.G. and Moffett, R.G. (1988) 'Outcomes of Work-Family Conflict Among Married Male and Female Professionals', *Journal of Management*, 14(3): 475–91.

Bittman, M. (1999) 'Parenthood Without Penalty: Time Use and Public Policy in Australia and Finland', *Feminist Economics*, 5(3): 27–42.

Bittman, M. and Pixley, J. (1997) *The Double Life of The Family*, St Leonards, Australia: Allen and Unwin.

Bittman, M. and Rice, J. (2002) 'The Spectre of Overwork: An Analysis of Trends Between 1974 and 1997 Using Australian Time-Use Diaries', *Labour and Industry*, 12: 5–26.

Buchanan, J. and Bearfield, S. (1997) *Reforming Working Time: Alternatives to Unemployment, Casualisation and Extended Hours*, Melbourne: Brotherhood of St Laurance.

Burgess, J. and Mitchell, W. (2001) 'The Australian Labour Market', *Journal of Industrial Relations*, 43(2): 124–47.

Campbell, I. and Charlesworth, S. (2004) *Background Report: Key Work and Family Trends in Australia*, Melbourne: Centre for Applied Social Research.

Campbell Clark, S. (2000) 'Work/Family Border Theory: A New Theory of Work/Family Balance', *Human Relations*, 53(6): 747–70.

Crompton, R. (2002) 'Employment, Flexible Working and the Family', *British Journal of Sociology*, 53(4): 537–58.

Dex, S. and Joshi, H. (1999) 'Careers and Motherhood: Policies for Compatibility', *Cambridge Journal of Economics*, 23: 641–59.

Edwards, J.R. and Rothbard, N.P. (2000) 'Mechanisms Linking Work and Family: Clarifying the Relationship Between Work and Family Constructs', *Academy of Management Review*, 25(1): 178–89.

Esping-Andersen, G. (1999) *Social Foundations of Postindustrial Economies*, Oxford: Oxford University Press.

Fox, M.L. and Dwyer, D.J. (1999) 'An Investigation of the Effects of Time and Involvement in the Relationship Between Stressors and Work-Family Conflict', *Journal of Occupational Health Psychology*, 4(2): 164–74.

Frone, M.R., Yardley, J.K. and Market, K.S. (1997) 'Developing and Testing an Integrative Model of the Work-Family Interface', *Journal of Vocational Behavior*, 50: 145–67.

Gershuny, J. and Robertson, J. (1994) 'Measuring Hours of Paid Work: Time Diaries Versus Estimate Questions', *Bulletin of Labour Statistics*, xi–xvii.

Glezer, H. and Wolcott, I. (1999) 'Work and Family Life: Reciprocal Effects', *Family Matters*, 52: 69–79.

Golden, L. (1998) 'Working Time and the Impact of Policy Institutions: Reforming the Overtime Hours Law and Regulation', *Review of Social Economy*, 56(4): 522–41.

Googins, B.K. (1997) 'Shared Responsibility for Managing Work and Family Relationships: A Community Perspective' in Parasuraman, S. and Greenhaus, J.H. (eds) *Integrating Work and Family: Challenges and Choices for a Changing World*, Westport, CT: Quorum.

Gray, M. and Stanton, D. (2002) 'Work and Family Life: Our Workplaces, Families and Futures', *Family Matters*, 61: 4–11.

Greenhaus, J.H. and Beutell, N.J. (1985) 'Sources of Conflict Between Work and Family Roles', *Academy of Management Review*, 10: 76–88.

Greenhaus, J.H. and Parasuraman, S. (1986) 'A Work-Non-work Interactive Perspective of Stress and its Consequences', *Journal of Organizational Behavior Management*, 8: 37–60.

Grzywacz, J., Ameida, D. and McDonald, D. (2002) 'Work-Family Spillover and Daily Reports of Work and Family Stress in the Adult Labour Force', *Family Relations*, 51: 28–36.

Gutek, B., Searle, S. and Kelpa, L. (1991) 'Rational Versus Gender Role Expectations for Work-Family Conflict', *Journal of Applied Psychology*, 76: 560–8.

Hakim, C. (1991) 'Grateful Slaves and Self-made Women: Fact and Fantasy in Women's Work Orientations', *European Sociological Review*, 7: 101–21.

Hakim, C. (2000) *Work-lifestyle Choices in the 21st Century: Preference Theory*, Oxford: Oxford University Press.

Hamilton, C. and Mail, E. (2003a) *Downshifting in Australia, A Sea-change in the Pursuit of Happiness*, Discussion Paper No. 50, Canberra: The Australia Institute.

Hamilton, C. and Mail, E. (2003b) *Downshifting in Britain: A Sea-change in the Pursuit of Happiness*, Discussion Paper No. 58, Canberra: The Australia Institute.

Hammer, L.B., Grigsby, T.D. and Woods, S. (1998) 'The Conflicting Demands of Work, Family, and School Among Students at an Urban University', *Journal of Psychology*, 132: 220–6.

Healy, E. (2000) 'The Shift to Long Working Hours: A Social and Political Crisis in the Making', *People and Place*, 8(1): 38–50.

Higgins, C., Duxbury, L. and Lee, C. (1994) 'Impact of Life-Cycle Stage and Gender on the Ability to Balance Work and Family Responsibilities', *Family Relations*, 43: 144–50.

Hochschild, A.R. (1997) 'The Time Bind', *Working USA*, 1(2): 21–9.

International Social Survey Programme (ISSP) (2002) *Family and Changing Gender Roles III*, Computer file and codebook, Koeln, Germany: Zentralarchiv Fuer Empirische Sozialforschung.

Kanter, R.M. (1977) *Work and Family in the United States: A Critical Review and Agenda for Research and Policy*, New York: Russell Sage.

Kossek, E.E. and Ozeki, C. (1998) 'Work-Family Conflict, Policies, and the Job-Life Satisfaction Relationship: A Review and Directions for Organizational Behavior-Human Resources Research', *Journal of Applied Psychology*, 83: 139–49.

Lewis, J. (1999) 'Gender and Welfare Regimes: Further Thoughts', *Social Politics*, 4(2): 160–77.

Markel, K.S. and Frone, M.R. (1998) 'Job Characteristics, Work-School Conflict, and School Outcomes Among Adolescents: Testing a Structural Model', *Journal of Applied Psychology*, 83: 277–87.

Mattingly, M.J. and Bianchi, S.M. (2003) 'Gender Differences in the Quantity and Quality of Free Time: The US Experience', *Social Forces*, 81(3): 999–1031.

McRae, S. (2003) 'Constraints and Choices in Mothers' Employment Careers: A Consideration of Hakim's Preference Theory', *British Journal of Sociology*, 54 (3): 317–38.

Morehead, A. (2002) 'Behind the Paid Working of Single Mothers: Managing Change and Constructing Support', *Family Matters*, 61: 56–61.

Nippert-Eng, C. (1996a) 'Calendars and Keys: The Classification of "Home" and "Work"', *Sociological Forum*, 11: 563–82.

Nippert-Eng, C. (1996b) *Home and Work: Negotiating Boundaries Through Everyday Life*, Chicago: University of Chicago Press.

Noon, M. and Blyton, P. (2002) *The Realities of Work*, 2nd edn, Basingstoke: Palgrave Macmillan.

Parasuraman, S., Greenhaus, J.H. and Granrose, C.S. (1992) 'Role Stressors, Social Support, and Well-Being Among Two Career Couples', *Journal of Organizational Behavior*, 13: 339–56.

Perlow, L.A. (1999) 'The Time Famine: Toward a Sociology of Work Time', *Administrative Science Quarterly*, 44: 57–81.

Probert, B., Ewer, P. and Whiting, K. (2000) 'Work Versus Life: Union Strategies Reconsidered', *Labour and Industry*, 11: 23–47.

Putnam, R. (1995) 'Bowling Alone: America's Declining Social Capital', *Journal of Democracy*, 6: 65–78.

Putnam, R. (2000) *Bowling Alone: The Collapse and Revival of American Community*, New York: Simon and Schuster.

Russell, G. and Bowman, L. (2000) *Work and Family: Current Thinking, Research And Practice*, Melbourne: Department of Family and Community Services.

Robinson, J.P. and Godbey, G. (1999) *Time for Life: The Surprising Ways Americans Use Their Time*, 2nd edn, Pennsylvania: Pennsylvania State University Press.

Rutherford, S. (2001) 'Are You Going Home Already?' *Time and Society*, 10(2/3): 259–78.

Schor, J.B. (1991) *The Overworked American: The Unexpected Decline of Leisure*, New York: Harper Books.

Simpson, R. (1998) 'Presenteeism, Power and Organisational Change: Long Hours as a Career Barrier and the Impact on the Working Lives of Women Managers', *British Journal of Sociology*, 9(3): 537–51.

Urry, J. (2000) 'Mobile Sociology', *British Journal of Sociology*, 51(1): 185–204.

Vanek, J. (1974) 'Time Spent in Housework', *Scientific American*, 11: 116–20.

Vanek, J. (1978) 'Household Technology and Social Status: Rising Living Standards and Residence Differences in Housework', *Technology and Culture*, 19: 361–75.

Wajcman, J. (1996) 'The Domestic Basis for the Managerial Career', *Sociological Review*, 44: 609–29.

Walby, S. (2003) 'Policy Developments for Workplace Gender Equity in a Global Era: the Importance of the EU in the UK', *Review of Policy Research*, 20(1): 45–64.

Warren, T. (2004) 'Working Part-Time: Achieving a Successful Work-Life Balance?' *British Journal of Sociology*, 55(1): 99–123.

Weston, R., Qu, L. and Sorinao, G. (2002) 'Implications of Men's Extended Work Hours for their Personal and Marital Happiness', *Family Matters*, Autumn: 18–26.

Wheelock, J. (2001) 'Don't Care was Made to Care: The Implications of Gendered Time for Policies towards the Household', *Capital & Class*, 75: 173–85.

Wooden, M. (2000) *The Transformation of Australian Industrial Relations*, Sydney: The Federation Press.

2
Work-Life Integration and the Changing Context of Work

Paul Blyton and Ali Dastmalchian

The increased prominence of issues relating to work-life balance has arisen partly as a consequence of significant developments taking place in the nature of society and economic activity. Specific aspects of these changes, and responses by trade unions, employers and the state, as well as different occupational and other groups, are considered in detail in many of the contributions to this volume. Here, we seek to provide a focused overview of relevant changes in patterns of labour market activity and employees' experience of work – and linked to the latter, the changing nature of work organisations themselves. Overall, space permits us only to note some of the most prominent developments in these areas, but hopefully we can achieve this in such a way as to anchor work-life issues a little more securely within their broader work and employment contexts.

Changes in economic activity, work patterns and work experiences

Patterns of economic activity

The most marked change in the overall pattern of economic activity in industrialised countries over the last half-century has been the increased participation of women in the labour market. In Britain, for example, between the early 1950s and 2001, the economic activity of women (that is those of working age active in the labour market) increased from 43 to 74 per cent, much of this concentrated in the second half of that period (Hakim, 2004: 60). Among married women with dependent children, the rise has been particularly marked. By 2004, almost 3 in 5 (58 per cent) married or cohabiting women with a dependent child under 5 years of age in the UK were in full or part-time employment; the proportion of married/cohabiting women in paid employment with older dependent children was even higher – 77 per cent for those whose youngest child was between 5 and 10 years, and 81 per cent for those with an 11 to 15 year-old youngest child (Office for National Statistics, 2005: 46–7; Twomey, 2002). Among lone mothers with dependent children, economic activity rates have also risen but remain lower than for their married counterparts (for example, an economic activity rate of 33 per cent among lone parents with pre-school children and 56 per cent among those with a child between 5 and 10 years in the UK in 2004; Office for National Statistics, op cit); the challenges facing lone parents in employment, however, bring issues of work-life balance into particularly sharp relief.

This pattern of growing proportions of women who are economically active is repeated, to a greater or lesser extent, in the vast majority of industrial countries, and the trend continues. Among the Organisation for Economic Co-operation and Development (OECD) member countries as a whole, for example, women's participation in the labour force increased from 56.4 to 59.6 per cent between 1990 and 2003, while male participation rates fell by over two per cent during the same period (OECD, 2004). Overall, and despite significant country variation in levels of male, and particularly female, economic activity, the picture is one of significant change in the composition of employment over the past generation.

A consequence of these trends in male and female participation rates is a change in the relationship between work and other aspects of society, with the result that a traditional source of 'balance' between paid work and other areas of individual activity has diminished. As a result of the rise in married women with children in the workforce, there has been a significant shift away from a family pattern based around a sole (generally male) 'breadwinner' and a sole (usually female) 'homemaker', towards a situation where a dual-earner pattern is the norm for the majority of families. Whatever its other (positive) effects, such a shift has undermined a form of balance created by one member of the household fulfilling income generating functions, while the other's sphere of responsibilities centred on childcare and domestic and related tasks.

The shift away from this sharp division of roles – a division which particularly characterised the majority of the 20th century – has been marked, and comparatively recent. If we take a country such as Canada for example, as Duxbury and Higgins (in this volume) report, in the late 1960s around one in three Canadian families were characterised by both husband and wife undertaking paid work outside the home; a generation later this proportion had increased to seven out of ten families where both worked outside the home for pay. Likewise in the UK, the number of households with all people of working age in employment grew by almost a million between 1997 and 2004, whilst the proportion of households with one (or no) persons in employment remained largely static (Office for National Statistics, 2005: 48–9).

This pattern of increased activity of women in paid employment outside the home, is predicted to continue. One estimate for the UK, for example, envisaged women filling more than four-fifths of the extra jobs created over the next decade (HM Treasury/DTI, 2003: 8). The high levels of female participation in the labour market in certain countries – notably in Scandinavia and particularly in Iceland, where the female labour force participation rate is well over 80 per cent (OECD, 2004: 296) – signals the potential for significantly higher proportions of women in paid employment elsewhere, should suitable conditions prevail.

There are many arguments adduced to account for this rise in female activity in paid work, ranging from rising female aspirations, changing social attitudes towards working mothers and the effects of the women's liberation movement, to the availability of suitable employment and maternity provision, the introduction or extension of equal pay legislation and the growing necessity of extra income for maintaining family expenditure patterns. One of the clearest links is between economic activity and rising educational qualifications among women, particularly among women with degree or equivalent qualifications. In the UK, women overtook men as a proportion of undergraduates in 1996–7, and currently almost 57 per cent of undergraduates in the UK are female. In 2004, 86 per cent of women with a degree were in employment, compared to 44 per cent with no qualifications (Office for National Statistics, 2005: 51).

Among the large numbers of women entering paid employment with dependent children, a principal means by which the two activities of work and childcare have been combined has been by working part-time. In the last decade, most (and in a number of countries, all) of the net increase in women's employment activity rates has been accounted for by a rise in part-time working. The typical dual-earner household comprises a male in full-time, and a female in part-time, paid work. While there has also been an increase in men working part-time (albeit from a low base) women continue to comprise the large majority of part-time job holders: on average in OECD countries, seven out of ten part-time jobs are held by women, and a quarter of women's jobs are part-time – both proportions significantly exceeded in a number of countries (OECD, 2004: 311).

Patterns of work hours

While the increase in women's labour market activity is probably the single most important factor stimulating the heightened interest in the issue of balancing work and non-work responsibilities, simultaneous developments in other aspects of work and employment are also exerting an influence. Of these, perhaps the major one is the evidence that many employees are increasingly spending long hours at work and taking additional work home. Despite reductions in the basic weekly hours of many groups since the early 1980s (Blyton, 1994), and the introduction or extension of maximum weekly hours legislation in Europe and elsewhere, the prevalence and growth of longer hours working has been noted in a number of industrial countries. Recent evidence for the UK, for example, indicates that almost one-third (32 per cent) of men and a tenth (10 per cent) of women in employment usually work more than 45 hours per week (Office for National Statistics, 2005: 54). Elsewhere among OECD countries, average annual hours are markedly higher in countries such as the Czech Republic, Greece, Korea, Mexico and Poland (OECD, 2004: 312)

So significant is the amount of hours worked in excess of basic hours that the average working time of many employees has increased over the past two decades. This has been the subject of much discussion, particularly in Australia (see for example, Bittman and Rice, 2001; and Campbell, 2002) and the United States (see for example, Schor's 1991 account of 'The Overworked American'). Particularly relevant to the present discussion is the analysis by Jacobs and Gerson (2001) who identify the increase in work time as being particularly apparent in the United States if family, rather than individual, work hours are considered. Elsewhere in North America, a similar picture is evident. In Canada, for example, a recent large-scale study found that the proportion of people reporting that they usually work in excess of 50 hours per week more than doubled between 1991 and 2001, rising from 11 to 26 per cent (Duxbury and Higgins, in this volume).

There are many possible reasons to account for this growth of long hours working. For some, it may represent the only means to earn enough income to achieve an acceptable standard of living. For others, it may reflect a particular attachment to work or a desire to show commitment and thereby improve job security or chances of advancement. For some, it may reflect a pressure to conform to a 'long hours culture' prevailing in many work organisations (Perlow, 1999). For others, as discussed in the following sections, it may reflect increased employer expectations and a growth in workload and work pressure.

Further, for a growing proportion of employees, some work hours (though for the most part, not officially recorded as work time) are worked at home. Where these come on top of hours already worked 'at work', this not only further contributes to longer work hours but also to a blurring of any boundaries between work and non-work lives. In the Canadian study referred to above, for example, whereas one in three workers took work home in 1991, by 2001 this proportion had risen to one in two (Duxbury and Higgins, in this volume; see also Tietze et al, in this volume). As discussed below, changes in technology have significantly extended this ability of employees to continue working while away from the workplace. Overall, more people in paid work – particularly the growth of dual-earner families – coupled with many people spending more hours at work and taking more work home, have fuelled debates about striking a satisfactory balance between time devoted to work and non-work spheres.

Changes in the experience of work

Yet it is not only the amount of time devoted to work that is changing for many individuals and dual-earner families, giving rise to more acute work-life balance issues. Among other relevant changes has been a rise in more precarious employment – characterised by an increased use of fixed-term contracts and temporary employment in several countries – and a heightened sense of job insecurity, fuelled by redundancy announcements, downsizing decisions, and continued high levels of unemployment in countries such as France, Germany, Poland and Spain (Burchell et al, 1999; Heery and Salmon, 2000; OECD, 2004: 296). Job insecurity, either objectively experienced through redundancy, a temporary contract or other form of short-term employment engagement, or subjectively experienced in the form of a perceived threat of job loss, potentially seriously undermines the opportunity for individuals to achieve work-life balance by restricting their ability to plan for the future, or make assumptions based on having a secure job and a predictable income. As Sennett (1998: 22) puts it, in the job insecure world of contemporary capitalism, there is 'no long term'.

In addition, for many in employment, problems arising from competing time demands have been further exacerbated by increasing work pressures and strains evident within the work sphere. Various analyses, based both on large-scale surveys as well as detailed case studies, report increasing numbers of employees feeling under growing pressure at work. In national and cross-national surveys, for example, this is reflected in a growing proportion of people reporting that they 'mostly' or 'always' work 'under a great deal of pressure', that their job involves 'working at high speed' or 'working to tight deadlines' (see for example, Green, 2004; Green and McIntosh, 2001). Factors found to be associated with increased work intensity include working with technology (those working with computers are more likely to report growing intensity) and those experiencing major work organisation change (Green, 2004). Both of these factors are prominent aspects of life in a growing number of contemporary work organisations, as managers seek improved performance partly by increasing the productivity of their workforce. The next section reviews the changing nature of organisations and how the changes evident are impacting on employers' expectations of their employees, and in turn on issues of work-life balance.

Changes in the nature of work organisations

Shifts in organisational boundaries

One of the biggest challenges facing organisations in recent years has been how to respond to a range of fundamental changes in how economies and societies are structured and function. Some of these changes are more subtle (like the effects of demographic change), others more visible in their effect on daily lives as well as longer-term concerns (e.g. the internet and the information age). In response, many work organisations are adopting a variety of innovative approaches to cope with these broader shifts in economy, technology and society. At their broadest these innovations involve fundamentally restructuring the nature of the work organisation itself. Such new organisational forms have been referred to as virtual organisations, cluster organisations, network organisations, ad hoc organisations, horizontal organisations, high performing work team organisations, reengineered organisations, and more. Ashkenas, Ulrich, Jick and Kerr (2002) summarise these developments by suggesting that the paradigm for organisational success has changed: from size, role clarity, specialisation and control to speed, flexibility, integration and innovation. In particular, organisations are increasingly expected to raise their speed of response to customers and outside stakeholders as if they were a small, fast moving entity, while maintaining their access to larger resource bases. In increasingly globalised markets, organisations are operating in environments characterised by greater uncertainty and less role clarity, and responding by managing more with task forces and teams rather than relying on traditional hierarchical structures. While there is a need to maintain specialisation, at the same time organisations are seeking to develop cultures and mechanisms among their employees to create collaboration and integrative solutions to market challenges. Organisations also need to create environments and processes that encourage innovation (and rewards it) in order to succeed, rather than relying on controls, double-checks and standard operating procedures to secure employee performance.

An implication of such a shift is that the boundaries of organisations both internally and externally are seen to be increasingly inappropriate and need to be revisited and removed, giving rise to the concept of the boundaryless organisation (Ashkenas et al, 2002; Bennis, 1967; Hatch, 1997). This could take the form of flattening *vertical* boundaries (e.g. removing levels in the hierarchy and people's ranks) and creating more integrative or cross-functional team-based structures. It could also relate to reducing *horizontal* boundaries by removing walls between departments and functions. The removal of the boundaries could also be *external* – more permeability with customers, suppliers and other agents in the environment, or *geographical* or *global*. With advances in information technology, people's increased mobility, and standardisation of products or services, international boundaries are rapidly disappearing in many of the world's regions. For some (particularly higher level) employees, the results of loosening or removing organisational boundaries leads to expanded work roles, more complex job designs and higher levels of skill and expectations. As organisations become more permeable and people's jobs and role expectations become more fluid and flexible, the pressure on work-life integration is likely to increase.

Changes in organisational roles and values

It is important to recognise that the above portrayal of organisational response to a rapidly-changing world is, according to several writers, accompanied by a substantial unfolding of new roles for individuals in organisations, changing values regarding the individual-organisation relationship, and a new reality for organisations in general. This perspective has implications equally for work and non-work lives.

One perspective would be that contemporary organisations are increasingly not just large bureaucracies or machines with human components; rather they are becoming communities of people with talent and with personalised contribution (Handy, 2001). Some have argued that increasingly in organisations, talent is being recognised and organisations are making room for the inclusion of knowledge and the skills of their employees and their customers in their existence and their systems. The direction of this change seems to be, according to Handy (1994; 2001), Drucker (2002) and others, in line with a notion of the personalisation of talent and knowledge. That is, there is less likelihood that large organisations and bureaucracies can utilise the knowledge of people as anonymous parts of organisations or market segments. An implication of this is that over time there will be more opportunities and a trend towards individuals providing such knowledge as independent brokers. This has, and will create fundamental changes in the role of organisations as a traditional employer, and will introduce new challenges for individuals in terms of work-life integration.

In this light, Drucker (2002) argues that a 'new workforce' is emerging that is substantially different from the old. This new workforce is different not only in terms of the nature of the contract with the employers (e.g. more contractors, part-timers, and so on) but also in terms of their orientation and expectation. Growing professionalisation, together with the rise of what are labelled 'knowledge workers' (those whose jobs require advanced formal training and schooling) form the basis of the new workforce. One way to imagine this shift is to consider the new knowledge workforce as the new capitalists – they collectively own the scarce resource (knowledge) and the means of production. At the same time, these knowledge workers also 'need' the organisation in order for their knowledge to be of value – they need a context to apply their knowledge. For Drucker (2002: 254) 'The knowledge society is a society of seniors and juniors, rather than of bosses and subordinates'.

From rigidity to more fluidity in organisations

As part of the response to changing economic environments, organisations are becoming more aware that the nature and quality of inter-organisational relationships they enter into, are perhaps more important for their capacity building and success than internal features such as size and technology (Clegg, Hardy and Nord, 1996). As a result, considerable attention has been paid in recent years to understanding inter-organisational collaborations (e.g. Astley, 1984; Gray, 1989) such as joint ventures and alliances (Harrigan,

1985; Kanter, 1990), network organisations and modular corporations in which core activities are contracted out (Alter and Hage, 1993; Tully, 1993), and virtual organisations (Byrne, 1993) which only exist as transient enabling structures connecting talents and resources in a temporary collaboration.

Network organisations can take many different forms, from loosely-coupled informal cellular structures, to more formal arrangements. They potentially offer various advantages compared with the traditional, bureaucratic form of organisations in that they allow for risk and resource sharing, offer considerable opportunities for knowledge sharing, and are more flexible compared to other structures that allow for integration of resources (e.g. mergers). Strategic alliances are another effective way for entering new markets and sectors, both domestically and globally, particularly where high levels of investment in technology are required. However, in order to achieve success in these new external environments, organisations are also increasingly looking to new internal organisational arrangements that allow for more radical innovation. Teamwork, cross-disciplinary collaborations and learning are central to this picture.

In order to make this transition, the nature of the processes needs to become much more decentralised, where power to make decisions moves to multiple teams. But teams also need more knowledge and rewards to remain motivated and successful. In short, decisions need to be made faster, control of quality needs to be moved closer to the point of origin, delivery of service to be moved to the point of contact with customers, and consequently decisions to be moved to lower levels in the organisation, leading to more distributed organisational structures, perhaps smaller organisations, and a reduction in the role of hierarchy (Galbraith et al, 1993). Coupled with the decentralisation trend is the existence of a distributed network of people and teams/divisions connected by means of intensive electronic communication. Overall in this picture, hierarchy becomes less central to control and coordination and is replaced by knowledge, teamwork and increased competencies of people in organisations that are more and more characterised by openness, trust and commitment (Fairtlough, 1994).

This is a very different organisation compared to one based on bureaucracy (Clegg et al, 1996; Greenwood and Lawrence, 2005), or even matrix organisation (Galbraith, 1973) or adhocracy (Minzberg, 1979). This networked form of organisation is fast becoming the norm in the new world of organisations, questioning the traditional assumption that large size is necessary or desired (Galbraith et al, 1993). But the key issue for our present discussion is that such fluid form of organisation is likely to have much more demanding job requirements and a very different array of impacts on individual ability, time and loyalty. We envisage that these 'new forms' of organisation are likely to be far more demanding on people's time and commitment levels and thus are likely to put additional pressures on individuals, potentially further exacerbating issues surrounding work-life balance.

Parallel developments in technology are likely to aggravate further this tendency for work organisations to become more 'greedy' institutions (Coser, 1974) in terms of their demands on employees' work time and energies. As we have noted, individual surveys already report an increased tendency for people to take work home to complete. Tecnological developments such as mobile phones, laptop computers and email mean that an increasing proportion of employees remain in touch with, and contactable by, their employing organisation even when they are physically away from the workplace (Fuchs Epstein and Kalleberg, 2001: 13). Working from home can, of course, positively contribute to achieving better work-life balance (see Tietze et al, in this volume) but being perpetually 'on call' can have the opposite effect, blurring boundaries between work and home, to the detriment of the latter.

Conclusion

The developments highlighted in the above discussion – changes in the profile of labour market participation, extensions in work hours, greater work pressure, and the prospect of more demanding and substantially more diffuse and boundaryless work organisations in the future – raise important questions about people's current and future ability to satisfactorily balance their work and non-work lives. Currently, some of these developments, particularly in the way organisations are developing, are only a reality for a proportion of employees. But the major changes identified seem not only to be enduring, but gathering pace. In addition, these are of course not the only contextual changes relevant to work-life balance discussions. Other wide-ranging social developments, ranging from the rise in single parent households and the decline of the extended family, to the growing emphasis on consumption and its impact on expenditure and debt levels, all pose critical questions for the integration of work into the lives of individuals and families, the support systems available to facilitate that integration, and more broadly the role and value of work and consumption in contemporary society (see for example, Ransome, 2005; and Schor, 1999). In combination, individual, organisational, economic and social developments raise important questions about how individuals and institutions should respond to these patterns of change. A number of these questions are dealt with in more detail elsewhere in this volume, but they also extend to broader areas of debate concerning the wider impact of current changes on the future for individuals, households, communities and society as a whole.

References

Alter, C. and Hage, J. (1993) *Organizational Working Together*, Newbury Park, CA: Sage.

Ashkenas, R., Ulrich, D., Jick, T. and Kerr, S. (2002) *The Boundaryless Organization: Breaking the Chains of Organizational Structures*, San Francisco: Jossey-Bass.

Astley, G. (1984) 'Towards an Appreciation of Collective Strategy', *Academy of Management Review*, 9(3): 526–35.

Bennis, W. (1967) 'Organization of the Future', *Personnel Administration*, September–October.

Bittman, M. and Rice, J. (2001) 'The Spectre of Overwork: An Analysis of Trends Between 1974 and 1997 Using Australian Time Use Diaries', *Labour and Industry*, 12: 5–26.

Blyton, P. (1994) 'Working Hours', in K. Sisson (ed.) *Personnel Management* (2nd edn) 495–526, Oxford: Blackwell.

Burchell, B.J., Day, D., Hudson, M., Ladipo, D., Mankelow, R., Nolan, J.P., Reed, H., Wichert, I.C. and Wilkinson, F. (1999) *Job Insecurity and Work Intensification*, London: Joseph Rowntree Foundation.

Byrne, J.A. (1993) 'The Virtual Corporation', *Business Week*, 8 February: 98–103.

Campbell, I. (2002) 'Extended working hours in Australia', *Labour and Industry*, 13(1): 91–110.

Clegg, S., Hardy, C. and Nord, W. (1996) *Handbook of Organization Studies*, London: Sage.

Coser, L. (1974) *Greedy Institutions: Patterns of Undivided Commitment*, New York: Free Press.

Drucker, P. (2002) *Managing in the Next Society*, New York: Truman Tally Books.

Fairtlough, G. (1994) *Creative Compartments: A Design for Future Organizations*, London: Adamantine Press.

Fuchs Epstein, C. and Kalleberg, A.L. (2001) 'Time and the Sociology of Work: Issues and Implications', *Work and Occupations*, 28(1): 5–16.

Galbraith, J.R. (1973) *Designing Complex Organizations*, Reading, MA: Addison-Wesley.

Galbraith, J.R., Lawler, E.E. and Associates (1993) *Organizing for the Future: The New Logic for Managing Complex Organizations*, San Francisco: Jossey-Bass.

Gray, B. (1989) *Collaborating: Finding Common Grounds for Multiparty Problems*, San Francisco: Jossey-Bass.

Green, F. (2004) 'Why Has Work Effort Become More Intense?' *Industrial Relations*, 43(4): 709–41.

Green, F. and McIntosh, S. (2001) 'The Intensification of Work in Europe', *Labour Economics*, 8: 291–308.

Greenwood, R. and Lawrence, T. (2005) 'The Iron Cage and the Information Age: the Legacy and Relevance of Max Weber for Organization Studies', *Organization Studies*, 26(4): 493–9.

Hakim, C. (2004) *Key Issues in Women's Work*, 2nd edn, London: Glasshouse Press.

Handy, C. (1994) *The Age of Paradox*, Cambridge, MA: Harvard University Press.

Handy, C. (2001) *The Elephant and the Flea*, London: Hutchinson.

Harrigan, K.R. (1985) *Strategies for Joint Venture*, Lexington, MA: Heath/Lexington Books.

Hatch, M.J. (1997) *Organization Theory: Modern, Symbolic and Postmodern Perspectives*, Oxford: Oxford University Press.

Heery, E. and Salmon, J. (eds) (2000) *The Insecure Workforce*, London: Routledge.

HM Treasury/DTI (2003) *Balancing Work and Family Life: Enhancing Choice and Support for Parents*, London: HMSO.

Jacobs, J.A. and Gerson, K. (2001) 'Overworked Individuals or Overworked Families?' *Work and Occupations*, 28(1): 40–63.

Kanter, R.M. (1990) 'When Giants Learn Cooperative Strategies', *Planning Review*, 18(1): 15–25.

Minzberg, H. (1979) *Structuring of Organizations*, Englewood Cliffs, NJ: Prentice-Hall.

OECD (Organisation for Economic Co-operation and Development) (2004) *Employment Outlook*, Paris: OECD.

Office for National Statistics (2005) *Social Trends No. 35*, London: Palgrave Macmillan.

Perlow, L.A. (1999) 'The Time Famine: Toward a Sociology of Work Time', *Administrative Science Quarterly*, 44: 57–81.

Ransome, P. (2005) *Work, Consumption and Culture: Affluence and Social Change in the Twenty-first Century*, London: Sage.

Schor, J. (1991) *The Overworked American: The Unexpected Decline in Leisure*, New York: Basic Books.

Schor, J. (1999) *The Overspent American*, New York: HarperCollins.

Sennett, R. (1998) *The Corrosion of Character*, New York: Norton.

Tully, S. (1993) 'Modular Corporation', *Fortune*, 8 February: 106–15.

Twomey, B. (2002) 'Women in the Labour Market: Results from the 2001 LFS', *Labour Market Trends*, March: 109–27.

3
Work-Life Balance Policies and Practices in the UK: Views of an HR Practitioner

Pauline Maybery

The issue of balancing paid employment with family life has been of interest in a number of domains including employing organisations and the human resource practitioners that work in those organisations. This chapter considers the question of work-life balance (WLB) practices and policies, their trend, and prevalence, in workplaces in the UK from an employer and HR practitioner perspective. It considers the social and economic context of WLB, and identifies a number of challenges with regard to the effectiveness of WLB policies: lack of take-up by employees; role of managers; formal versus informal policies; size of the organisation; and equality and diversity. The chapter then reviews a number of case studies, particularly in Wales, and further discusses the challenges and implementation barriers for WLB policies and practices.

The context of work-life balance in the UK

There are a number of demographic trends that have a major impact on the role and importance of work-life integration and WLB issues in the UK. For example, there will be a significant skill shortage in the future, the population is aging and workforces are older (e.g. the number of elderly dependents will outnumber young dependents in the UK during the next 20 years). There are increased numbers of women in the paid workforce (69 per cent of women of working age were in employment in 2003, and lone parent employment in the UK rose from 46 per cent in 1997 to 54 per cent in 2002). There are fewer young workers in the workforce and there is some evidence that those that are in paid employment have rejected the traditional work ethic and are looking to balance work commitments with outside work activities (http://www.roffeypark.com/research/wlb.html).

Economic changes, as is highlighted elsewhere in this collection, have led to an increase in the number of hours of work, particularly for women. Increased hours of work do not necessarily translate into working smarter or more productively and have been shown to have negative consequences on work productivity and health and well-being. Stress, often due to work-life imbalance, is the biggest cause of absence in the UK and has significant financial liabilities for organisations. Additional legislation covering working families was introduced in April 2003 in the UK with the introduction of paid paternity leave and adoption leave, increased maternity leave provisions and the statutory right to request flexible working for parents of children under the age of six years. It was the view of the Secretary of State for Trade & Industry that legislation was required as organisational 'good practice' would take 20 years to reach the same point and skill shortages could not sustain this approach. In particular, there is ongoing concern at the loss of skilled females in the workforce.

Socially and culturally, there is growing recognition of the positive role model of the male parent on children, in particular boys, and the positive impact for many children of spending more time with their parents. A Chartered Institute of Personnel and Development (CIPD) (2003) report highlights the benefits to patterns of socialisation of children. There is increased pressure on males to be involved in childrearing and increased pressure on parents to spend quality time with their children. In addition, Corporate Social Responsibility and concerns about societal social capital have gained high prominence on the social agenda and WLB policies provides workers more opportunity to contribute to their communities. In some areas in the UK 'Better Communities' is high on the policy agenda and WLB policies and working practices can have a significant impact on the opportunity for civic engagement and volunteering.

Recruitment and retention are major concerns in the workplace. WLB can reduce the stress caused by competing demands on employees and so lead to increased focus, reduced absenteeism, increased commitment and morale, all of which can have a positive impact on productivity and organisational performance. There is also the potential to provide enhanced customer service. Being an 'Employer of Choice' is increasingly an important target for organisations and WLB features prominently here. According to research findings from the Roffey Park Institute (2004) (http://www.roffeypark.com/research/wlb.html), 38 per cent of a sample group of employees were considering leaving their current organisation in the near future to gain a better WLB. The emphasis on family-friendly policies has resulted in concerns about equity in the workplace, as reflected in the transition from a concern with 'equal opportunities' to 'diversity' in the workplace.

Work-life balance policies

This chapter focuses on WLB policies in the UK based on my experiences of working within organisations as a human resource (HR) practitioner. 'WLB' is a wider concept than flexible working, and its strategies can encompass a wide variety of areas. A list of such areas together with business benefits generally suggested for WLB (replacing the former focus on 'family-friendly') are shown in Table 3.1.

The UK Department of Trade and Industry's (DTI) (2004) web site states that 'Increasingly, employers are developing a wide range of work-life balance options, covering flexible working arrangements and flexible benefit packages' (www.dti.gov.uk/work-lifebalance). Twelve of the thirteen options it cites relate to working-time/workplace arrangements, with one mention of flexible working and one of cafeteria benefits.

The DTI advocates the benefits to both employers and employees from WLB practices and comments on the savings and profits for business (acknowledging the costs, but indicating these are outweighed by the benefits) through improvements in the quality of people's work. A review of the 'business case' for policies addressing WLB, however, highlights that 'it seems difficult to reach a general judgement about the salience of the business case on the basis of current knowledge' (Evans, 2001: 26, see also Dex, 2004). For example, there is agreement on the need to retain qualified staff and the costs associated with losing hard-to-replace employees. But, there is less agreement on the benefits flowing from improved morale, since this is more difficult to quantify. However, the DTI states that whilst there has been an increase in the number of employers adopting flexible working arrangements, there was little evidence of employees using them, apart from flexi-time and part-time work. This raises the question of the lack of take-up of such practices, discussed below.

Research has examined the organisational and policy-oriented aspects of WLB in the UK (see Evans, 2001 for detail on the UK experience and

Table 3.1 WLB policies, strategies and benefits

WLB policies	WLB strategies	WLB business benefits
Flexible working	Working patterns	Improved recruitment and retention
Working families leave	Personal WLB	Staff motivation and commitment
Childcare and carer	Leave provision	Improvements in productivity
support	Career support	Reduced overheads
Sabbaticals	Well-being	Reduced stress and absenteeism
Sick leave	Advisory services	Improvements in employee
Flexible benefits	Financial services	relations
Volunteering		Improvements in employee health
opportunities		and well-being
Employee care		
Counseling		
Flexible training and		
development		
Flexible retirement		

selected international comparisons). Many of the studies have argued that work-family policies are a necessary but insufficient strategy to help employees effectively manage work and family demands (Batt and Valcour, 2003). They argue that employers must consider a broad range of HR practices as components of systems that together shape employee capacity to meet work and family demands in an integrated manner. Furthermore, they point out that the effectiveness of formal WLB policies depends, in large part, on whether front-line supervisors support their implementation. Studies have shown that where supervisors support work-family balance, job satisfaction is higher and work-family conflict is lower.

Work-family policies affect organisational commitment, but only to the extent that employees feel they can use them without negative consequences. There is also some difference reported on the effects of supportive supervisors on men and women. Support from supervisors has been associated with reduced turnover and decreased work-family conflicts for women but not for men, while flexible work policies decreased turnover intention for men but not for women. Batt and Valcour (2003) conclude that flexibility is not a complete solution, and its effectiveness depends on who has control of that flexibility, the employee or the supervisor. Wood, Menezes and Lasaosa (2003) further conclude that organisations that show more adaptability have a better chance of success with family-friendly HR policies than those that are less adaptable. Therefore, it appears that family-friendly and flexible working arrangements are related. Eaton (2003) too found a positive relationship between family-friendly and flexible policies and organisational commitment. However, such a relationship also depends on the culture of the organisation. This study showed that perceived usability of flexible work-family policies is important to employees, more so than the presence of either formal or informal policies alone, to achieve the desired outcomes of commitment and productivity.

A study by Berg, Kalleberg and Applebaum (2003) shows that a high commitment environment – characterised by high-performance work practices, intrinsically rewarding jobs and understanding supervisors – positively influences employees' perceptions that the company is helping them achieve WLB. The authors reinforce the view that helping workers balance work and family responsibilities is more complex than the benefits to be gained from formal family-friendly policies, pointing out that characteristics of jobs within the organisations also has an effect on work-life issues.

CIPD Studies on work-life balance

The CIPD has carried out a number of surveys during recent years which, directly or indirectly, have looked at WLB issues in the UK workplace (CIPD 2000; 2001; 2002; 2003; 2004a,b). Although detailed examination of the findings is beyond the scope of this chapter, the following section is an attempt to highlight some of the key findings of the various surveys as they relate to WLB.

Legislation was introduced in the UK in 2003 requiring employers to create flexible work arrangements for employees with young children. Since that time, one-half of all the requests received are being implemented, and nine out of ten employers report no difficulties in implementing them.

Flexible and more family-friendly policies have entered a new phase in UK organisations. The vast majority of employers (91 per cent) are prepared to consider requests and to work with the new statutory right, and about half of the employers surveyed expressed intentions to expand this practice to larger groups of employees. The surveys have shown that when the options are available, the take-up is high (81 per cent). It is also interesting to note that such arrangements have been more prevalent in public service and government industries than in the private sector.

The critical importance of line managers in effectively implementing people-management policies, and the difference this makes to organisational performance, is an issue highlighted in a number of CIPD research studies published in the last few years. This is consistent with the points made earlier that supervisor support of policies is essential to their take-up and success.

The findings from the surveys indicate that from the employer perspective first, there is not a strong business case for WLB policies. Secondly, cultural and structural factors, for example, a firm's size and administrative history, pose serious constraints. Third, employers fear the increased cost of WLB policies and practices. In the surveys, managers were one of the key groups resisting WLB policies, as they were reluctant to accept variations in standard working hours and patterns. In contrast, case studies reported by CIPD (2000) demonstrate significant business benefits of WLB policies and practices and improved motivation and commitment by employees. Some of the key findings from the case studies include:

- The need to formalize working practices into specific policies and criteria
- Guidance on the practical arrangements of flexible working practices to dispel assumptions about the difficulties of implementing such practices
- The need for research into demand, accurate costing and evaluation to make the business case for large-scale initiatives
- More needs to be done to encourage take up of the family-friendly arrangements and to reduce the negative attitudes of managers and staff.

The Trades Union Congress (TUC) has been heavily involved in promoting WLB (see Heery, in this volume). Its publication *Changing Times: a TUC Guide to Work-Life Balance* (TUC, 2001) refers to a number of case studies where unions have worked in partnership with staff and organisations to introduce WLB initiatives in both the public and private sectors. Again the major focus is on a range of flexible working options – shift patterns, annualised hours, home working and special leave; but also included are retirement schemes, training opportunities and reductions in supervision. The publication includes findings from a Baseline Study conducted by the Institute for Employment Research at the University of Warwick (Hogarth et al, 2001) which assessed the extent to which employers operated WLB practices and whether employees felt existing practices met their needs.

A key finding of this Baseline Study is the underlying high level of support for the idea of WLB from both employers and employees. Overall, the views of employers and employees were fairly similar. Around 62 per cent of employers and 80 per cent of employees agreed with the statement that: 'everyone should be able to balance their work and home lives in the way they want'. Employers almost always held the view that 'the employer's first responsibility has to be to ensure that the organisation meets its goals'. Forty-three per cent of employers thought that WLB practices were unfair to some staff and 26 per cent of employees thought that WLB practices were unfair to people like them. People without caring responsibilities, however, were no more likely to see WLB practices as unfair to them compared with people with caring responsibilities.

Overall the key findings of Hogarth and colleagues (2001) were:

- A high level of support for WLB from both employers and employees. Employers and employees agreed that while organisational goals have priority, employers have a responsibility to help employees balance work and other aspects of their lives.
- In 62 per cent of workplaces at least some staff were allowed to vary their usual hours (such as start late and make time during lunch break). Other than part-time working, only a modest proportion of employers operated flexible working-time arrangements such as flexi-time, term-time contracts and reduced hours. Approximately 20 per cent of employees worked from home at least occasionally. Of those employees not currently working from home, around a third said they would like to.
- The extent of consultation over WLB between employer and employees varied across workplaces and workforces. Other than consultation over hours of work, employers reported that management tended to decide alone about issues relating to leave or working at home. Where consultation took place, the incidence of flexible working practices was greatest.
- Generally, the incidence of WLB practices and their take-up by employees was greatest in the public sector. The more people employed in a workplace the more likely that WLB practices would be provided and taken up by employees.
- There was a consensus amongst employers that WLB practices improved certain aspects of work – work relations and staff motivation/commitment – and helped retain female employees and lowered labour turnover.

The challenges

Lack of employees' take-up of WLB

Despite support from top-level management and demand for the availability of WLB working practices, the lack of employee take-up of work-balance options comes through as a central issue in the debates, and this continues to be an issue for HR practitioners. The employee survey that was undertaken as part of the Baseline Study discussed above (Hogarth et al, 2001) indicates that there is little evidence of significant take-up of flexible working-time arrangements amongst employees, with the exception of flexi-time and part-time working. This issue is also referred to in the CIPD Research Report (2000) where the main reasons for the lack of take-up were suggested to be:

- employees may not be at the stage in their lives in which they need to make use of such provisions
- employees may have chosen other solutions to meet their needs
- employees' inability to afford to reduce their income by taking up reduced hours or career breaks
- employees may feel there is some stigma or career penalty attached to taking up such policies
- line managers or organizational culture may implicitly or explicitly discourage take-up. This is likely to be more pronounced during recessions when there is a context of downsizing making employees feel vulnerable.

Line manager influence

Line managers' influence comes out consistently as having a major impact on the success of WLB in the workplace. The CIPD Research Report (2000) found that all case study organisations had difficulties in convincing managers of the value of flexible working, and that the main constraint on the wider adoption of such practices was managers' beliefs about the problems of accommodating flexibility with operational and business needs. In the CIPD publication, *Managing Work-Life Balance*, Clutterbuck (2003) highlights the difficulty of convincing of managers that:

- the business genuinely wants them to put in place good WLB practice
- failure to deliver a culture of WLB is a black mark on their career
- they, themselves, can have a better WLB without damaging their career prospects
- that they can have the best of both worlds – by thinking flexibly and working with the team as a whole they can develop more effective ways of working that will benefit the employee, the company and themselves.

Many line managers are caught between pressure from above to improve productivity and pressure from below for greater understanding and flexibility. Managers frequently have to work to meet tighter deadlines with fewer staff, so the task of enabling a better balance for their remaining employees is often an unwelcome burden. However, the different research surveys also suggest that there is a considerable amount of ad hoc informal WLB practices existing in the workplace.

Formal versus informal policies

The prevalence of informal practices or special arrangements where a few individuals negotiate to work non-standard hours, in contrast to company-wide policies and practices, is another area of research and policy interest. The CIPD (2004b) survey refers to examples where managers who had part-time and other flexible arrangements did not experience the difficulties that were anticipated. In most cases, information on the benefits and practicalities was not disseminated well to other managers. One of the conclusions of the CIPD Research Report (2000) is the need to formalise flexible working practices into specific policies and criteria, to help ensure that there is consistency between departments and to make it easier for employees to take advantage of the opportunities without feeling that they have to individually negotiate. However, the CIPD made a distinction between different sized organisations in that small organisations may not need to enact formal policies but many implement family-friendly working practices through informal and individually-specific arrangements. The differences between types of organisations, such as large and small, is consistently cited as an important issue in developing appropriate policies and practices and in their implementation.

The ad hoc approach adopted by some organisations may be beneficial to some employees but it poses significant challenges in promoting examples of good practice and the business benefits of WLB, especially amongst small and medium-sized organisations which tend to have less exposure to management training and development and benchmarking of best practices. The lack of formal policies and a reliance on managerial discretion, pose significant challenges for human resources in promoting and implementing the application of WLB within organisations.

Organisational size

An initial premise of the CIPD Research Report (2000) was that small firms lack the flexibility required for varying working hours, working-time and leave arrangements. Evans (2001) has highlighted that formal family-friendly arrangements in the UK are more prevalent in large and unionised organisations and the public sector. However, the case studies included in the CIPD Report found that the benefits (if not the prevalence) of implementing family-friendly policies were found equally in the small and medium-sized firms in the study. When taking into account the opportunity for ad hoc, individualised arrangements, Dex (2004: 9) notes that 'Many smaller organizations were found that did not have any formal policies offering flexible working arrangements to their employees, but which nonetheless allowed individuals who came forward with requests to change their working arrangements'.

Equity and diversity

The focus on 'family-friendly' features strongly in research and is of particular concern from an equity and equality perspective. According to one CIPD Research Report (2000: 13) 'most family-friendly practices in the case studies have focused on the needs of women with young families. Broader questions of WLB were being considered by only a few, more prescient-minded employers'. It was also reported that that some of the case study organisations were not open-minded about the possibilities of extending family-friendly arrangements to existing staff (ibid). However, this view was not reflected in a later CIPD Survey Report (2004b) which reported a greater willingness to extend the right to request flexible working.

The current government is using the term 'work-life balance' rather than 'family-friendly'. The CIPD is also of the view that the term 'work-life balance' is more inclusive and might encourage the recruitment of more part-time workers, including older people, and other forms of flexibility such as using short-term contracts for covering business peaks and that it has a wider appeal because it benefits men and women at a number of stages in the life course, rather than just parents with dependent children.

Evidence from the field

The preceding sections have provided a brief overview of the context of the WLB debate in the UK and drawn attention to the challenges that lie ahead for organisations and for HR practitioners. In the following sections these ideas are illustrated using evidence and case study material from the UK (Wales). The case study material and examples have been gathered through my work in organisations as an HR practitioner over the last several years. The conclusion of this chapter reflects on what the case studies illuminate about the WLB challenges employers and HR practitioners face in the UK today. My experience of WLB polices and practices is as a HR practitioner with over 15 years of experience in a large voluntary organisation, followed by more than two years as an independent HR consultant working mainly with SMEs. Wales is particularly interesting because 99 per cent of its businesses are small businesses and 95 per cent are microbusinesses. It is also notable because of the high profile given to entrepreneurship and self-employment. As highlighted throughout this chapter, there are particular issues for small business owners in achieving WLB.

My impression, from working with SMEs, is that the case for any policies and practices is generally made on the business benefits, and at compliance level, rather than at the best practice level. Generally, provisions are based on the statutory minimum in relation to sickness as well as the working families' provisions. Movement beyond that is generally limited to some provision for compassionate leave. However, there are some notable exceptions.

A large proportion of workers in SMEs are paid at or near the minimum wage. This means that provision of flexible benefits and, indeed, the ability to work reduced hours is likely to have limited application. A significant proportion of workers are working long hours at basic pay; willingness to work long hours is seen as the acid test of commitment and is frequently referred to in discussions about reward.

A very interesting feature I have come across in working with SMEs, particularly in some areas/sectors in Wales, which impacts on WLB in a surprising way, is the so-called 'benefits trap'. It can be uneconomic for males as well as females to work more than 15 hours a week. This causes a tension with some traditional employers who only want to employ full-time workers. The employees are achieving WLB, but counter to the organisation's needs, and not by a model that is sustainable in the long term. Further, it is frequently uneconomic for women to return to work because of low wages and the high costs of childcare. Where women do return to work, childcare is frequently undertaken by members of the family for cost reasons. This can be less reliable than professional childcare and means that informal arrangements relating to flexible working prevail.

Case study 1

This organisation employs 70 staff in the social housing sector. It is a group organisation with four companies with some differences in culture and operating practices between the companies. The Group is regulated by the Wales Assembly Government (WAG). The business imperative for the Group in progressing WLB was recruitment, retention and also impact in the community. As part of my work with the company, a survey was carried out questioning employees' attitudes towards work-life issues and their preferences for specific WLB provisions.

Employees in the survey group reported a strong degree of satisfaction with their ability to achieve WLB in the organisation, although there were some significant differences in responses on management style in one particular part of the Group. The Group had an extensive flexi-time system which very few staff were using; the majority of staff were working a standard work pattern. However, the most significant responses concerned removing core hours and introducing late start/early finish working patterns (a high proportion of staff had childcare responsibilities). The demand to remove core hours was accepted by the Management Team.

However, there was resistance by staff to the proposal that they would need to sacrifice the full range of flexi-time options if they wanted to adopt a customised working pattern. There appeared to be a resistance to give up anything, even if it was not being utilised.

A limited flexible benefits package was also offered and the provision of well-being was being promoted strongly by the HR Manager. A particular issue raised by staff in one of the companies was that the current flexi-time system did not allow them to attend classes in the local leisure centre. The case is also interesting in that it demonstrated lack of consistency even though there were formal procedures in place. It was evident from focus group discussions that informal arrangements and inconsistency in the application of managerial discretion were causing a degree of resentment among staff between the different companies.

One of the most interesting features of this case was that at the time of the initial survey there was an extremely positive response to the issue of job security (a basic tenet of WLB). Subsequently there have been two redundancy exercises and an office move that has had significant travel to work implications for staff. It could be anticipated that the extremely high level of satisfaction reported by staff on WLB achievement might be adversely affected by these events. It also demonstrates the susceptibility of higher level employee relations initiatives to other business priorities.

Case study 2

This organisation was a newly set-up social care organisation employing initially three part-time staff. It is owned by a husband and wife team, the latter with a background in social care. The company offers a domiciliary care service within the local authority area. It is regulated through the WAG.

The organisation is able to offer a number of flexible working patterns through a fortnightly rotation which is produced by the manager and any amendments are negotiated within the team. The flexibility of its working patterns has allowed it to recruit (it is now employing 15 staff) and retain staff in a sector with retention problems. It also offers a significant amount of training to its staff and also arranges regular team meetings and social activities. It has built up a very good reputation, both with clients and the local authority. It has a detailed handbook concerning all its working procedures and is also producing a Staff Handbook. We have recently worked together on formalising a WLB policy that was aimed at underlining the company's general support for the principles of WLB, rather than having detailed procedures.

The company is also interesting from the entrepreneurship and WLB perspective in that the female owner is striving to, and currently achieving, her own WLB. One of the findings that emerged from the CIPD research was that the self-employed work some of the longest hours, but that they have choice. However, for some of the start-up companies there is little choice about the necessity to put in long hours, exacerbated by the cost and lack of availability of employees to work the hours the business needs.

Case study 3

I have recently been working with a retailer in a tourist area in North Wales. The company has been in business for 20 years and has built an enviable reputation for its products within North Wales. The company has a number of long-serving female staff who work in the shop. Several of these staff now have childcare responsibilities and the owner has accommodated requests for family-friendly working on an ad hoc basis. During the previous year's tourist season, he experienced problems of adequate staffing to cover this peak trading period.

During our discussions on this, he indicated initially that he would take a very strong line with all new staff and require them all to work every Saturday. We discussed the impact this might have on recruiting and retaining staff. The company is already using self-rostering for holidays and we discussed whether adopting a problem-solving approach with the staff would work. The owner was able to persuade the staff of the difficulties he faced and to come to a compromise whereby they agreed to work Saturdays at peak trading times.

This case is interesting because it demonstrates the prevalence of ad hoc informal arrangements where the business case has not been addressed. It also demonstrates success in achieving business and individual goals. This issue is advocated in all the promotional literature on WLB.

Conclusions

There is mounting evidence, supported by research and demonstrated in case studies, of the business benefits that can accrue from implementing WLB policies – benefits such as greater flexibility, service improvements, holiday and sickness absence cover, and more motivated, adaptable and committed staff. It is apparent that there is support for practices that enhance WLB from both employers and employees, although this does vary. It frequently appears that the biggest constraint in the implementation of WLB practices is at line manager or supervisor level. It is clear that these managers need support from senior management, from HR through training and information, and from their peers, to ensure the implementation of diverse working arrangements to cater for diversity and equity in organisations.

Interestingly, there is evidence, particularly in earlier studies of a lack of take-up of WLB practices: that although employees are glad that they are in place they do not take full advantage of the opportunities. Questions remain about why take-up is fairly low. Lack of take-up could be interpreted as a lack of interest from staff in changing the way they work and taking advantage of the policies; but this may be a misinterpretation. Best practice advocates piloting initiatives and being prepared to modify and adjust policies and practices, based on feedback from staff. There remain significant gender differences in terms of preferred working patterns. Part-time working is the favoured option for female returnees to the workplace, while flexi-time is more valued by men. I find it interesting that job-sharing continues to be an unpopular choice compared to part-time working.

The evidence points to more extensive WLB provisions in the public and service sectors. However, there are some examples of progressive initiatives in the private sector and some particularly noteworthy practices in multinationals where there is a significant proportion of female employees. Size continues to be a factor with larger organisations tending to have more progressive WLB initiatives. However, there are some innovative practices amongst some SMEs in England and Wales. A lack of continued funding may make these practices unsustainable in the longer term however, and this is likely to have a bigger effect in Wales because of the high proportion of microbusinesses.

Overall, the value of WLB amongst employers and employees is perceived differently and implementation of WLB practices is mixed and ranges from reluctant compliance to positive development. Continued research is needed to monitor the development and implementation of WLB initiatives and to measure the effectiveness of such practices for organisations and for employees.

References

Batt, R. and Valcour, P.M. (2003) 'Human Resource Practices as Predictors of Work-Family Outcomes and Employee Turnover', *Industrial Relations*, 42(2): 189–230.

Berg, P., Kalleberg, A.L. and Applebaum, E. (2003) 'Balancing Work and Family: the Role of High-Commitment Environments', *Industrial Relations*, 42(2): 168–88.

CIPD (2000) *Research Report: Getting the Right Work-Life Balance: Implementing Family-Friendly Practices*, London: Chartered Institute of Personnel and Development.

CIPD (2001) *Survey Report: Married to the Job?* London: Chartered Institute of Personnel and Development.

CIPD (2002) *Survey Report: Work, Parenting and Careers*, London: Chartered Institute of Personnel and Development.

CIPD (2003) *Survey Report: A Parent's Right to Ask: A Review of Flexible Working Arrangements*, London: Chartered Institute of Personnel and Development.

CIPD (2004a) *Overview of CIPD Surveys 2003–04*, London: Chartered Institute of Personnel and Development.

CIPD (2004b) *Survey Report: Working Time Regulations: Calling Time on Working Time?* London: Chartered Institute of Personnel and Development.

Clutterbuck, D. (2003) *Managing Work-life Balance; A Guide for HR in Achieving Organizational and Individual Change*, London: Chartered Institute of Personnel and Development.

Dex, S. (2004) 'Flexible (or Family-Friendly) Working Arrangements in the UK: Where are we Now?' Paper Presented at the Work-Life Balance Across The Life Course Conference, Centre for Research on Families and Relationships, Edinburgh University, Scotland, July.

DTI (2004) *Achieving Best Practice in your Business: Flexible Working*, (www.dti.gov.uk/work-lifebalance).

Eaton, S. (2003) 'If You Can Use Them: Flexibility Policies, Organizational Commitment, and Perceived Performance', *Industrial Relations*, 42(2): 145–67.

Evans, J.M. (2001) *Firms' Contribution to the Reconciliation between Work and Family Life*, Labour Market and Social Policy Occasional Papers, OECD: Paris.

Hogarth, T., Hasluck, C. and Pierre, G. (2001) *Work-Life Balance 2000: Results from the Baseline Study*, Warwick: Institute for Employment Research, University of Warwick.

Roffey Park Institute (2004) (http://www.roffeypark.com/research/wlb.html).

Trades Union Congress (2001) *Changing Times: a TUC Guide to Work-Life Balance*, London: TUC.

Wood, S.J., de Menezes, L.M. and Lasaosa, A. (2003) 'Family-Friendly Management in Great Britain: Testing Various Experiences', *Industrial Relations*, 42(2): 221–50.

4

Bargaining for Balance: Union Policy on Work-Life Issues in the United Kingdom

Edmund Heery

Introduction

Securing a better integration of work and home life is often viewed by policy makers as a matter of persuading employers of the business case for change or of endowing individuals with new legal rights (DTI, 2003). Collective action through trade unions, however, may furnish an alternative or supplementary means of effecting change. In the connected field of equal opportunities it has been observed that trade unions can play an important mediating role, ensuring that legal entitlements to equal treatment are given genuine effect at the workplace (Dickens, 1988: 170–1; see also Bewley and Fernie, 2003). It has also been noted that unions can make employer policy on equality more inclusive, extending provisions to those in lower graded work and ensuring practice bends to a social justice, not purely a business logic (Dickens, 2000: 28–33). The object of this chapter is to establish if trade unions generate similar effects in the field of work-life balance. It examines the nature and significance of attempts by British unions to restore balance between paid employment and other spheres of social life, using documentary, interview and survey data collected since 2000.

The examination is conducted in three stages. At the first stage there is a review of national union policy on work-life issues, particularly within the Trades Union Congress (TUC). This focuses on the development of the union position on working time. It is argued that there has been a significant shift in union policy objectives with regard to working time since the early 1990s, in which the traditional union concern to reduce working hours (Arrowsmith, 2002) has been overlain with a new desire to provide opportunities for choice and variation in the scheduling of paid work. This objective has been expressed under the rubric of 'positive flexibility'.[1] It is also argued that there have been significant changes in union method. The main developments here have been greater emphasis on legal regulation, reflecting the juridification of British industrial relations, and a movement from distributive to integrative bargaining that has formed part of the TUC's broader espousal of labour-management partnership (Taylor, 2000: 263–5).

The second stage is concerned with the implementation of union policy on work-life balance. A repeated theme in the literature on trade unions and equality is that there is a frequent mismatch between national policy and the actions of union representatives who deal with employers at enterprise or workplace level in the UK's fragmented system of industrial relations; that there is poor articulation of policy and the on-going work of representation (Terry, 2003: 269; see also McBride, 2001). To examine the extent of union engagement with the question of work-life balance a large survey of paid union officers was carried out that gathered systematic data on the pattern of collective bargaining on working time and work-life issues. This was designed to test whether a traditional agenda, focused on hours-reduction and improvements to annual leave, was giving way to or being supplemented by negotiation on family-friendly practices and other aspects of work-life balance. It was also designed to measure the amount of bargaining and the extent to which unions are recording success in negotiating on a work-life agenda.

The third stage makes further use of the survey and is concerned with the influences on the bargaining behaviour of paid officers. The aim here is to establish the conditions under which union bargainers pursue, or fail to pursue, work-life balance. Three potential influences are considered: that bargaining is a function of worker demand and reflects the characteristics of employees serviced by officers, that it is a function of the characteristics of officers themselves, and that it is a function of individual unions, the policies they adopt and their internal systems for managing bargaining activity. The initial assumption behind the analysis was that unions can play an important, independent role in promoting work-life balance within the economy, akin to their role in narrowing gender, ethnic and other differences at work (Turnbull, 2003). Given this assumption, it is important to establish the characteristics of unions, their members and representatives that allow this influence to be exerted.

National policy – objectives

For much of the 20th century British unions pursued three main objectives with regard to working time. They sought to reduce basic working hours in order to extend leisure time and generate employment and were reasonably successful in doing so: basic weekly hours were brought down over the course of the 20th century in a series of union campaigns (McKinlay and McNulty, 1992: 206). Unions also sought to extend paid holidays and, again, were reasonably successful (Green, 1997), though notably less successful than their counterparts in other European countries, at least in securing statutory provision for paid leave. Finally, unions sought to obtain premium rates of compensation for work beyond basic working hours and for unsocial and shift working. Success on this dimension frequently cut across the objective of cutting work hours per se as wage premiums provided an incentive for long hours working: protecting and regulating the distribution of institutionalised overtime became common features of workplace industrial relations in male-dominated union employment (Clegg, 1972: 276–80).[2] This compensation model of union activity focused on the achievement of a series of 'quantitative' (Hyman, 1997: 318) bargaining objectives that strove to improve the time-payment exchange for unionised workers. At its heart was an assumption of work as a disutility, Adam's curse (Thompson, 1968: 205).

Much of this traditional policy remains in place and the TUC is committed to securing further reductions in working time and extending paid leave. Since the early 1990s, however, there have been significant changes in emphasis and new themes have emerged in union policy on working time. With regard to hours reduction, the main change has been a switch from campaigning to reduce basic hours towards a focus on total hours. The TUC has targeted the substantial proportion of British men and growing percentage of British women who persistently work long hours and campaigned for a pattern of working time similar to that seen in other western European countries. The main recent focus of this campaign has been the provision in the working time directive that allows British workers to opt out of the 48-hour maximum week through an individual agreement with their employer. The TUC has argued that workers are placed under duress to accept long hours and that these agreements typically are not voluntary in any meaningful sense. To date, however, success has been limited and the TUC failed to persuade the European Commission that the opt out be withdrawn in its recent review of the directive (*People Management*, 30 September 2004: 13).

There has also been a change in policy on paid leave. The TUC continues to campaign for a universal increase in paid leave and has argued both for an increase in public holiday provision and for a legal guarantee that public holidays be excluded from the statutory entitlement to paid holiday contained in the Working Time Regulations (TUC, 2004).[3] The main thrust of recent policy, however, has focused on introducing or strengthening special leave for those with caring responsibilities. The TUC was an architect of statutory maternity leave through its Social Contract with the Labour Government of the 1970s and since then has pressed with considerable success for improved provision. This traditional concern has been supplemented in recent years by lobbying at both European and domestic levels for rights to parental, paternity, adoptive and special leave to be taken in circumstances of family emergency (TUC, 2001b). All of these rights have been established in UK law since Labour's return to power in

1997, partly through the recommendations of the Government's Work and Parents Task Force on which the TUC was represented (Dickens and Hall, 2003: 133).The unions' prime concern since has been one of strengthening rights, particularly by ensuring that entitlements to leave are given real effect by an entitlement to payment.

The most novel feature of recent policy on working time has been a focus on choice, on securing rights for workers to increase or decrease their hours or alter their schedule of working time in order to better integrate work and non-work activities. This policy has been pursued in two ways. First, the TUC has pressed for an end to discrimination against those on non-standard employment contracts, particularly part-time workers. The primary achievement of this campaign has been the negotiation of a European framework agreement on part-time work,[4] which formed the basis of the part-time workers' directive and the regulations that transposed it into UK law in 2001. The latter are deeply unsatisfactory from a union point of view and have become a focus of TUC lobbying and campaigning (TUC, 2000) but nevertheless they have established the principle of equal treatment for part-time workers. The significance of this principle is that part-time work should become more attractive and be freely chosen by a broader range of workers if the disadvantages of low pay and poor conditions, with which it has traditionally been associated, are removed. 'Part-time work or job-sharing which gives employees the rights and pay levels of full-time workers', the TUC argued in its evidence to a Parliamentary inquiry into part-time work, 'allows employees to choose different patterns of work at different times of their lives' (House of Commons Education and Employment Committee, 1999: 243). An officer in the TUC Equal Rights Department reinforced this position, arguing that stronger rights for part-timers permitted the 'mainstreaming' of part-time work, such that 'it loses its stigma...and people move in and out of it more' (Interview, December 2000).

Second, the TUC has argued for a positive right to adjust working time in order to accommodate caring responsibilities (TUC, 2001b). It wants, 'to extend the choice and control that individual employees have over their working hours to ensure that choices can reflect changing priorities and needs – whether the need to work part-time arises from family responsibilities, managing a disability or preparing for retirement' (TUC, 2000: 1). As this quotation suggests the right to work part-time in the light of changing domestic circumstances has lain at the heart of TUC policy: there has been a particularly strong insistence that women returning after childbirth should have a right to part-time work. But policy extends beyond choosing reduced hours to embrace movement back to full-time work and changes to the scheduling of hours. Again, this policy has borne fruit through the TUC's participation in the Work and Parents Task Force. From April 2003, parents with children under six years have a right to request flexible working, with the employer obliged to give such a request serious consideration (TUC, 2002). Current TUC policy is focused on strengthening this right, such that employers can only refuse a request on objective grounds and must do so in writing (TUC, 2001b: 12).

These shifts in union objectives suggest that the traditional compensation model of policy on working time has been overlain with a choice model. The key elements of this are removing the right of employers to coerce long hours working through closer regulation, the harmonisation of conditions across different types of employment to facilitate free choice, a positive right to vary the amount and scheduling of hours in the light of changing domestic circumstances and improved paid leave for those with caring responsibilities. Underpinning the model is a more favourable conception of work but also a perception that the demands of paid employment impinge too frequently on other aspects of social and domestic life and in cases of long hours working are injurious to health (TUC, 2001b). Also underpinning the model are developments in union equality policy and it is notable that recent proposals on working time have originated primarily in the TUC's Equal Rights Department. In important respects work-life policy represents an, albeit guarded, embrace by unions of the theme of 'managing diversity'. Thus, on the one hand there is an emphasis on reaching beyond formal equal treatment and matching or tailoring working patterns to the specific needs of working women. On the other hand, work-life balance has been framed as an issue for all workers and not just women: positive flexibility is meant to benefit working fathers, men approaching retirement, those wishing to combine work and study and those with disabilities; indeed anyone who is burdened with excessive working time.

National policy – methods

For much of the 20th century union attempts to reduce working time were characterised by two features. There was primary reliance on collective bargaining with working time being regulated through a series of industry level agreements on basic hours, overtime and shift premiums and paid leave (Arrowsmith, 2002). The TUC continued to call for the statutory regulation of working time and the introduction by law of a maximum working week (Rubery et al, 1994: 227; Taylor, 2000: 54). But the main thrust of policy from the end of the First World War was pursued through free collective bargaining. There was also an assumption that hours reduction was an issue for distributive bargaining. The basic week was shortened in Britain through a series of trials of strength, major disputes that established a new template for the regulation of hours, usually in the engineering industry, which was subsequently applied elsewhere. The two most recent disputes of this kind were the 1979 engineering strike to establish the

39-hour week and the coordinated company-level strikes in engineering in 1989–90 for 37 hours (McKinlay and McNulty, 1992).

This traditional pattern of action has changed in recent years in a number of ways. Collective bargaining on working time continues to be significant, as is shown below, but the method of legal regulation has become more central and TUC pronouncements in its favour less rhetorical. Recent union action on working time has included the following: negotiation at European level, under the auspices of the European Trade Union Confederation, of framework agreements on part-time and fixed-term work and parental leave that have been adopted as European directives (Marginson and Sisson, 2004: 85); participation in the UK Government's tripartite Work and Parents Task Force; direct lobbying of the UK Government and European Commission; formal responses to Parliamentary inquiries and Green Papers; and the sponsorship of test cases on a variety of aspects of working time in both UK and European courts. The main reason for this switch in method has been that state institutions have provided an opportunity for unions to exert influence.[5] The European Commission has sought to develop social dialogue and provided opportunities for the social partners to influence regulatory processes at the European level, including those concerned with working time and non-standard work. The transposition of European law into national regulations has then provided another opportunity for influence as the UK Government has attempted to generate a consensus between stakeholders on at least some aspects of working time regulation (e.g. the entitlement to request flexible working). Finally, unions have learnt to use judicial review and test cases to flesh out, clarify and extend the law, often by challenging the minimal interpretation of European directives favoured by the British Government. In recent years there have been significant union-sponsored cases that have strengthened the leave entitlements of non-standard workers, extended the principle of equal treatment for part-timers and produced revision of both the part-time and parental leave regulations (Heery et al, 2004: 147).

Reflecting the theme of social partnership, the TUC has also presented working time as an issue suited to integrative bargaining. The template here has been the *Time of Our Lives* project at Bristol City Council. This project was sponsored by the European Union and brought together a range of interest groups, including the TUC, council unions (GMB, TGWU and UNISON), Bristol City Council and the Employers' Organisation for Local Government to generate a schedule of flexible working time that was beneficial to all stakeholders, including users who gained through longer opening hours for council services (TUC, 2001a: 7–9). Subsequently the TUC has tried to extend this process and there have been other experiments elsewhere in the public sector and the development of a TUC guide to work-life balance, *Changing Times*, which proposes a partnership methodology for the management of working time within employing organisations. Much of this TUC literature uses a business case to frame the issue of work-life balance. A better deal for working carers is justified in terms of employee motivation and an increased ability to retain workers, while the case against long hours working has been made in terms of its inefficiency and contribution to a low pay, low productivity dynamic in UK business (TUC, 2001a: 31). The title to another TUC report, however, is *Rights not Favours*, and it would be a mistake to exaggerate the degree to which the organisation believes that a voluntary consensus on work-life balance can be achieved. The TUC wants stronger regulation of employer behaviour and stronger rights for workers. What is notable, however, is that these appeals have also been framed in integrative terms, as serving a general, not just a sectional interest. The union movement has argued for legislation on work-life balance in terms of improving public health and the quality of child and eldercare, supporting fertility, allowing the integration of single parents in paid work and promoting civil participation, a factor that is perhaps particularly significant for an institution that labels itself 'Britain's largest voluntary organisation' (TUC, 2000; 2001b; 2004).

A final theme that has been apparent in recent union policy on working time has been a willingness to work in concert with other organisations. The TUC's campaign on part-time work of the mid-1990s included as one of its objectives 'to build alliances with organisations which support TUC campaign goals' (TUC, 2000) and involved particularly close cooperation with the Citizen's Advice Bureaux (Heery, 1998). More recently, the TUC has worked closely with the Maternity Alliance to press the UK Government to strengthen family-friendly legislation and has also cooperated with the Equal Opportunities Commission and Women's Budget Group (TUC, 2001b: 10). In certain respects this activity represents a step back to the 19th century cross-class campaigns on child labour and the length of the working day that established initial state regulation of working time (Arrowsmith, 2002: 88–91). What is distinctive about the current phase of coalition-building, however, is that the TUC has built 'coalitions of influence' (Frege et al, 2004: 144), in which unions seek alliances with 'insider' organisations that possess expertise and legitimacy and which can advance union policy in direct dealings with government. Rather like the attempts to build partnership with employers and frame the issue of working time in non-sectional terms, the aim has been to generate a broad authoritative consensus that accepts stronger regulation of work-life issues.

Bargaining for work-life balance

Although there has been an emphasis on legal regulation in recent union policy, the TUC and its affiliates remain committed to bargaining on working time and work-life issues: the *Changing Times* methodology developed by the TUC is intended to result in the signing of a conventional collective agreement with an employer or employers. To explore the extent to which union negotiators were in fact bargaining on work-life issues, a large survey of paid union officers was conducted in 2002. The initial aim was to apply the survey in all TUC-affiliated unions with more than 100,000 members, together with a selection of smaller unions organising particular occupations (e.g. lecturers, journalists, physiotherapists) or in particular industries (e.g. clothing and footwear, telecommunications, media). In the event, 19 unions took part (see Table 4.1) which reported employing 1,406 officers engaged either in organising or bargaining on behalf of union members. A total of 585 officers responded to the survey (42 per cent) and of these, 538 (92 per cent) reported that their job involved collective bargaining. It is this subset of the survey population that forms the basis of the analysis below.

Table 4.1   Union participation and responses to the paid officer survey, 2002

Trade union	Members 2001	Number of officers	Number of responses	Response %
Association of University Teachers (AUT)	42,709	10	6	60
Broadcasting, Entertainment, Cinematograph and Theatre Union (BECTU)	25,799	30	12	40
Connect	17,616	20	7	35
Chartered Society of Physiotherapy (CSP)	32,576	13	7	54
Communication Workers' Union (CWU)	284,422	32	11	34
British Actors' Equity Association (Equity)	35,246	24	10	42
GMB – Britain's General Union*	692,147	111	62	56
Graphical Paper and Media Union (GPMU)	200,676	94	44	47
National Union of Knitwear, Footwear and Apparel Trades (KFAT)	20,650	7	6	86
NATFHE – The College Lecturers' Union	65,031	43	23	53
National Union of Journalists (NUJ)	22,930	9	5	56
Public and Commercial Services Union (PCS)	267,644	90	37	41
Prospect	103,942	53	29	55
Transport and General Workers' Union (TGWU)	858,804	300	58	19

Table 4.1 Union participation and responses to the paid officer survey, 2002 – *continued*

Trade union	Members 2001	Number of officers	Number of responses	Response %
Transport Salaried Staffs Association (TSSA)	31,494	18	12	67
Union of Construction Allied Trades and Technicians (UCATT)	123,000	50	31	62
UNIFI	160,267	108	38	35
UNISON	1,272,470	283	103	36
Union of Shop, Distributive and Allied Workers (USDAW)	310,222	111	84	76
Total	4,567,645	1,406	585	42

* In the GMB the survey was restricted to four of the union's constituent regions, Northern, Wales and South West, London and Liverpool, North Wales and Northern Ireland.

The officers surveyed in unions differed slightly as a result of variation in organisational size, structure and the pattern of industrial relations in different industries. In the smaller unions plus GPMU, TGWU and USDAW all officers were included below general secretary, including full-time elected branch officials in the case of the GPMU. In CWU, PCS, and UNIFI a small number of seconded officers were included in the survey; that is senior lay officials who were working for their unions in a similar capacity to paid staff. For other unions the survey was confined to regional organisers and their equivalents, largely as a condition of access. This was true of GMB, KFAT, TSSA, UCATT and UNISON. Despite the different patterns of response, the survey can be viewed as broadly representative of paid union officers in the UK.[6]

The survey questionnaire asked union officers if, 'In the past three years', they had attempted to negotiate on a list of 20 issues that could result in improved 'work-life balance' for the workers they represented. The list included traditional items on the union bargaining agenda on working time, such as reduced basic hours for full-time employees, changes to leave entitlements, such as the introduction of paid parental leave, and opportunities for greater choice over the scheduling of working hours. It also contained items relating to discouragement of long hours working, such as 'measures to reduce unpaid overtime working'. In addition to asking officers if they had raised issues in bargaining with employers, the questionnaire asked if they had been successful in negotiating at least one collective agreement for each item listed. The survey therefore generated measures both of union activity and of union success.

The descriptive results from the survey are shown in Table 4.2. This suggests that work-life issues have registered on the bargaining table to a considerable degree: 50 per cent or more of officers report negotiation on nine of the 20 items. On only one item, moreover, the introduction of retainer payments for workers on term-time only contracts, does less than one in five officers report bargaining. It is common amongst commentators on British industrial relations to report that collective bargaining has become a hollow shell and that the range of issues negotiated has narrowed dramatically (Millward et al, 2000: 167–73). On the evidence presented here, however, there is still dynamism in the system of collective industrial relations and a capacity to encompass new themes.

The table also indicates that bargainers have continued to pursue traditional union objectives, such as extended leave, reduced hours and enhanced

Table 4.2 Negotiation on work-life balance in the past three years (percentages)

Work-life issues	Attempt at negotiation	At least one success in negotiation
Paid parental leave	71	77
Improvements to annual leave	69	79
Paid paternity leave	61	77
Right to *request* flexible or reduced hours	59	85
Written policy on work-life balance or family-friendly work	54	85
Reductions in basic (contractual) hours for full-time employees	54	62
Entitlement to reduced working hours	53	83
Introduction or improvements to special leave for care of dependents	53	75
Entitlement to flexible hours	50	80
Enhanced maternity provisions	49	77
Employer support for childcare (e.g. crèche or vouchers)	42	56
Career break or sabbatical scheme	38	77
Joint statement with management to discourage long hours working	38	77
Measures to reduce paid overtime working	37	65
Introduction or revision of a job-sharing scheme	36	72
Pre-retirement counselling	35	87
Measures to reduce unpaid overtime working	34	60
Arrangements for workers to work from home to cope with domestic responsibilities	30	73
Introduction of pay for overtime to discourage long hours working	20	62
Retainer payment for term-time working	16	48

maternity provisions, while also embracing newer themes, such as the nego-tiation of family-friendly policies, parental and special leave and a right to reduced hours. The raw data presents a picture of the overlaying of the tradi-tional compensation with the newer choice model of union policy on working time. A third thing to note about the table is that the items on which bargaining is most frequently reported tend to be those that corre-spond to developments in public policy and changes in employment law. At least eight of the ten most frequently bargained issues relate to recent changes in law, such as the working time regulations (e.g. reduced basic hours, improvements to leave), the Employment Relations Act 1999 (e.g. enhanced maternity provisions, special leave) and the Employment Act 2002 (e.g. the right to request flexible hours). The pattern shows the interaction of legal and joint regulation that arguably has become an increasingly marked feature of UK industrial relations (see also Heery et al, 2004). It is also perhaps indicative of the increased dependence of unions on legislation as a lever to open up negotiations with employers (for similar Australian findings see Whitehouse, 2001: 114).

The items for which less bargaining is reported tend to fall into two categories. On the one hand, there are issues such as pre-retirement coun-selling and arrangements for home-working which seek to promote work-life integration but without the support of public policy. On the other hand, there are items that seek to reduce long hours working and, while there are substantial minorities of officers reporting negotiation on reducing paid and unpaid overtime, it is notable that negotiation at this end of the working time spectrum is less visible. This suggests that there is a continuing ambiva-lence in union policies on working time: seeking reduction on the one hand but anxious to preserve earnings opportunities on the other. The final thing to note in the table is that on all but one item (retainers for term-time working) a majority of officers who report bargaining also report at least one negotiating success. Indeed, for most items more than three-quarters of bar-gainers report success. Unions, on this evidence, are a positive force pushing for improved work-life balance in British workplaces. The high success rate probably reflects the pragmatism of union negotiators: items are only placed on the bargaining agenda where there is a likelihood of achieving a success-ful outcome. Nevertheless, the findings indicate that unions make a differ-ence on this as on other dimensions of their members' working conditions; a finding that has also emerged from recent analysis of the UK's Workplace Employee Relations Survey (Budd and Mumford, 2004).

Influences on bargaining

Further analysis of the data presented in Table 4.2 was undertaken in order to identify the situations in which union negotiators were likely to be most active in raising the issue of work-life balance. The aim was to identify the relative importance of membership characteristics, officer characteristics and the characteristics of unions themselves in shaping bargaining activity in this area. The initial stage in conducting this analysis was to reduce the information in the table to two statistically reliable scales. The first scale measured bargaining activity on the types of issue that have lain at the heart of recent 'positive flexibility' policies of unions and has been labelled the 'choice' scale. This comprised ten items: officer responses to all of the questions on maternity and other forms of leave for carers, all of the questions on choosing different or flexible patterns of work and the items on written policy and childcare. The second scale consisted of responses to the two items in the table that related to traditional union objectives on working time: reducing basic hours for full-timers and raising paid holiday entitlement. This has been labelled the 'compensation' scale.[7] On both of these scales there was considerable variation. Half of the union officers reported negotiating on five or fewer of the positive flexibility and family-friendly practices, 13 per cent reported no negotiations and 14 per cent reported negotiation on all of them. The percentage reporting no negotiation increased to 26 per cent for the compensation scale but 25 per cent of officers reported bargaining on both items. Clearly union negotiators have differed substantially in the degree to which they have engaged with both types of work-life issues.

Table 4.3 presents choice and compensation scores for different sub-groups of union officers and indicates the kinds of factors that have encouraged bargaining on work-life balance. Clearly, the characteristics of members for whom the officer is responsible emerge from the table as significant influences. With regard to bargaining on both choice and compensation issues, there is notable variation across members concentrated in particular industries and occupations. For the choice scale there is also a slight tendency for officers responsible for mainly women members (but not part-timers) to report more bargaining and those responsible for mainly men members to report less.

Table 4.3   Influences on bargaining activity

	Number of cases	Choice %	Compensation %
All bargainers	513, 514	53	49
Industry			
More than 75% of members in industry			
Healthcare	31	70	48
Public administration	73	68	64
Financial services	26	60	30
Transport & communications	36	49	47
Manufacturing	50	45	44
Education	25, 26	40	31
Distribution	44	37	38
Construction	26	23	40

Table 4.3   Influences on bargaining activity – *continued*

	Number of cases	Choice %	Compensation %
Occupation			
More than 50% of members in occupation			
Managers & administrators	25	71	70
Clerical & secretarial	61	69	57
Associate professional	20	61	53
Personal service workers	16	54	47
Operatives	78	52	49
Professional workers	55, 56	48	36
Sales workers	56	40	42
Craft workers	58	31	45
Identity			
More than 50% of members in identity/ status group			
Majority female	260	58	52
Majority male	247, 248	48	47
Majority part-time	82	47	47
Officer commitment			
Officers reporting 'high' personal commitment to each goal			
Partnership	107	61	57
Work-life balance	250, 251	58	52
Improvements for part-timers	308, 309	57	52
Officer characteristics			
Senior position	41	66	50
Women	115	57	47
Men	395	51	50
Management systems			
Bargaining objectives	202	59	51
Training in work-life issues	109	58	51
Training in WTR	259	53	48
Training in PTR	149, 150	54	49
Trade unions			
Unions with 20 or more responses			
PCS	33	81	79
Prospect	24	75	67
UNIFI	27	62	31
UNISON	98	61	54
GMB	52	56	55
TGWU	54	55	49
GPMU	36	56	43
USDAW	78	41	45
UCATT	29	24	42

The highest scores on both measures are recorded in two public service industries: healthcare and public administration. It is probable that this association reflects the policy of the employer as much as the characteristics of union members. It is a well-established finding that equality and diversity initiatives are more likely to be found and more likely to have substance in the public services (e.g. Hoque and Noon, 2004: 488, 495) and these findings point in the same direction. The public services, with the exception of education, seem to have provided a more receptive context for union bargaining on work-life issues (see also Whitehouse, 2001: 117). It has been common in recent years to identify the collapse of the 'model employer' commitment in public service and emphasise its displacement by hard-edged new public management (Carter and Fairbrother, 2004). The pattern in these data suggests this change may have been exaggerated: that there is still life in the model employer tradition.

In the private sector less bargaining tends to be reported: only financial services has a higher than average score and then only for the first measure. Particularly low levels of bargaining are recorded on the newer work-life issues in distribution and construction. In the latter case this may reflect the fact that it is male-dominated and it is notable here that the emphasis in bargaining has been placed on more traditional aspects of working time. In the former, it may reflect the preponderance of part-time work in the sector (Marginson and Sisson, 2004: 280), which provides an alternative means of integrating paid and unpaid activities. It could also reflect a relatively conservative bargaining orientation on the part of USDAW, the primary retail union.

The findings on occupation indicate that bargaining on work-life issues has been targeted mainly at white-collar workers; particularly managers and administrators, secretarial, clerical, technical and associate professional employees. Only the professional group – made up largely of teachers and lecturers in the sample – does not score highly. This pattern undoubtedly reflects the earlier sectoral pattern: unionised managers are mainly found in public service. It also reflects a wider pattern in which access to family-friendly practices increases up the occupational scale (Hoque and Noon, 2004: 492; Wood et al, 2003: 246). One of the benefits of union bargaining is that it can extend access to benefits of this kind to a broader range of employees and in many cases union representatives have negotiated on work-life issues of both a traditional and non-traditional kind for operatives, personal service and sales workers. It is clear, however, that more effort has been directed at white-collar workers, again probably reflecting employer policy and the fact that there is more scope to negotiate successfully on these issues for these groups of workers. The other main finding with regard to occupation is that for the male-dominated craft group, the traditional core of UK trade unionism, bargaining on traditional working time issues is more common than bargaining on flexibility and family-friendly practices.

Associations with officer characteristics are less pronounced. There is a slight tendency for women officers to report more bargaining on choice issues, suggesting that the identity of officers can sensitise them to a particular negotiating agenda (Heery, 2003: 294). A stronger association is found, however, with occupancy of a senior position in a trade union. Why this might be the case is not clear but it may be that senior officers, responsible for higher profile negotiations are more susceptible to influence from national conference and national policy. At the least it suggests that bargainers do not become more conservative in their orientation as they climb the bureaucratic hierarchy within unions.

Most of the officers surveyed (69 per cent) reported that they exercised a 'great deal' of autonomy in 'deciding the bargaining agenda with management'. This implies that their commitment to particular issues will shape the incidence of bargaining activity. The table provides modest support for this belief. Those declaring a strong commitment to work-life issues and to improving the position of part-time workers are marginally more likely to report bargaining on working time. The strongest connection, however, is with a declared commitment to working in partnership with employers. Only a minority of officers report a commitment of this kind but those that do, declare that they are more likely to have negotiated on both traditional and newer working time agendas. There is support here for the belief, advanced by the TUC, that the regulation of working time can be a matter for integrative bargaining.

The bottom rows in Table 4.3 show the influence of union characteristics. With regard to internal management systems, two elements seem to produce a slight upward increase in the incidence of bargaining. Officers who report that they set formal bargaining objectives, that they are subject to performance management, report more negotiation on a new working time agenda, while the same is true of those who have been trained in work-life issues. A major theme in recent discussion of trade unions is the importance of the articulation of union activity at workplace and higher levels (Heery, 2003: 288). The descriptive findings from the survey suggest that union management systems may provide a modest but significant degree of articulation, linking union policy on working time to bargaining practice at single employer level.

The strongest associations in the table are found for individual unions. The pattern here largely reproduces that for industry, in that it is the three public service unions (PCS, Prospect and UNISON) which emerge as having above average levels of bargaining on both types of working time issue. The levels of reported bargaining are particularly high for PCS and Prospect, the two civil service unions and this probably reflects the fact that the UK Government itself has prioritised family-friendly issues and so has provided a favourable bargaining context in that branch of the public service that it most directly controls.[8] The pattern, that is, reflects the opportunity structure facing trade unions. Other notable findings are the relatively low propensity of USDAW officers to negotiate on work-life issues and the tendency of officers in UCATT, the construction union, to prioritise a traditional working time agenda. In UNIFI, in contrast, the reverse set of priorities is seen with about two-thirds of officers reporting negotiation on choice issues while only a third report bargaining on compensation issues.

The final thing to note about Table 4.3 is that the pattern of findings for the newer positive flexibility agenda largely reproduces that for the traditional working time agenda.[9] There are exceptions as with UNIFI and UCATT where bargainers have privileged either new or traditional issues. In most cases, however, this is not the case and the evidence suggests, again, that we have seen an overlaying, not a supplanting, of one policy framework with another. The reason for this is probably that there are incentives in public policy for unions to continue to develop the traditional agenda alongside the newer. The Working Time Regulations have given unions an opportunity to bargain on hours reduction and increases in paid leave, just as the regulations on parental leave or flexible hours have done. Once again, therefore, the evidence points to the shaping of union activity by bargaining context and the openings this provides for pragmatic negotiators to initiate collective bargaining (see also Heery et al, 2004).

To complete the analysis of influences on bargaining, OLS regressions were performed on the choice and compensation scales, using all of the variables listed above apart from the dummies for individual unions. The latter were excluded because several are highly correlated with the industrial and occupational characteristics of union members. The results are shown in Table 4.4. The first thing to note about the table is that the level of variation explained in both tests is low: in combination the independent variables are not strongly related to either of the bargaining scales. Nevertheless, the process helps identify the relative significance of different influences. What emerges most strongly is that the most powerful influence on bargaining is the characteristics of union members and in particular the sector in which they work. The receptiveness of public administration and health to bargaining on work-life issues is confirmed, as are the distinctive pattern of retail, construction and craft employment. The main additional finding with regard to membership characteristics is the fact that bargaining on the new working time agenda is relatively common for factory and machine operatives when other factors are controlled for. There is evidence here of unions acting in the manner suggested above: extending access to working time benefits to those at the lower end of the occupational hierarchy.

The measures of officer and union characteristics entered in the regression explain relatively little. There is a weak association between a declared

Table 4.4 Relative strength of bargaining influences (OLS Regression)

	Choice	Compensation
	Standardised Beta Coefficients	
Industry:		
Manufacturing	−.011	.121
Construction	−.049	.123#
Retail trade	−.232**	−.028
Transport	.017	.093#
Financial services	.053	−.044
Public administration	.158*	.232***
Education	−.087	−.076
Health	.105#	−.067
Occupation:		
Managers	.057	.058
Professionals	.023	−.048
Assoc. professional & technical	.068	.134*
Clerical & secretarial	.062	−.013
Craft & related	−.141*	−.094
Personal service workers	.025	−.008
Sales workers	.085	−.031
Operatives	.135*	−.052
Contract & gender:		
Part-timers	.032	−.016
Women	−.001	.068
Officer training:		
Working time regulations	.007	−.044
Part-time regulations	−.015	.036
Work-life issues	.013	.022
Bargaining objectives	.098*	−.024
Characteristics:		
Sex (female = 1)	.012	−.046
Senior position	.092*	.019
Commitment:		
Work-life balance	.053	−.031
Part-time work	.092#	.103#
Partnership	.012	.087
Summary statistics	Adjusted R Square .163	Adjusted R Square .080
	F 4.485***	F 2.557***
	N = 482	N = 483

= .1; * = .05; ** = .01; *** = .001

commitment to improving conditions for part-time employees and bargaining on both new and old working time agendas. There are also weak associations between occupying a senior position and setting bargaining objectives and negotiation on flexible and family-friendly practices. There is support here for the arguments of the 'articulation school'. The inclusion of new items on the bargaining agenda is seemingly more likely at the centre of unions and where management systems are in place to encourage their diffusion. It must be emphasised, however, that factors of this kind tend to be secondary. The overall pattern suggests that the internal configuration of unions is not the primary influence on officer bargaining behaviour. Rather, it is the external opportunity structure and the receptiveness of (mainly public sector) employers that shapes bargaining on work-life issues.

Conclusion

The purpose of this chapter has been to review the development of UK union policy on work-life balance. Three main findings emerge. First, the British trade union movement has adjusted its policy on working time to encompass the theme of work-life balance and in the past decade we have seen the overlaying of a traditional concern to reduce basic hours and extend paid leave with a focus on family-friendly benefits and worker choice over the scheduling and duration of working time. This development, moreover, is visible at both national (policy development) and local (policy implementation) levels. There has been an uneven but not insignificant attempt to include the issue of work-life balance on the negotiating agenda, and the research, contrary to the view of pessimists, indicates that the latter is responsive to new issues in union policy.

Second, there is evidence of unions making a difference in the sense of registering negotiation success and concluding agreements on work-life issues. There is also evidence that unions have targeted bargaining activity at receptive employers but nevertheless the steady but unspectacular work of the labour movement in refining conditions of employment (cf. Flanders, 1975: 39) is visible in the study. There is also evidence of unions extending access to family-friendly and positive flexibility policies down the occupational hierarchy to the particular benefit of manual workers in manufacturing and other machine operating roles. This in itself could be taken as an indicator of unions promoting work-life policy on social justice grounds but there is also direct evidence of unions framing the issue of working time in this way. Unions have repeated the business case favoured by the UK Government but they have also developed a health and safety, gender equality and 'social utility' case for the regulation of working time. The latter emphasises the broader social and familial benefits that accrue from work-life policy and unions have been quite successful, operating in conjunction with other pressure groups, in framing the issue as serving a general, not particular or narrowly economic, set of interests.

Third and finally the research has identified some of the factors within and beyond unions that encourage the inclusion of items on the bargaining agenda. Within unions, there is evidence that supports the arguments of the articulation school. Bargaining on work-life issues is more common amongst senior officers, closer to the heart of union policy and is also found where there is a system of performance management encouraging the diffusion of the issue amongst negotiators. Beyond unions, the key factor seems to be the structure of opportunity. There has been most negotiation on topics where there has been recent legislation, suggesting that unions have used the law as a lever to open bargaining with employers; in many cases to go beyond statutory minimum entitlements. There has also been a concentration of bargaining in the public services and in the civil service in particular. The continuing distinctiveness of the public sector emerges from this research and there is evidence of the state continuing to use public sector employment, notwithstanding the new public management, as a model for employer practice elsewhere.

Notes

1. The TUC's guide to work-life balance, *Changing Times*, defines positive flexibility as a situation, 'where working people have more autonomy and choice, and the employer invests in development and training and works in partnership with the workforce. This version of flexibility produces a skilled and adaptable workforce, meeting the employers' needs for competitiveness, whilst also increasing workers' security' (TUC 2001a: 4). This position was reinforced in interview. A TUC policy officer said that in the past 'flexible working' had been 'dirty words' for unions but now, 'flexibility is all about giving people choices over how they work, work-life balance' (Interview, May 2001).
2. This list is not exhaustive and there have been other significant union policies on working time, including attempts to harmonise basic hours and leave entitlements across the manual/non-manual status divide (Price and Price, 1994) and secure earlier retirement.
3. The UK's Working Time Regulations 1998 implement the EU's Working Time Directive. They have endowed British workers with a statutory entitlement to paid leave for the first time, which currently stands at four weeks per annum (Dickens and Hall, 2003: 132).
4. In interview it was reported that the British and Dutch trade union movements played the most active roles in pressing for and negotiating the framework agreement.
5. Other reasons have also probably been significant. The decline of union bargaining power in the UK means that primary reliance on collective bargaining to secure changes in working time is less feasible as a union strategy (Terry, 2003). The break up of industry bargaining in much of the country since the early 1980s (Brown et al, 2003: 198–201), moreover, means that bargaining cannot be used in the manner it was in the past, with industry agreements providing a common framework of working time that applied across much of the economy. In a context of weakened unions and fragmented bargaining structures, employment law is more attractive to unions as a means of pursuing the common rule of developing minimum standards with very broad coverage.
6. The research was funded by the Economic and Social Research Council under the *Future of Work* programme (Award No. L212252023). Thanks are due to Melanie

Simms for help in administering the survey and to the TUC and to all unions and
union officers that cooperated with the research.

7. Cronbach's alpha, the measure of statistical reliability for the scales, was 0.88 for
   the choice scale and 0.63 for the compensation scale. The latter figure is low but
   the scale comprised only two items.
8. Diversity policy is a central theme in government policy for the civil service,
   outlined in its statement *Modernising Government*. A manager who was interviewed in a civil service agency in 2001 explained that greater scope for reduced
   and flexible hours working had been introduced with union agreement partly
   because, 'We do have to respond to the views of the centre...We have to do it for
   business reasons but it helps to have someone chivvying us along as well'.
9. The two scales are correlated: $P = 0.570$, sig. 000.

Acknowledgement

Thanks are due to Paul Blyton and Ali Dastmalchian for comments on an earlier
draft. The usual disclaimer applies.

References

Arrowsmith, J. (2002) 'The struggle over working time in nineteenth and twentieth
century Britain', *Historical Studies in Industrial Relations*, 13: 83–118.

Bewley, H. and Fernie, S. (2003) 'What do unions do for women?', in Gospel, H. and
Wood, S. (eds) *Representing Workers: Union Recognition and Membership in Britain*,
London: Routledge, 92–118.

Brown, W., Marginson, P. and Walsh, J. (2003) 'The management of pay as the
influence of collective bargaining diminishes', in Edwards, P. (ed.) *Industrial
Relations: Theory and Practice*, second edition, Oxford: Blackwell, 189–213.

Budd, J.W. and Mumford, K. (2004) 'Trade unions and family-friendly policies in
Britain', *Industrial and Labor Relations Review*, 57 (2): 204–22.

Carter, B. and Fairbrother, P. (2004) 'The transformation of British public sector
industrial relations: from 'model employer' to marketised relations', *Historical
Studies in Industrial Relations Journal*, 7: 119–46.

Clegg, H.A. (1972) *The System of Industrial Relations in Great Britain*, enlarged edition,
Oxford: Basil Blackwell.

Dickens, L. (1988) 'Women – a rediscovered resource?' *Industrial Relations Journal*,
20 (3): 167–75.

Dickens, L. (2000) 'Promoting gender equality at work – a potential role for trade
union action', *Journal of Interdisciplinary Gender Studies*, 5 (2): 27–45.

Dickens, L. and Hall, M. (2003) 'Labour law and industrial relations: a new settle-
ment?', in Edwards, P. (ed.) *Industrial Relations: Theory and Practice*, second edition,
Oxford: Blackwell, 124–56.

DTI (2003) *Flexible Working: The Business Case*, London: Department of Trade and
Industry.

Flanders, A. (1975) *Management and Unions: The Theory and Reform of Industrial
Relations*, London: Faber and Faber.

Frege, C.M., Heery, E. and Turner, L. (2004) 'Trade union coalition-building', in
Frege, C.M. and Kelly, J. (eds) *Varieties of Unionism: Strategies for Union Revitalization
in a Globalizing Economy*, Oxford: Oxford University Press, 137–58.

Green, F. (1997) 'Union recognition and paid holiday entitlement', *British Journal of
Industrial Relations*, 35 (2): 243–55.

Heery, E. (1998) 'Campaigning for part-time workers', *Work, Employment and Society*,
17 (3): 351–66.

Heery, E. (2003) 'Trade unions and industrial relations', in Ackers, P. and Wilkinson, A. (eds) *Understanding Work and Employment: Industrial Relations in Transition*, Oxford: Oxford University Press, 278–304.

Heery, E., Conley, H., Delbridge, R., Simms, M. and Stewart, P. (2004) 'Trade union responses to non-standard work', in Healy, G., Heery, E., Taylor, P. and Brown, W. (eds) *The Future of Worker Representation*, Basingstoke: Palgrave Macmillan, 127–50.

Hoque, K. and Noon, M. (2004) 'Equal opportunities policy and practice in Britain: evaluating the "empty shell" hypothesis", *Work, Employment and Society*, 18 (3): 481–506.

House of Commons Education and Employment Committee (1999) *Part-time Working in the UK: Education and Employment Second Report*, London: House of Commons.

Hyman, R. (1997) 'The future of employee representation', *British Journal of Industrial Relations*, 35 (3): 309–36.

Marginson, P. and Sisson, K. (2004) *European Integration and Industrial Relations: Multi-level Governance in the Making*, Basingstoke: Palgrave Macmillan.

McBride, A. (2001) *Gender Democracy in Trade Unions*, Aldershot: Ashgate.

McKinlay, A. and McNulty, D. (1992) 'At the cutting edge of new realism: the engineers' 35 hour week campaign', *Industrial Relations Journal*, 23 (3): 205–13.

Millward, N., Bryson, A. and Forth, J. (2000) *All Change at Work? British Employment Relations 1980–1998, as Portrayed by the Workplace Industrial Relations Series*, London: Routledge.

Price, L. and Price, R. (1994) 'Change and continuity in the status divide', in Sisson, K. (ed.) *Personnel Management: A Comprehensive Guide to Theory and Practice in Britain*, second edition, Oxford: Blackwell, 527–61.

Rubery, J., Deakin, S. and Horrel, S. (1994) 'United Kingdom', in Bosch, G., Dawkins, P. and Michon, F. (eds) *Times are Changing: Working Time in 14 Industrialised Countries*, Geneva: International Institute for Labour Studies, 261–88.

Taylor, R. (2000) *The TUC: From the General Strike to New Unionism*, London: Palgrave.

Terry, M. (2003) 'Employee representation: shop stewards and the new legal framework', in Edwards, P. (ed.) *Industrial Relations: Theory and Practice*, second edition, Oxford: Blackwell, 257–84.

Thompson, E.P. (1968) *The Making of the English Working Class*, Harmondsworth: Penguin Books.

TUC (2000) *Response to DTI Consultation on Implementation of Part-time Work Directive*, London: Trades Union Congress.

TUC (2001a) *Changing Times: A TUC Guide to Work-Life Balance*, London: Trades Union Congress.

TUC (2001b) *Rights not Favours: Submission to 'Work and Parents' Green Paper*, London: Trades Union Congress.

TUC (2002) *General Council Report*, London: Trades Union Congress.

TUC (2004) *General Council Report*, London: Trades Union Congress.

Turnbull, P. (2003) 'What do unions do now?' *Journal of Labor Research*, 24 (3): 492–526.

Whitehouse, G. (2001) 'Industrial agreements and work/family provisions: trends and prospects under enterprise bargaining', *Labour and Industry*, 12 (1): 109–30.

Wood, S., de Menezes, L.M. and Lasoasa, A. (2003) 'Family-friendly management in Great Britain: testing various perspectives', *Industrial Relations*, 42 (2): 221–50.

5

State Policy and Work-Life Integration: Past, Present and Future Approaches

Betsy Blunsdon and Nicola McNeil

Introduction

The difficulties experienced by individuals in managing their many social roles (worker, partner, parent, carer, homemaker and so on) have been the subject of growing interest in academic, political and media circles. As noted elsewhere in this volume, the dialogue surrounding the integration of these different spheres of life has been further stimulated by significant macro-level shifts in Western countries – in particular, the growing insecurity of labour markets, the abandonment of Keynesian employment policies, increasing levels of consumption, the intensification of work and leisure activities, and the increasing engagement of women in part-time and full-time employment. These factors have brought into question the conventional notions of a labour market and welfare state, in favour of a dual-income, household approach to social policy.

Few commentators have challenged the importance of the state's role in facilitating work-life integration. Moreover, the policy frameworks employed by governments to promote work-life balance have been subject to relatively little scrutiny. The majority of research and discussion has focused on understanding the role overload and conflict faced particularly by working mothers. There has been limited critical attention given to the role and effectiveness of government in two main areas of work-life balance policy – first, in providing a policy framework that assists and enhances the integration of work, leisure and domestic activities for both men and women, and second, in employing policies to redefine some of the normative and structural constraints faced by individuals negotiating their life course.

Western governments have to date typically utilised a variety of mechanisms to address the experienced tension between work and family life. This has been delivered most often through a combination of state-provided and market-regulated services and the regulation of terms and conditions of employment. However, changes towards family-responsive workplaces have typically remained slow and sporadic. This has lead to questions about whether the common strategy of devolving control over determining the terms and conditions of employment to the enterprise level, coupled with market-based provision of services, will deliver effective or equitable outcomes for individuals and families in the future. Further, commentators have argued that current approaches to policy formulation have neglected adequately to consider ways in which individuals within a family or household context make choices about how to spend their time and resources, given the normative and structural pressures that create or constrain available options (Crompton, 2002; Hakim, 2000; McRae, 2003).

This chapter considers first the broad question of the role of government in work-life balance. Secondly, it discusses the macro-level policy responses to work-life balance, both through welfare regimes and through industrial relations systems. Thirdly, it outlines arguments concerning the need to consider household structures and individual preferences in social policy frameworks in more detail. To conclude, we argue that one requirement for a more comprehensive policy development is greater multi-level research that will enable a better understanding of how institutions, households and individuals interact and impact on work-family outcomes.

What is the role of government in work-life balance?

As discussed in more detail elsewhere in this collection, there has been a series of social and economic changes that have impacted on working time and the time available to engage in other aspects of life including leisure, personal care, domestic and caring responsibilities. The increase in female participation in paid employment and the growth of dual-earner households are but two examples of changes that have increased the challenges associated with balancing the demands of work, family and other activities. This situation has ensured that debates continue about the most appropriate means to address the problems associated with work-family conflict amongst various stakeholders – the state, employers, families, households and individuals. 'Work-family' issues are now found in the policy discourse of most Western nations and expressions such as 'family-friendly workplaces', the 'flexible workplace' and 'work-life balance' are now commonplace in the lexicon of industrial relations and welfare policy.

The role and extent of state involvement in the work-family arena rests on the issue of whether the ends to be achieved and interests to be served are of 'public' interest, therefore implying that collective rather than individual action is required for their attainment (Mayer, 1985). In the area of work and family, this involves concerns about whether work-family issues, such as accessible and affordable childcare, maternity and paternity leave provisions, and access to domestic support are 'public' matters, to be addressed by government, rather than private issues, to be considered by individuals, families and households. In most Western countries, work-family issues are considered to be of public concern and are increasingly being discussed and debated in public forums and are legitimately recognised by government. In addition, there is some agreement that certain issues belong on the policy agenda if they involve an element of 'social risk', the idea that individual situations or decisions can impact on the overall welfare of society.

Although there is general agreement that work-family issues are important societal concerns and therefore belong in the public policy discourse, uncertainties characterise the best way of providing the goods and services appropriate for work-family balance. Much of the discussion centres on the amount of public monies that go towards the provision of work-family support services, compared to the level of private benefits that accrue to individuals as a result of engaging in these activities (Burstein and Bricher, 1997). These debates around the role of government in the provision and funding of support services are not new. Such issues have been widely contested, particularly in relation to the provision of education to primary, secondary and tertiary students. Mayer (1985: 70) illustrates the arguments in relation to education, explaining that:

'education is a communalistic interest, that is, an individual interest shared by all members of society. It would be easy to conclude from this recognition that public schools are necessary to meet this need, that is that a system of public education constitutes a public interest. On closer inspection this turns out not to be the case, as education could be attained through individual action; each child could be educated in his or her own home by private tutors'.

Similar arguments are now at the forefront of debates concerning the role of government in alleviating some of the role conflict experienced by individuals. For example, in relation to childcare, we may agree that society has a moral obligation to ensure that children are adequately supervised and receive care, and that enormous benefits will accrue to society if this occurs. However, there is far less agreement about where the responsibility for providing and financing childcare lies. Does the responsibility rest with parents and households, communities, employers, or the market (as in private childcare services), and what role, if any, should the government play in the provision of care for children?

Governments and policy-makers at different times have offered varying solutions to work-life balance questions in their approaches to welfare systems and industrial relations. Such responses are driven in part by an ideological agenda, underpinned by widely held societal values and based on perceived needs within the community. The next section reviews this variation and illustrates the different roles that governments around the world play in work and family life.

Macro-level policy responses: The state

Macro-level economic and social policies, by their very nature, are employed by governments to set the broad policy agendas during terms in administration. Policy-makers are primarily concerned with the betterment of society as a whole, and therefore tend to define the population as a homogeneous set of actors with commonly-held needs and desires (Crompton, 2002; Hakim, 2000; McRae, 2003). The reality, of course, is that society consists of a complex amalgam of actors and institutions, with varying requirements. As a result, there is often only a loose coupling between the economic and social policies enunciated by governments and the actual needs of constituents. This is due, in part, to the complex role of economic and social policy-making in determining both the current and future direction of nation states and the inherent difficulties in identifying 'real' needs and implementing a policy framework to adequately fulfil the requirements of both individuals and society as a whole. These tensions are clear in the area of work and family balance, as the wants of individuals are weighed against the needs of society as a whole.

As a way to overcome this individual-collective challenge, governments have tended to adopt unitarist perspectives to policy-making in the work-life area. Policy outcomes have targeted broad groups, such as working women or single parents, without recognising variations in need within these groups (see Hakim, 2000 for her critique on 'universal' policies). In some cases, there has been criticism of work-life balance policies based on the lack of consumption of government incentives. In the UK, for example, lack of take-up of 'family-friendly' options has been observed in both quantitative and qualitative studies (Cully, Woodland, O'Reilly and Dix, 1999; Dex and Smith, 2002; Houston and Walmsley, 2004) though there are some signs of change in certain initiatives (Holt and Grainger, 2005). A pluralist policy perspective would require the identification of the widespread and diverse needs of the population. In addition, the development of policies and practices to alleviate some of the specific challenges faced by individuals and households in balancing their work and non-work life poses a mounting challenge. The increasing differentiation evident in individual and household circumstances (such as the growth in lone-parent households) has made this criticism of past approaches more salient (these issues will be considered in the latter sections of this chapter). However, the cost and administration of complex policy initiatives, coupled with concerns about the perceived equity of such programmes, have represented major obstacles to change. Variations in state approaches to work-family assistance are related to differences in welfare regimes and industrial relations frameworks, as described in the next section.

Macro-level policy responses to role conflict: welfare states

The welfare policies implemented by governments are a public attempt to manage, and minimise, social risk (Esping-Andersen, 1999). Governments have sought to provide forms of assistance to individuals and households who are at social risk arising from role conflict, through a variety of different means: the provision of welfare support and services (either state provision, market provision or a combination of both); labour market reform, generally aimed at making working conditions more flexible; and through an often 'silent' reliance upon the family to meet the increasing needs and expectations of individuals (Lewis, 1992, 1999; Walby, 2003). The notion of 'social risk' refers to the aggregate of the risks faced by individuals in everyday life, which manifest as 'social risks' when the fate of individuals has consequences for the welfare of society in general – for example, when risks faced by individuals negatively impact on health, quality of life, the care of children or the safety of the community. The risks faced by individuals may also evolve into social risks when the issues involved are considered by the wider society as worthy of public deliberation. Further, it may be argued that part of the role conflict experienced by individuals is a consequence of macro-level pressures, such as increasing levels of consumption, the intensification of work and the increasing engagement of women in part-time and full-time employment (Lewis, 2003). However, individuals' responses to such pressures can be mediated, to some degree, by macro-level intervention.

The role conflict experienced by individuals as they juggle work and family responsibilities is a social risk to post-industrial society. Indeed, there is increasing evidence demonstrating the inability of individuals and households to adequately address the inherent tension between work and family life (and the subsequent outcomes of such tension). This creates a social risk which is having significant consequences at a societal level. These effects include poor health outcomes (Sparks, Cooper, Fried and Shirom, 1997); decreased quality of life and lower levels of life satisfaction (Adams, King and King, 1996; Edwards and Rothbard, 2000; Smith Major, Klein and Ehrhart, 2002); decreased fertility rates; and the absence of parental supervision of children (the so-called 'latch-key kid' generation) and other dependents (Albrecht, 2003).

Esping-Andersen (1990) argues that the central tenet of a welfare state is the creation of 'equality' amongst all citizens. However, varying understandings and applications of equality has led to the development of divergent welfare regimes throughout the world. Different welfare states emphasise different egalitarian justice principles and advocate differing forms of social cohesion. Governments endeavour to find institutional responses to the issue of social solidarity by creating rules and regulations to govern who should have equal rights, what kind of shared protection, and who should fund such schemes (Arts and Gelissen, 2001). Korpi (1983) further suggests that there are fundamental questions that need to be addressed when analysing the way in which welfare states provide support for the reconciliation of work and family life. The first question concerns the treatment of gender inequality within the welfare system. Should the state take an active role in articulating welfare policies to address perceived gender inequities within society, or should this be a matter for the family and the market? Bittman (1999: 40) in his comparison of gender differences in domestic labour in Finland and Australia, for example, argues that social policy can make a difference. He notes that, 'The Scandinavian experience shows that entitlements to generous parental leave, high quality child care, and to family-friendly hours of paid work are all necessary components of an equitable solution to the difficulties of combining work and family in the twenty-first century.' An issue implicit in such discussions is the extent to which domestic labour (including child rearing), still primarily borne by women, should be considered as a public good and worthy of recognition by the welfare state. A related question concerns the extent to which models of family income should be promoted by government policy; for example, should welfare policy actively promote a male breadwinner or dual-income model for families?

Esping-Andersen (1990) identifies three models (or ideal types) of welfare states: liberal, conservative and social-democratic. In creating this typology, he suggests that welfare states should be classified according to two main characteristics: the degree of decommodification of the welfare state, and the extent to which the welfare state contributes to patterns of social stratification, both in terms of state- and market-provided services. 'Decommodified welfare states' typically administer welfare systems through the implementation of a labyrinth of rules and standards. This includes the regulations governing access and eligibility, income replacement levels, and the range of protections against social risks (Esping-Andersen, 1999). Hence, decommodification is essentially a measure of the degree to which individuals are able to maintain their livelihood independent of labour market participation. The basic elements of Esping-Andersen's welfare systems, and their approach to easing role conflict within society, are listed in Table 5.1.

Table 5.1   A summary typology of welfare states and their role in alleviating role conflict

	Liberal	Social-democratic	Conservative
Welfare State:			
Unit of analysis	Individual	Society	Family / Corporatism
Providers of welfare services	Market	State	Family
Degree of decommodification	Low	High	High (for breadwinner)
Importance of institutions in addressing work-life balance:			
Family	Minor	Minor	Paramount
Market	Paramount	Minor	Minor
State	Minor	Paramount	Ancillary
Examples	USA	Sweden	Germany

Adapted from Esping-Andersen (1999: 85)

Liberal Welfare States

Liberal welfare states emphasise notions of equality, both in terms of equal opportunity for social actors and individualistic equity (Esping-Andersen, 1990, 1999). Liberal welfare states are characterised by a minimalist approach to the provision of welfare by the state. Individuals are considered to be responsible for their own welfare, and their ability to 'take care of themselves' and their kin is ostensibly determined by the market, through monetary rewards for both performance and endeavour (Esping-Andersen, 1999). The reliance on the market as a surrogate for the state's provision of welfare generally benefits only individuals whose daily activities are valued by the market, and does not, for example, provide an allocation for domestic labour or the care of children (Wheelock, Oughton and Baines, 2003). Castles (1993) notes that Anglo-Saxon nations generally adopt a liberal welfare model, including the US, the UK, Canada and Australia.

The provision of welfare is based upon a 'targeted social assistance' model rather than a model based on welfare as an absolute right. This approach relies upon a narrow definition of the term 'social risk', and upon means testing as a criterion for eligibility (Esping-Andersen, 1999). It is not uncommon in liberal states for there to be an absence of comprehensive national healthcare, sickness and maternity benefits and parental leave provisions, due to the market's failure to adequately provide such provisions and services (Myles, 1998). Liberal regimes typically respond to such a gap by implementing targeted policies to provide a minimum safety net for those in absolute need.

In the absence of state-provided initiatives, individuals are required to enter into private market-based arrangements with providers, with the assumption that an economic behaviour model drives decision-making (Wheelock, 2001). Families are generally left to their own devices to resolve problems of care of dependents, work and the distribution of domestic labour. For example, childcare is generally provided in the marketplace by private, commercial providers, with only part of the costs associated with the services being provided by governments, in the form of vouchers, subsidies or tax credits. The Australian Government, for example, currently sponsors parental uptake of childcare through subsidies to parents and providers, but on a sliding scale (Wooden, 2002). Despite this, the Australian Government's expenditure on childcare is amongst the lowest in the OECD (Pocock, 2003). Similarly, the US federal income tax code contains a (non-refundable) income tax credit to working parents for expenses associated with necessary childcare (Gustafsson and Stafford, 1995). In Canada, provincial governments provide subsidised childcare for some low income families (Mahon, 2000).

It has been argued that the liberal approach to employment policy and reliance on market forces has led to an increased emphasis on providing a business case for the provision of work-family arrangements (Lewis, 1999).

Access to parental and carer's leave and other benefits in liberal states is frequently determined by a process of decentralised bargaining between collective agencies and employers (this issue will be discussed further in the next section). For example, in the US, relatively few employees are provided with paid parental leave when a child is born or ill, with such benefits provided by employers on a voluntary basis (unpaid leave for the birth or sickness of a child has been mandatory since 1994) (Kuhlen, 2004). In Australia, whilst a maximum of 52 weeks unpaid maternity leave is guaranteed by statute to women, the provision of paid leave is determined by enterprise-level agreements. Five days of leave is also guaranteed in Australia for the care of family and household members, either as annual leave, make-up time, time-in-lieu of overtime, rostered days off or unpaid leave (Evans, 2001).

Conservative welfare states

Esping-Andersen (1999) identifies a second type of welfare regime which is termed a 'conservative welfare state'. Conservative welfare states exist in Italy and Germany, and are generally premised upon the preservation of equity within society. Welfare institutions and programmes are designed to reinforce and conserve the hierarchy and status differentials. Conservative or corporatist welfare states are characterised by high degrees of familialism and a tendency towards the pooling of social risk within occupational bands (Esping-Andersen, 1990, 1999). The welfare state is defined by interest group cooperation rather than social competition. The provision of welfare, in the form of fiscal benefits (in particular, health and pensions), is delivered through corporatist schemes consisting of employer and employee contributions, and is therefore provided along occupational classes. There is a strong bias towards the 'male breadwinner' model of the family within these societies (Duncan, 1996). The family is viewed as the central provider of welfare, in terms of caring and financial support for the young, elderly and unwell. The state provision of welfare benefits occurs principally when there is a 'family breakdown'.

Policy responses in conservative regimes to the issue of work-life balance are primarily based on general family support, founded upon the male wage-earner model. Broadly speaking, governments provide limited fiscal support to families, through child cash allowances and family tax benefits. Consequently, such schemes may deter mothers of young children from engaging in paid work. For example, the policies put in place by successive Italian governments emphasise the importance of familial responsibilities and support a male breadwinner model (Duncan, 1996). Some assistance is provided to individuals and families through a system of grants, parental leave and childcare support to improve work-family outcomes. Fiscal assistance for families is provided to families with low incomes. However, the amount of the benefit is inversely related to the income of the family (defined as the income of the claimant, spouse and sons under the age of 18 years).

There are increasing efforts in Italy to ensure there is adequate childcare and nurseries for all children over the age of three years, with priority being given to the children of single parents and parents on low incomes. In 2002, six per cent of children under the age of three and 75 per cent of children aged between three and six years of age were enrolled in publicly-funded childcare facilities in Italy (Kuhlen, 2004). In terms of support for parental leave, maternity leave benefits include three months mandatory paid maternity leave post-birth (individuals receiving 80 per cent of earnings during this time). Parents are also given the option of sharing up to six months paid parental leave (receiving 30 per cent of their salary) for care of children under the age of three years, and six months unpaid parental leave for care of children under the age of eight years (ibid). Some organisations are entitled to apply for a government grant to assist in the provision of flexible working conditions for parents with young children (including flexible working time arrangements and teleworking, for example). However, it is argued that the lack of specific support for females with child-rearing responsibilities in the workplace is a major deterrent to workforce participation in Italy (Haas, 2003).

In Germany, there are several welfare initiatives in place to assist individuals and families in reconciling work and family roles. The Germany welfare model provides financial support for the 'stay-at-home' parent with child-rearing responsibilities, with some provision for publicly-funded day care for older children (O'Hara, 1998; Trzcinski, 2000). These provisions include guaranteed child-rearing leave of approximately three years per child, with recipients receiving a flat rate of compensation. Parents are permitted to share this leave entitlement, although the uptake rate for fathers in Germany is very low (approximately two per cent) due in part to the low levels of compensation offered. Mothers are entitled to a paid maternity leave period of 14 weeks on full pay (subsidised by social insurance and employer contributions) although during this time payments are not subject to tax or social security contributions. In terms of childcare, every child aged three years and over is entitled to kindergarten care. Parents are also entitled to a statutory maximum of ten days leave per year to care for ill children (Kuhlen, 2004). The policies aimed at reducing role conflict in conservative welfare states invariably reinforce the view of the family as the primary provider of care, with the state intervening only when family funds have been expended.

Social-democratic welfare states

Esping-Andersen (1999) identifies the social-democratic welfare state as being predicated upon ideas of universal solidarity and egalitarianism. This means equality in outcomes for all: all citizens enjoy the same rights and benefits, irrespective of class or status (Esping-Andersen, 1990, 1999). Social assistance through the welfare system is seen to be an individual's right of citizenship. The state is totally responsible for social welfare, guaranteeing a minimum standard of living and undertaking to prevent social exclusion, coupled with relatively generous benefits and a high expectation of meeting the needs of constituents. These welfare states attempt to reduce reliance on private welfare (i.e. the market provision of welfare) and are characterised by high levels of decommodification. The Nordic countries of Norway, Denmark, Sweden and Finland fall into this cluster of welfare regimes (O'Hara, 1998).

Social-democratic welfare regimes have approached the problem of work-life balance by promoting policies that transfer the provision of care from the family to the public sector, thereby supporting gender equality through encouraging the independence of women from family responsibilities (Williams and Cohen Cooper, 2004). The Swedish welfare system, for example, provides a variety of types of assistance for families, including financial grants, parental leave and subsidised childcare. State-supported parental leave provisions in Sweden allow for up to 64 weeks of paid leave, with the at-home parent receiving up to 80 per cent of their usual salary during the first 52 weeks leave and 60 per cent of their usual salary for the remaining 12 weeks (Kuhlen, 2004). Such policies require a significant revenue base in order to finance such commitments, to the extent that in countries such as Sweden, full employment is almost necessary to maintain the required taxation base.

Fiscal assistance is provided to families in Sweden in the form of a universal child allowance for children under 16 years of age (20 years of age for students), with increasing levels of support for larger families. Single parents are guaranteed monthly support either from child support payments from the other parent or advanced maintenance allowance from the state (Kuhlen, 2004). Up to 450 days of paid parental leave is available to be shared by parents; days can be transferred to the other person except for a minimum of 30 days per parent (Haas, 2003). Parental leave payments are the same as sickness insurance (80 per cent of usual salary) with special conditions regarding membership, previous work and minimum payments. Furthermore, mothers can draw upon a special allowance (80 per cent of normal wage) to account for reduced work ability 60 days before confinement for a maximum of 50 days. There is also a temporary parental allowance of 60 days per child per year for the care of sick children under the age of 12. The various forms of public childcare in Sweden today are available to children aged one to 12 years. Children who have yet to start school can attend pre-school activities, while school children have access to school-age childcare outside school hours. The costs for public childcare are met by state grants, local tax revenue and parental fees (which are capped at between one and three per cent of the family's income, depending on the number and age of the children) (Haas, 2003). There have been two major outcomes of this policy platform worth noting – first, a sharp increase in the number of women participating in the labour market in Sweden, from 53 per cent in 1963 to 86 per cent in 1990 and second, a relatively high fertility rate (Hirdman, 1989).

Criticisms of the typology

Typologies of welfare states provide an interesting point of contrast for varying welfare regimes, and how the various ideologies and latent values influence work-family balance policies. However, it is important to note that the typology of welfare states offered by Esping-Andersen has attracted criticism, particularly from feminist theorists who argue that the idea of decommodification fails to account for the welfare work provided by women within the household (Figart and Murari, 2000; Lewis, 1992; Orloff, 1993; Sainsbury, 1994; Wheelock, Oughton and Baines, 2003). Domestic chores and the care of dependents (including children, the elderly and infirm) occur outside the boundaries of welfare systems and are not regulated by market forces (Sainsbury, 1994). In this way, Esping-Andersen's typology, which relies upon classifying the constitution of welfare regimes in terms of the decommodified state and commodified market provision, does not account for the unpaid welfare work undertaken by both women and men. Nor does it account for the idea that an element of social risk for women is their ability to engage in or withhold these domestic duties. In a later analysis, however, Esping-Andersen (1999) acknowledges that such domestic work is performed on a decommodified basis, and outside the jurisdiction of existing welfare or market regimes. Reflecting this, the concept of familialisation was subsequently included as an element of the classification scheme – that is, the extent to which policy is predicated on the expectation that families are the main providers of family members' welfare. Subsequent theorists have argued that Esping-Andersen's typology of welfare states requires expansion to include additional welfare state types, in particular to include states with welfare systems based upon high levels of familialism (such as Southern Mediterranean countries) (Arts and Gelissen, 2001).

Macro-level policy responses to role conflict: industrial relations

Industrial relations systems complement the welfare state as the primary institutional framework that underpins most of the policies aimed at addressing role conflict. There is a close nexus between types of welfare states and industrial relations systems. Inclusive welfare states, such as the social-democratic system, tend to develop in conjunction with centralised, coordinated employee bargaining systems (as is the case with most Nordic countries) (Esping-Andersen, 1999). On the other hand, residual welfare states, such as liberal regimes, are associated with decentralised bargaining systems and weak unionism (Esping-Andersen, 1999). Industrial relations systems play an important role in the provision of policies to assist individuals and families in combining the spheres of work, family and leisure. The literature pertaining to work-life integration is dominated by references to the need to foster 'family-friendly workplaces'. This includes the need for increased flexibility in terms and conditions of employment and supervisory support to assist in alleviating the role pressures experienced by workers (Aldous, 1990; Fox and Dwyer, 1999; Strachan and Burgess, 1998). Centralised, coordinated bargaining systems have tended to deliver more comprehensive, homogeneous and egalitarian terms and conditions of employment for all labour market participants (Esping-Andersen, 1999). Guaranteed uniformity with respect to maternity, paternity and carer's leave entitlements and flexible working time models have been the hallmark of such systems.

Industrial relations systems based on a decentralised model of bargaining have generally devolved the negotiation of terms and conditions of employment from the state to the company or enterprise-level, with organisations negotiating employment contracts with collective agencies and in some cases, with individual workers. The state generally will legislatively provide for a minimum 'safety net' of terms and conditions of employment (for example, minimum wages, annual and unpaid parental leave entitlements). Advocates argue that decentralised bargaining models can provide workers with access to more targeted, innovative benefits, as enterprises are more able to respond to the needs of their particular group of employees than the state (Blau and Ehrenberg, 1997; Lewis and Lewis, 1996). In Australia and the UK, there is evidence to suggest that enterprise-level agreements have provided for flexible working arrangements, including school-term-only work, telework, on-site childcare facilities, up to 12 days additional leave per year in lieu of overtime, a fiscal contribution to the provision of a carer for an ill child while the principal carer is at work, and guaranteeing the availability of part-time work to mothers returning to the organisation after maternity leave (Evans, 2001).

There has been debate about the merits of a decentralised bargaining system, particularly with respect to the treatment of women and part-time workers, and the danger of creating inequity within the labour market. Access to employer-provided family-friendly initiatives are a function of a bargaining process, and will inevitably lead to inequitable outcomes for workers in different occupations and industries. Furthermore, critics have cited evidence suggesting that decentralised bargaining has not been conducive to the provision of basic work-family measures (such as parental leave). In a longitudinal study of the content of industrial agreements within Australia for example, Whitehouse (2001) concluded that such agreements typically demonstrate a low incidence of family-friendly measures, but also notes the increasing prevalence of measures relating to working time flexibility within industrial agreements. Whilst this may provide some workers with flexibility over their working hours, such agreements also serve to permit employers to vary working hours and hinder the capacity of employees to predict and manage their working time (Whitehouse, 2001; Strachan and Burgess, 2000). Furthermore, there is evidence to suggest that decentralised bargaining has facilitated access to family-friendly benefits being traded for higher rates of remuneration, and also that minority groups may not be adequately represented or provided for within such agreements (Eveline, 1999).

The industrial relations framework and the power of individual organisations to set the terms and conditions of employment for their employees provides an important context for understanding issues of work-family integration. However, at the core of a complete understanding of the mechanics of social policy in this area is an appreciation of how individuals will respond to the opportunities and constraints provided to them by work-life integration policies. As we now go on to discuss, the identification of family and household structure and individual choices are also essential in framing relevant and appropriate work-life integration policies.

The problem with work-life balance policy: addressing family, household and individual needs

The design of social policy is a complex and multi-faceted task, contingent upon a great many considerations – political ideology, economic position, characteristics of the population and some presumptions about human motivation and behaviour, to name a few. The enactment and ultimate success of these policies in achieving the goals of government depends upon an intimate understanding of how units within society (organisations, families, households or individuals) will respond to policy initiatives, based on their needs and wants (Le Grand, 1997). In the area of work-life balance, this translates into a need to understand how families, households and individuals will respond to and effectively utilise childcare policies, family benefit payments, parental leave policies and other policies enunciated by governments. As discussed in the preceding section and elsewhere in this collection, there is increasing evidence to suggest that whilst governments are providing different types of assistance through their welfare and industrial relations systems, the lack of uptake of such provisions by families, households and individuals, is compromising the success of work-life integration policies (Cully, Woodland, O'Reilly and Dix, 1999; Dex and Smith, 2002; Holt and Grainger, 2005; Houston and Walmsley, 2004). Moreover, policy-makers have been criticised for adopting a view of society as consisting of a homogeneous set of actors, with policies targeting perceived, generic needs (Crompton, 2002; Hakim, 2000; McRae, 2003).

There is no question that successful policy development in the area of work-life balance has been complicated by the increasing variation in both household types and individual preferences that has resulted from the social and economic changes that have characterised most Western societies since the 1960s. The social changes documented throughout this collection – the increased participation of women in paid employment, rising divorce rates, control over fertility, and the rise in different types of households, for example – have resulted in greater social heterogeneity. The standard breadwinner model of households that characterised social policy prior to this period assumed a homogeneity of the family and sex roles which, it can be argued, is becoming increasingly irrelevant. Hakim (2000: 251) notes that 'most governments are biased towards social uniformity rather than diversity, towards a single model of the family and sex-roles rather than a plurality of models'. This was the case prior to the 1960s and is a continuing criticism of work-family policies that are argued to favour one group in society over another (Hakim, 2000). Bittman (1999: 29) also argues that the focus on family-friendly workplaces is only one facet of a multi-dimensional problem and results in 'focusing on what happens at the factory, the sales counter or the office and neglecting what happens at home.' Hakim (2000) argues that unitary government policies fail to recognise the variation in individual preferences and that policies in Western societies have tended to favour women who prefer to work rather than those that wish to exercise their choice to stay at home to care for their children.

Households also provide an important context in which individuals exercise choice to realise their own preferences. Increasing variation in household structure such as the rise in single-parent households, dual-income households and single-occupant households also bring complexity to the work-family policy arena. Rahilly and Johnston (2002: 482) argue that in the UK, single-parent and dual-income households 'share common problems of attempting to combine the care and maintenance of their children' but that the UK government's tendency in recent years to focus on childcare for full-time workers is limiting to those with different childcare needs such as single parents who wish to combine part-time employment with the care of their children.

The household, as distinct from the family, has been identified as the crucial unit of analysis in understanding social and economic change (Jacobs and Gerson, 2001; Wheelock and Oughton, 1996). Wheelock and Oughton (1996:143–4) argue that:

'For consumption as well as labor supply decisions, the crucial unit is not the individual, but the household. Indeed, the term "individual" is misleading because it conjures up the idea of isolation from the social and historical setting. Nor does it distinguish between men and women.

Also, once we look at people in households, it becomes apparent that they have a variety of motivations besides narrow economic gain; actions may be based on traditional or patriarchal reasoning, people have a need for dignity and self respect, and a need to care and nurture. Actions can also be based on reciprocity or cooperation between people'.

Therefore, policy-makers in the area of work-life balance need to consider two main issues. First, individual preferences and an individual's ability to act on those preferences need to be considered when devising policy; and second, there needs to be some acknowledgement that an individual's role within the family and the structure of the households in which they live will also impact on behavioural responses to work-life balance policies. Support for the importance of understanding the context within which individual actors make decisions is found in a study by Jacobs and Gerson (2001), where it is argued that changes to an individual's working time patterns were largely determined by changes in family composition, part-icularly in dual-income families. Further, Morehead (2002) studied the difficulties in achieving work-life balance in single-mother households, and concluded that single mothers would benefit from the implementation of a series of policy initiatives that may not necessarily be useful to women in different situations. Therefore, whilst women and men may prefer to combine paid employment and domestic duties, family and household responsibilities may constrain one's ability to act upon this preference. Families and households provide an important context to understanding individual lives, preferences and decision-making, by constraining or enhancing available courses of action open to individuals. Thus, the challenge for policy-makers is to disentangle the interplay between individual needs and preferences, household and family constraints and the wider policy arena.

Hakim (2000) argues that 'preference theory' can provide a foundation on which to develop more appropriate work-family policies for the 21st century. Preference theory recognises that women display different preferences for combining work and family life. Hakim identifies three 'types' of women: home-centred, adaptive and work-centred and argues that fiscal, social, family and welfare policy initiatives have a different impact on these groups. Further, she argues that the common governmental bias in favour of social uniformity rather than diversity, has lead to generic policy solutions which do not target groups with specific needs or preferences. Whilst such generalisations may simplify the policy-maker's task, the outcomes are inadequate social policies that do not adequately address variation in individual preferences.

Critics of Hakim (for example, Crompton, 2002; McRae, 2003; Probert, 2002; Probert and Murphy, 2001) have argued that understanding variation in women's lifestyle choices needs to involve investigation of more than just what women want. They should also take into account the female's scope or ability to act on these preferences. McRae (2003) for example, highlights that variation in preferences needs to be understood in the context of the normative and structural constraints that create variation in the ability to act on preferences. Normative constraints are the cultural norms and expectations and social influences that impact on gender relationships and attitudes to work and family. Structural constraints are macro-level institutional and societal conditions that enable or inhibit choices and action. As McRae (2003:329) explains 'perhaps the most immediate structural constraints affecting mothers' choices are job availability and the cost and availability of childcare, but the outcomes of different social origins also curtail choice more sharply for some women than for others, acting either through poor educational qualifications, early pregnancy, poor health, or culture'. Government policy therefore plays an important role in shaping the opportunities or constraints that individuals face in exercising choice over their lifestyle preferences through the allocation of resources for social support and services (Probert, 2002).

Conclusion

Providing a framework to facilitate the integration of the spheres of work, family and civic life for individual citizens is a multifarious and challenging problem for policy-makers. The issues generated transcend the requirements and actions of individual actors, and involve the consideration of the needs of households and the wider community in considering adequate social and economic policy responses. It has been argued that macro-level policy formulation in this area has improperly viewed society as a homogeneous group of actors with similar requirements, with little consideration of the true needs of individuals and of households, or an acknowledgement that needs within a society are likely to vary according to situation. This has resulted in policy responses to role conflict which are non-specific and target extremely broad sections of society, which in some cases has served to reinforce the normative constraints faced by individuals (particularly women). This has created a detachment between the goals of policy on the one hand, and the realities faced by individuals and families in daily life, on the other. What is therefore required is a multi-level approach to policy formulation, which accounts for the differing needs of individuals, households and society.

In other areas, multi-level approaches are increasingly being employed to inform social policy development, for example in understanding the neighbourhood, family, and peer effects on children's development and drug use, and the effects of welfare reform at the neighbourhood level (for further information, see for example http://www.lasurvey.rand.org/ and http://www.hms.harvard.edu/chase/projects/chicago/). Multi-level approaches to study these phenomena are necessary due to the complexities of the social problems being investigated and the ramifications for families and communities. A greater understanding of how different actors and units within society interact, tempered by the varying ideologies and values underpinning societies, will inevitably lead to a more comprehensive and suitable array of policies to govern the integration of work and family life for the advancement and prosperity for all. Increasingly, governments have a pivotal role to play in articulating policy frameworks to achieve better work-life balance outcomes for citizens. Current policy responses would be further enhanced by the recognition of the need for more differentiated and versatile solutions to what is a highly complex and multi-dimensional issue.

References

Adams, G.A., King, L.A. and King, D.W. (1996) 'Relationships of Job and Family Involvement, Family Social Support and Work-Family Conflict with Job and Life Satisfaction', *Journal of Applied Psychology*, 81(4): 411–20.

Albrecht, G. (2003) 'How Friendly are Family Friendly Policies?' *Business Ethics Quarterly*, 13(2): 177–93.

Aldous, J. (1990) 'Specification and Speculation Concerning The Politics of Workplace Family Policies', *Journal of Family Issues*, 11(4): 335–67.

Arts, G. and Gelissen, J. (2001) 'Welfare States, Solidarity and Justice Principles: Does the Type Really Matter?' *Acta Sociologica*, 44: 283–99.

Bittman, M. (1999) 'Parenthood Without Penalty: Time Use and Public Policy in Australia And Finland', *Feminist Economics*, 5(3): 27–42.

Blau, F.D. and Ehrenberg, R.G. (eds) (1997) *Gender and Family Issues in the Workplace*, New York: Russell Sage Foundation.

Burstein, P. and Bricher, M. (1997) 'Problem Definition Public Policy: Congressional Committees Confront Work, Family and Gender 1945–90', *Social Forces*, 76(1): 135–68.

Castles, F. (1993) *Families of Nations*, Dartmouth: Aldershot.

Crompton, R. (2002) 'Employment, Flexible Working and the Family', *British Journal of Sociology*, 53(4): 537–58.

Cully, M., Woodland, S., O'Reilly, A. and Dix, G. (1999) *Britain At Work: As Depicted By The 1998 Workplace Employee Relations Survey*, London: Routledge.

Dex, S. and Smith, C. (2002) *The Nature And Patterns Of Family-Friendly Employment Policies In Britain*, Bristol: Policy Press for the Joseph Rowntree Foundation.

Duncan, S. (1996) 'The Diverse Worlds of European Patriarchy', in Garcia-Ramon, M. and Monk, J. (eds) *Women Of The European Union*, London: Routledge, 74–110.

Edwards, J.R. and Rothbard, N.P. (2000) 'Mechanisms for Linking Work and Family: Clarifying The Relationship Between Work and Family Constructs', *Academy of Management Review*, 25(1): 178–99.

Esping-Andersen, G. (1990) *The Three Worlds Of Welfare Capitalism*, Cambridge: Polity Press.

Esping-Andersen, G. (1999) *Social Foundations Of Post-Industrial Economies*, Oxford: Oxford University Press.

Evans, J.M. (2001) *Firms' Contribution to the Reconciliation Between Work and Family Life*, Occasional Paper no. 48, Directorate for Education, Employment, Labour and Social Affairs, Paris: Organisation for Economic Co-operation and Development.

Eveline, J. (1999) 'Men, Work and Family: Australian Scenes', 7th International Congress of Women's Research, Tromso, Norway.

Figart, D.M. and Murari, E. (2000) 'Work Time Regimes in Europe: Can Flexibility and Gender Equity Co-Exist?' *Journal of Economic Issues*, 34(4): 847–71.

Fox, M.L. and Dwyer, D.J. (1999) 'An Investigation of the Effects of Time and Involvement in the Relationship Between Stressors and Work-Family Conflict', *Journal of Occupational Health Psychology*, 4(2): 164–74.

Gustafsson, S.S. and Stafford, F.P. (1995) 'Links Between Early Childhood Programs and Maternal Employment in Three Countries', *Long-Term Outcomes of Early Childhood Programs*, 5(3): 161–74.

Hakim, C. (2000) *Work-Lifestyle Choices In The 21st Century: Preference Theory*, Oxford: Oxford University Press.

Haas, L. (2003) 'Parental Leave and Gender Equality: Lessons from the European Union', *Review of Policy Research*, 20(1): 89–125.

Hirdman, Y. (1989) 'The Swedish Welfare State and the Gender System: A Theoretical and Empirical Sketch', *The Study of Power and Democracy in Sweden*, English Series, Report no. 9, Stockholm.

Holt, H. and Grainger, H. (2005) *Results Of The Second Flexible Working Employee Survey*, Employment Relations Research Series no. 39, London: Department of Trade and Industry.

Houston, D. and Walmsley, J. (2004) *Family-Friendly Working Arrangements: Attitudes and Uptake in Men and Women*, Bristol: Policy Press.

Jacobs, J.A. and Gerson, K. (2001) 'Overworked Individuals or Overworked Families? Explaining Trends in Work, Leisure and Family Time', *Work and Occupations*, 28(1): 40–63.

Korpi, W. (1983) *The Democratic Class Struggle*, London: Routledge.

Kuhlen, M. (2004) (ed.) 'International Reform Monitor: Social Policy, Labour Market Policy, Industrial Relations', Issue 9, Germany: Die Seutsche Bibliothek.

Le Grand, J. (1997) 'Knights, Knaves or Pawns? Human Behaviour and Social Policy', *Journal of Social Policy*, 26(2), 149–69.

Lewis, J. (1992) 'Gender and the Development of Welfare Regimes', *Journal of European Social Policy*, 2(3): 159–73.

Lewis, J. (1999) 'Gender and Welfare Regimes: Further Thoughts', *Social Politics*, 4(2): 160–77.

Lewis, S. (2003) 'The Integration of Paid Work and the Rest of Life. Is Post-Industrial Work the New Leisure?', *Leisure Studies*, 22(4): 343–54.

Lewis, S. and Lewis, J. (eds) (1996) *The Work-Family Challenge*, London: Sage.

Los Angeles Family and Neighbourhood Survey (L.A. FANS) <http://www.lasurvey.rand.org>, accessed on 8th of August 2005.

Mahon, R. (2000) 'The Never-Ending Story: The Struggle For Universal Child Care Policy in the 1970s', *Canadian Historical Review*, 81(4): 582–616.

Mayer, R. (1985) *Policy And Program Planning: A Development Perspective*, Englewood Cliffs: Prentice Hall.

McRae, S. (2003) 'Constraints and Choices in Mothers' Employment Careers: A Consideration of Hakim's Preference Theory', *British Journal of Sociology*, 54(3): 317–38.

Morehead, A. (2002) 'Behind the Paid Working Hours of Single Mothers: Managing Change and Constructing Support', *Family Matters*, 61: 56–61.

Myles, J. (1998) 'How to Design a Liberal Welfare State: A Comparison of Canada and The United States', *Social Policy and Administration*, 32(4): 341–64.

O'Hara, K. (1998) *Comparative Family Policy: Eight Countries' Stories*, Canada: Canadian Policy Research Networks.

Orloff, A. (1993) 'Gender and the Social Rights of Citizenship: A Comparative Analysis of Gender Relations and Welfare States', *American Sociological Review*, 58: 303–28.

Pocock, B. (2003) *Work Life Collision*, Sydney: Federation Press.

Probert, B. (2002) '"Grateful Slaves" or "Self-Made Women"': A Matter of Choice or Policy?' *Australian Feminist Studies*, 17 (37): 7–17.

Probert, B. and Murphy, J. (2001) 'Majority Opinion or Divided Selves? Researching Work and Family Experiences', *Journal of People and Places*, 9(4): 25–33.

Project on Human Development in Chicago Neighbourhoods (PHDCN) <http://www.hms.harvard.edu/chase/projects/chicago>, accessed on 8th of August 2005.

Rahilly, S. and Johnston, E. (2002) 'Opportunity for Childcare – The Impact of Government Initiatives in England upon Childcare Provision', *Social Policy and Administration*, 36(5): 482–95.

Sainsbury, D. (1994) *Gendering Welfare States*, London: Sage.

Smith Major, V., Klein, K.J. and Ehrhart, M.G. (2002) 'Work Time, Work Interference with Family and Psychological Distress', *Journal of Applied Psychology*, 87(3): 427–36.

Sparks, K., Cooper, C., Fried, Y. and Shirom, A. (1997) 'The Effects of Hours of Work on Health: A Meta-Analytic Review', *Journal of Occupational and Organizational Psychology*, 70(4): 391–408.

Strachan, G. and Burgess, J. (1998) 'The Family Friendly Workplace', *International Journal of Manpower*, 19(4): 250–65.

Strachan, G. and Burgess, J. (2000) 'The Incompatibility of Decentralised Bargaining and Equal Employment Opportunity in Australia', *British Journal of Industrial Relations*, 38(3): 361–81.

Trzcinski, E. (2000) 'Family Policy in Germany: A Feminist Dilemma?', *Feminist Economics*, 6(1): 21–44.

Walby, S. (2003) 'Policy Developments for Workplace Gender Equity in a Global Era: The Importance of the EU in the UK', *Review of Policy Research*, 20(1): 45–64.

Wheelock, J. (2001) 'Don't Care Was Made To Care: The Implications Of Gendered Time For Policies Towards The Household', *Capital and* Class, Autumn: 173–5.

Wheelock, J. and Oughton, E. (1996) 'The Household as a Focus for Research', *Journal of Economic Issues*, 30: 143–59.

Wheelock, J., Oughton, E. and Baines, S. (2003) 'Getting By With A Little Help From Your Family: Toward A Policy-Relevant Model Of The Household', *Feminist Economics*, 9(1): 19–45.

Whitehouse, G. (2001) 'Industrial Agreements and Work Family Provisions: Trends and Prospects Under Enterprise Bargaining', *Labour and Industry*, 12(1): 109–30.

Williams, J.C. and Cohen Cooper, H. (2004) 'The Public Policy of Motherhood', *Journal of Social Issues*, 60(4): 849–65.

Wooden, M. (2002) *Childcare Policy: An Introduction And Overview*, Melbourne, Australia: Melbourne University, Institute of Applied Economic and Social Research.

6

Work-Life Balance in Canada: Rhetoric versus Reality

Linda Duxbury and Christopher Higgins

Introduction

Traditionally, work and family life have been treated as mutually exclusive domains, segregated by both geography and gender. Organisations have had little reason to be concerned with an employee's family or personal situation or the negative consequences of work-life conflict on their employees or on the organisation. Ambitious employees worked long hours and were easily relocatable for the right opportunity within the organisation. Family duties, such as childcare, cooking and housework were the domain of the employee's wife and not a concern for the organisation.

Dramatic demographic, social and economic changes of the past few decades have, however, led to a work and lifestyle 'revolution' (Vanderkolk and Young, 1991). There are now more: (1) dual-income families, (2) working heads of single-parent families, (3) working women of all ages, (4) working mothers, (5) men with direct responsibility for familycare, (6) workers caring for elderly relatives, and (7) workers in the sandwich generation with responsibility for both childcare and eldercare (Statistics Canada, 2000).

These substantial changes in the Canadian workforce are creating a new emphasis on the balance between work and family life as employees are now coping with care-giving and household responsibilities that were once managed by a stay-at-home spouse. Such employees are not well served by traditional 'one size fits all' human resource policies which can impose rigid time and place constraints on employees and reward long work hours at the expense of personal time. Clearly, the old model of coordinating work and family, which assumes that one's work role is separate from, and takes precedence over, one's family role (referred to by Kanter, 1977, as the 'myth of separate worlds') is no longer valid for the majority of the Canadian labour force. Employees in dual-income families no longer have the option of a gendered division of labour when it comes to the organisation of work and family. Women are increasingly being forced to deal with job-related demands which place limits on the performance of their family role. Men

82

are becoming more involved with their family and are experiencing a shift in their priorities away from work. The new reality has had a marked effect on what is required of each family member and on what employers can expect from employees. As the US Bureau of National Affairs notes:

> 'Caring for elder parents, children or both is not new. Combining it with a career is' (BNA, 1997: 7).

As in most transition periods, changing behaviours often outpace social and organisational structures. Such appears to be the case for today's working parents who have experienced the burden of both working and caring for dependents in a world that has been largely unresponsive to their realities. The evidence suggests that both governments and employers have been slow to respond to the changing social and economic pressures on employees (Scott, 2000). In the absence of supportive government policies and organisational practices, families have struggled to accommodate job demands at the expense of their family role obligations and their own well-being (Scott, 2000).

Difficulties associated with balancing work and family responsibilities have been compounded by a diffusion of responsibility in which each part of the system believes that it is someone else's problem. Management often holds the view that it's a workers' problem, men think it's a women's issue, and older parents and/or those without children believe it's a concern for younger parents. Workplaces have tended to act as if wives were still at home managing the multiple roles of homemaking and child rearing. Governments, as legislators and policy-makers, have reacted cautiously to the changing workplace. A study done by the US Government over a decade ago, for example, noted that:

> 'Many politicians have talked a lot about family but few have made the crucial issues, childcare, job security, family leave, flexibility, a legislative priority' (BNA, 1997: 5).

Research questions

This chapter reports survey data from two Canadian national studies to answer the following questions:

1. How prevalent was high work-life conflict (overload, work interferes with family, and family interferes with work) in 2001? How has the prevalence of each of these forms of work-life conflict changed over the past decade?
2. How much time did employees spend in work-related activities (i.e. working at the office, paid and unpaid overtime, job-related education) in 2001? How have these work demands changed over the past decade?

3. How much time did employees spend in family-related activities (i.e. childcare, eldercare, home chores) and leisure in 2001? How have these non-work-related time demands changed over the past decade?
4. What is the link between work demands, family demands and the various forms of work-life conflict?
5. How does gender, job type, and dependent care status affect work demands, non-work demands and the prevalence of the various forms of work-life conflict?

Literature review

What is work-life conflict?

We all play many roles: employee, boss, subordinate, spouse, parent, child, sibling, friend, and community member. Each of these roles imposes demands on us which require time, energy and commitment. Work-family conflict occurs when the cumulative demands of these work and non-work roles are incompatible in some respect so that participation in one role is made more difficult by participation in the other role. There are three components of work-life conflict. One component, role overload exists when the total demands on time and energy associated with the prescribed activities of multiple roles are too great to perform the roles adequately or comfortably. Interference from work to family, a second component, occurs when work demands and responsibilities make it difficult to fulfil family role responsibilities. Family interference with work, the final component, occurs when family demands and responsibilities make it difficult to fulfil work role responsibilities.

Changes in the prevalence of work-life conflict over time

The face of the Canadian workforce has changed dramatically over the past several decades. The key demographic and social changes which have been linked in the literature to increased work-life conflict include the following:

The growing involvement of Canadian women in the paid labour force. Between 1977 and 1996, women's labour force participation rate increased from 43 per cent to 57 per cent. In 1998, 58 per cent of women over the age of 25 worked for pay outside the home (Statistics Canada, January, 1999). In 1998 women comprised 45 per cent of Canada's total labour force.

The growth in labour force participation rates for women with children (especially young children). Between 1976 and 1998 labour force participation rates for mothers with children under age three doubled from 32 per cent to 64 per cent (Vanier Institute, 2000). During the same time period the participation rate of women with a youngest child aged six to 15 increased from 50 per cent to 72 per cent. In 1998, two-thirds of Canadian mothers of young children (i.e. at least one under 6) were in the paid labour force (Scott, 2000).

Women's patterns of employment are becoming like those of men. Traditionally, Canadian women left the workforce once they started their families. In the 1990s this was no longer true as the majority of women (55 per cent) returned to work within two years of giving birth (Fast and de Pont, 1997; Scott, 2000).

The dual-income family has replaced the traditional male breadwinner/ homemaker wife as the prototypical Canadian family type. Both husband and wife work for pay outside the home in seven out of ten Canadian families (up from one in three in 1967) (Statistics Canada, 1997a). In 1976, almost three million mothers stayed home to care for their children. This number had declined to 1.1 million mothers by 1997 (Statistics Canada, 2000).

Lone-parent households became more prevalent in the 1990s. In 1996 the number of lone-parent families in Canada reached 1.1 million, up 19 per cent from 1991 and 33 per cent from 1986 (Statistics Canada, 1997b). Although these figures include both male- and female-headed households, lone parenthood is largely the domain of women. In 1996, lone-parent families headed by women outnumbered those headed by men by more than four to one (Johnson et al, 2001).

Canadian fathers are spending more time in 'family' labour. Although Statistics Canada only began to include unpaid labour in the 1996 census, the data which are available suggest that in the 1990s men spent more time in unpaid work activities than was the case a decade earlier (Vanier Institute, 2000).

More Canadian employees have elderly dependents. Canada's population is aging (Foot, 1996) which has a number of implications for the country, not the least of which is a greater proportion of Canadian employees responsible for the care of elderly dependents (Scott, 2000). A recent report by Statistics Canada (1999) dedicated to the topic of eldercare noted that in 1996, about 2.1 million Canadians (both male and female) looked after older family members or friends.

The percentage of Canadians who have responsibility for both childcare and eldercare (the so-called 'sandwich generation') has increased as 'baby boom' and 'baby bust' generations assume responsibility for both dependent children and aging parents (Scott, 2000). It has been estimated that while one in four Canadians are currently part of the sandwich generation (Duxbury and Higgins, 2001), this per cent will increase over the next decade as Canadians delay family formation and childbirth (CCSD, 1996).

Smaller family size means that children will be required to provide support for a larger number of elderly family members. Declining fertility rates mean that Canadian families are smaller today than they were thirty years ago. The average family size in 1995 was 3.01, down from 3.67 in 1971 (CCSD, 1996).

The literature also suggests a number of economic factors that may have contributed to an increase in work-life conflict for Canadian employees. These factors include:

Unemployment due to downsizing and restructuring. Changes in the Canadian economy and the need to compete globally led many Canadian organisations to downsize and right-size aggressively (Stone and Meltz, 1993). During the 1990s layoffs burgeoned and in 1994 alone, one in four Canadian families experienced a period of unemployment for at least one family member (Vanier Institute, 1997).

A growth in non-standard forms of work and a decline in perceived job security. Concomitant with the restructuring and downsizing that occurred in Canada in the 80s and 90s was a growth in the use of non-standard forms of work that are low in quality and offer few benefits and little flexibility (Scott, 2000; Lowe and Schellenberg, 1999). Employees in such positions are likely to experience greater conflict between work and family. Job insecurity also has relevance to work-life conflict in that for many employees, work-life conflict takes second place to securing permanent full-time employment. In 1998 one in five Canadians said they were worried about losing their job (Lowe and Schellenberg, 1999).

Technological advances have blurred the boundary between work and non-work and increased the pace of work. Technological changes can be linked to the following antecedents of work-life conflict: (1) increases in unemployment/underemployment for those without the skills to compete in today's labour market, (2) a blurring of the boundaries between work and life as it becomes increasingly easy for employees to work any time and anywhere, and (3) increased workloads and greater job stress.

Organisational inertia has exacerbated work-life conflict issues. While the rhetoric of management throughout the 1990s was one of 'putting people first', 'human capital' and 'competitive advantage through people,' the data would suggest that management practices throughout the past decade tended to move in the opposite direction (i.e. massive downsizing, restructuring) (Lowe, 2000).

Who is more likely to report high levels of work-life conflict?

To fully appreciate how employees' ability to balance work and non-work demands have changed over the past decade it is necessary to recognise that factors such as gender, job type, and dependent care responsibilities may have a strong impact on their experiences. Consequently, we extended our analysis by considering the following demographic variables that may have an impact on the attitudes and outcomes being examined: (1) gender, (2) job type and (3) dependent care responsibilities. While this list is by no means exhaustive, it does focus on those factors which previous research has shown influence both the nature of an individual's participation in work and family roles and/or shape the meaning individuals give to family and work and the identities they develop.

Gender constitutes the socio-demographic characteristic most frequently examined with respect to the prevalence of work-life conflict (Guerts and Demerouti, 2003; Hammer et al, 2000). Haas (1995: 115) defines gender as a 'system of socially constructed boundaries that define what is considered to be appropriate masculine and feminine behaviours, attitudes, values, personalities, roles and occupations.' Similarly, Milkie and Peltola (1999) define gender as a hierarchical structure that 'infuses everyday relations in the family and the workplace.' Both of these definitions assume that employed women and men have different role expectations and demands.

There is a large body of literature to attest to the fact that women experience higher levels of work-life conflict than do men. Some suggest that women may be biologically 'programmed' to respond differently to stressors (Jick and Mitz, 1985). This hypothesis is borne out by differences in symptomatology shown by women versus men. Others argue that gender differences in the stress response are attributable to differences in socialisation processes and role expectations that expose women to a higher level of stressors. In the home, women, irrespective of their involvement in paid work, are significantly more likely than men to bear primary responsibility for home-chores and childcare (Statistics Canada, 2000). In the workplace, women are disproportionately represented in occupations with 'built-in strain' such as clerical work, which couples high work demands with little discretionary control (Statistics Canada, 2000). Although it is difficult to determine which of these mechanisms is most responsible for women's differential response to stress, there is little doubt that women are exposed to different stressors than men at both work and at home.

Several bodies of research (e.g. Duxbury and Higgins, 1994; Quick et al, 1997) suggest that the type of job an individual holds will affect their ability to balance work and family demands. This research points out that managers and professionals are more likely to occupy occupations which afford better flexibility and personal control over the timing of work and offer greater extrinsic rewards. It is believed that this increase in flexibility, control and income make it easier for managers and professionals to balance work and family demands and offset some of the 'costs' that demanding jobs entail. Higher incomes, for example, permit employees to purchase goods and services to help them cope while increased flexibility makes it easier to coordinate work and non-work activities. Non-professional employees, on the other hand, are more likely to work in high demand, low control jobs. Seminal work by Karasek (1979) indicates that employees in these types of positions typically report higher levels of stress and poorer physical and mental health.

The decision to look at job type differences within gender is supported by recent data (Statistics Canada, 2000; Lowe, 2000) that show that Canadian women are compressed into lower paying positions within organisations. For example, in 1999, 70 per cent of all employed women (versus 29 per cent of employed men) worked in occupations in which women have traditionally been concentrated such as teaching and nursing. One in four women worked in a clerical or administrative position (Statistics Canada, 2000).

A large body of research links the parental responsibilities of working couples to the incidence of work-family conflict (see Duxbury and Higgins, 2001). This research suggests that parents will have more difficulties with respect to balance than non-parents as they have more demands and less control over their time.

In the new millennium dependent care is not just a question of care for children. Concerns over eldercare responsibilities are now increasing as the parents of baby boomers enter their sixties, seventies and eighties. Demographic projections suggest that society has yet to feel the full effects of eldercare problems as the per cent of the workforce involved in eldercare is expected to increase from one in five to one in four in the next decade (Statistics Canada, 2000).

Gender and dependent care status are considered simultaneously in this analysis to accommodate the literature which suggests that 'motherhood' is different from 'fatherhood' (i.e. Statistics Canada, 2000; Hochschild, 1989). Virtually all of the literature in the work-life arena notes that working mothers assume a disproportionate share of family responsibilities and that even in the new millennium society judges women's worth by their performance of family roles while men's merit is judged by their success as a 'breadwinner.' As Vanderkolk and Young (1991: 45) note:

> Even as women's attitudes and needs have changed regarding the world of work, corporate America has by and large been stuck in the 50s with a TV image of 'Harriet' keeping the home together while 'Ozzie' goes off to the office or the plant. The fact of the matter is that 'Harriet' has now taken on both roles.

Methodology

In 1991 we conducted a national study on work-life balance and supportive work environments in Canada that was funded by Health Canada. Just over 25,000 Canadians participated in this study. In 2001 we replicated the 1991 study with a sample size of over 31,000 employees who worked for 100 medium to large (i.e. 500 or more employees) public (federal, provincial and municipal governments), private and not-for-profit organisations. Both samples, while not random, can be considered to be representative of the population of employees working for medium and large Canadian organisations.

Survey questionnaire

A 12-page survey instrument was developed for use in the 2001 study. Just over 31,000 useable surveys were returned for a response rate of approximately 26 per cent. Virtually all of the scales used in the 2001 questionnaire are psychometrically sound measures from the research literature. To allow comparisons over time, many of the survey measures that were used in our 1991 national work-life study were incorporated into the 2001 questionnaire. A full discussion of the methodology and measures used in the 1991 (Duxbury et al, 1991) and 2001 studies (Duxbury and Higgins, 2001) are readily available.

As noted in the literature review, job type has been shown to theoretically influence the nature of an individuals' participation in work and family roles (i.e. demands) as well as shape the meaning individuals give to family and work, the identities they develop and their work environment. It is, therefore, highly likely that job type will confound most of the relationships between the dependent and independent variables considered in this analysis. Thus, to examine the impact job type has on work demands, non-work demands and work-life conflict we divided our respondents into two groups as follows:

- professionals: defined to include employees who held either managerial and/or professional positions, and
- non-professionals: defined to include employees who worked in technical, clerical, administrative, and production positions.

To gain a better appreciation of how dependent care influences the demands faced by employed Canadians and their ability to balance work and family we compared the responses given by individuals who had dependent care responsibilities (defined as an individual who spends at least one hour a week caring for a child and/or an elderly or disabled dependent) to those without any type of dependent care.

Data analysis

One of the key objectives of this study was to estimate the prevalence of the various forms of work-life conflict in the Canadian workforce. Work-life conflict data are reported in two ways in this paper. For comparisons over time we use percentages to report the prevalence of high, moderate and low levels of the various forms of work-life conflict. To determine who scored high versus low on each of these constructs we calculated overall role overload, work to family interference and family to work interference scores and then used population norms to divide the sample into three groups (high, moderate and low) on the basis of the respondent's overall role overload, work to family interference and family to work interference score.

Changes over time in the amount of time spent in work and non-work activities were estimated by comparing the mean amount of time spent in such activities in 1991 to the amount of time spent in 2001.

To make the comparisons over time consistent we limited the comparison to employees who worked full-time (i.e. 37 hours per week) and who had some form of dependent care responsibilities. Over 20,000 respondents in both the 1991 and 2001 samples met these criteria. Statistical analysis indicates that differences of 1 per cent or more between the two time periods are statistically significant ($p = .000$) and substantive (see Duxbury and Higgins, 2001 for a full reporting of these data).

Examination of the impact of gender, job type and dependent care responsibilities on the prevalence of work-life conflict as well as time spent in work and non-work activities was done using the 2001 data only. In this case we report means and standard deviations and between group differences were tested using Scheffe's post hoc procedures.

Regression analysis was used to meet research objective number four. The three different measures of work-life conflict were used as the dependent variables in these regressions. Work demands were used as the independent variables in the first set of regressions while non-work demands were used as independent variables in the second set of regressions.

To determine the importance of each independent variable in a significant regression equation we used a technique described by Thomas et al (1998). This technique involves multiplying each standardised regression coefficient by its correlation with the dependent variable and dividing each product by the overall R^2. These products, which sum to one, are called Pratt's measures. By rank ordering Pratt's measures we can determine variable importance.

Two sets of regression equations (one for men, one for women) were run to examine how gender influences the relationship between demands and work-life conflict. Job type was included in all regression equations as a control variable.

Finally, it should be noted that all of the differences discussed in this paper meet two criteria: they were statistically significant and substantive (i.e. the differences matter in a practical sense). This second requirement was necessary as the large sample sizes meant that very small differences were often statistically significant.

Profile of the survey respondents

A comparison of the 1991 and 2001 samples is given in Table 6.1. These data show that, with a few exceptions, the samples are quite similar. Approximately the same proportion in each sample were female, parents, managers and technical employees. The age data are also quite similar though not directly comparable as different categories were used in 1991 compared to 2001.

Table 6.1   Comparison of 1991 and 2001 samples

Variable		1991	2001
Number in sample		31,228	28,394
% Female		56%	56%
Job Type:			
➜ % Managers		11%	16%
➜ % Professionals		22%	38%
➜ % Technical		15%	16%
➜ % Clerical/Administrative		34%	20%
% Parents		64%	69%
% With Eldercare		6%	25%
Personal Income:			
➜ % under $40,000		58%	40%
➜ % $40,000 to $60,000		28%	38%
➜ % $60,000 +		14%	22%
Family Income:			
➜ % under $40,000		15%	8%
➜ % $40,000 to $60,000		18%	16%
➜ % $60,001 to $100,000		42%	45%
➜ % 100,000 +		25%	32%
Age: 1991	Age: 2001		
➜ under 30	➜ under 35	22%	27%
➜ 30 to 39	➜ 35 to 45	38%	37%
➜ 40 to 49	➜ 46 to 54	28%	30%
➜ 50 +	➜ 55+	21%	7%

Note: only full-time employees included in comparison

A greater proportion of the 2001 sample had eldercare responsibilities (one in four employees in the 2001 sample versus 6 per cent in 1991). This finding is consistent with Statistics Canada (2000) data showing that the proportion of the Canadian population over 65 has increased over the last decade. It also supports our contention that the per cent of Canadian employees at risk for high work-life conflict has increased over time. When comparing the 1991 and 2001 samples we also observe that the per cent of respondents working in professional positions has increased while the proportion of the sample working in clerical/administrative positions has declined. This change is consistent with the increase in the knowledge sector and changes in the gender composition of the Canadian workforce reported by Statistics Canada (2000) (i.e. more female professionals in 1999 than in 1987).

Research findings

Key findings pertaining to each of the research questions are discussed below.

Prevalence of the various forms of work-life conflict

One of the primary objectives of this study is to quantify the extent to which work-life conflict was a problem in Canada in 2001 and to examine changes in the prevalence of high work-life conflict over the past decade (Research Question One). Data on the incidence of the various forms of work-life conflict are shown in Table 6.2 (means and standard deviations for 2001 data) and Table 6.3 (per cent high data for 1991 and 2001 samples).

Examination of data in Table 6.4 leads to the following observations with respect to the prevalence of work-life conflict in Canada 2001:

- The distribution of role overload shows a positive skew with the majority of the respondents (58 per cent) reporting high levels of role overload. Only 12 per cent reported low levels of role overload.
- The distribution of work interferes with family is normally distributed with a plurality of the working Canadians in our sample (38 per cent) reporting moderate levels of work interferes with family. While 29 per cent reported high interference from work to family, 33 per cent were experiencing relatively low levels of interference.
- The majority (58 per cent) of the sample reported that their family demands did not interfere with their work demands. While one in three of the respondents reported moderate levels of interference, very few Canadians (10 per cent) indicated that their family demands interfered with the their ability to meet demands at work.

Table 6.2 The incidence of work-life conflict in 2001

	Male				Female			
	No dependent care n = 4,298		dependent care n = 6,595		No dependent care n = 7,337		dependent care n = 8,565	
	_	sd.	_	sd.	_	sd.	_	sd.
Overload	3.39	0.012	3.61	0.015	3.61	0.011	3.88	0.011
W ≻ F	2.90	0.017	3.11	0.014	2.77	0.013	3.01	0.012
F ≻ W	2.04	0.016	2.41	0.013	2.04	0.012	2.45	0.011
	Mgr./Professional n = 5,945		'Other' n = 4,959		Mgr./Professional n = 6,877		'Other' n = 9,075	
	_	sd.	_	sd.	_	sd.	_	sd.
Overload	3.61	0.013	3.43	0.013	3.85	0.012	3.68	0.016
W ≻ F	3.15	0.015	2.88	0.015	3.11	0.013	2.73	0.011
F ≻ W	2.29	0.014	2.24	0.015	2.3	0.013	2.23	0.011

Key:
W ≻ F   Work Interferes with Family
F ≻ W   Family Interferes with Work
Note: Scheffe's post hoc test determined that all but the following between group differences were statistically significant at p > .000:
• *Role Overload:*
• Male dependent care compared to female no dependent care (α = 1.00)
• *Work Interferes with Family*
• Female manager/professional compared to male manager/professional (α = .557)
• *Family Interferes with Work*:
• Male no dependent care compared to female no dependent care (α = 1.00)
• Female dependent care compared to male dependent care (α = .027)
• Male manager/professional compared to male 'other' (α = .234)
• Male manager/professional compared to female manager/professional (α = .757)
• Male 'other' compared to female 'other' (α = 1.00)

Table 6.3 Changes in the prevalence of work-life conflict: 1991 versus 2001
a. Total sample

% Reporting high	1991	2001
Role Overload	47	58
Work Interferes with Family	26	29
Family Interferes with Work	3	10

Table 6.3 Changes in the prevalence of work-life conflict: 1991 versus 2001 –
continued

b. Breakdown by gender, job type and dependent care status

% Reporting high	Men				Women			
	Professional		Non-professional		Professional		Non-professional	
	1991	2001	1991	2001	1991	2001	1991	2001
Role Overload	46	55	33	50	58	67	51	59
Work Interferes with Family	28	33	24	31	31	33	24	29
Family Interferes with Work	2	10	0	9	4	11	2	8

	Dependent care		No dependent care		Dependent care		No dependent care	
	1991	2001	1991	2001	1991	2001	1991	2001
Role Overload	45	54	34	48	65	74	42	52
Work Interferes with Family	30	35	20	31	29	40	22	29
Family Interferes with Work	6	16	0	1	13	23	0	1

Changes in the prevalence in work-life conflict over time

Data on the percentage of the sample reporting high levels of work-life conflict in 1991 and 2001 are shown in Table 6.4. These data allow us to compare the prevalence of the various forms of work-life conflict in 2001 to that reported in 1991. The following observations can be made.

First, the proportion of working Canadians with high role overload has increased dramatically in the past ten years (47 per cent in 1991 versus 58 per cent in 2001). Other data from the 2001 survey (Duxbury and Higgins, 2001) suggest that much of this increase in role overload can be linked to increased time in work, new information and communication technologies (i.e. laptops, e-mail, cell phones), organisational norms that reward long hours at the office rather than performance, and organisational anorexia (downsizing has meant there are too few employees to do the work).

Second, these data suggest that the proportion of Canadians with high work interferes with family has remained fairly constant over the decade. While in some senses this is a positive finding, in others it is cause for concern as it indicates that little has been done to address this issue.

Finally, the data also indicate that the percentage of Canadian employees reporting high levels of family interference with work has increased over the past decade. In 1991, only 3 per cent of respondents reported high levels of family interferes with work. In 2001 the percentage had increased to 10 per cent. In other words, a greater percentage of the working Canadians are putting family ahead of work than was the case a decade ago. Analysis of the data (Duxbury and Higgins, 2003) suggests that much of this increase can be attributed to an increased need to supply care to elderly dependents.

Work demands

The second objective of this study was to examine how much time Canadians devoted to work-related activities in 2001 and to estimate how work demands have changed over the past decade. Data on the work demands reported by the respondents to this survey are shown in Table 6.4 (means and standard deviations for 2001 data) and Table 6.5 (percentage data for 1991 and 2001 samples).

The typical full-time respondent to the 2001 survey spent 42.2 hours in work per week. The sample is fairly well distributed with respect to hours spent in work per week with one in four respondents spending 35 to 39 hours per week and one in four spending 50 or more hours. One in three respondents spent between 40 and 44 hours in work per week. The following key observations can be drawn from the data on overtime given in Table 6.4:

- respondents were more likely to work unpaid overtime than paid overtime,
- employees donate a significant proportion of unpaid time to their employer: the amount of time per month spent performing supplemental work-at-home (SWAH) and unpaid overtime is considerable and greater than the amount of time spent in paid overtime, and
- while the type of employees performing paid and unpaid overtime are slightly different (managers and professionals are more likely to perform unpaid overtime while non-professionals are more likely to perform paid overtime), substantial proportions of all employees in the various job types worked paid and unpaid overtime.

These observations are consistent with data on overtime work collected by Statistics Canada (1997c) which noted that in the first quarter of 1997 one-fifth of the Canadian workforce – roughly two million employees – reported working approximately nine hours of overtime a week. Six in ten of these employees received no pay for these hours (Statistics Canada, 1997c).

Table 6.4 Work demands: 2001

	Professionals		Non-professionals		Dependent care		No Dependent care	
	Men	Women	Men	Women	Men	Women	Men	Women
Hours in work per week	45.8	42.6	41.4	39.1	48.7	43.6	46.5	43.7
% who perform SWAH	70%	60%	44%	27%	60%	47%	51%	43%
Hours in SWAH per week	6.7	6.5	6.2	6.6	6.6	6.1	6.5	6.8
% working paid overtime	27%	29%	37%	35%	31%	30%	30%	31%
Hours per month paid OT	10.9	9.6	12.7	9.5	11.1	10.9	10.8	11.3
% working unpaid overtime	69%	61%	40%	33%	68%	66%	54%	48%
Hours per month unpaid OT	22.4	17.7	17.2	11.4	18.6	18.1	17.5	17.7

Table 6.5 Time spent in work: 1991 versus 2001

Total hours in work per week	Men				Women			
	Professionals		Non-professionals		Professionals		Non-professionals	
	1991	2001	1991	2001	1991	2001	1991	2001
35 to 39	23%	11%	41%	23%	38%	18%	66%	48%
40 to 44	28%	25%	40%	39%	30%	34%	26%	34%
45 to 49	21%	19%	10%	15%	16%	17%	5%	9%
50 or more	28%	45%	9%	23%	16%	31%	3%	9%
% Performing SWAH	56%	70%	25%	44%	45%	60%	14%	27%

	Dependents		No dependents		Dependents		No dependents	
	1991	2001	1991	2001	1991	2001	1991	2001
35 to 39	31%	16%	33%	15%	60%	34%	57%	32%
40 to 44	34%	30%	33%	32%	27%	34%	26%	34%
45 to 49	16%	17%	16%	17%	7%	12%	10%	13%
50 or more	19%	37%	18%	36%	6%	20%	7%	21%
% Performing SWAH	42%	60%	38%	51%	29%	47%	26%	43%

Change in work demands over time

Comparisons done using the 1991 and 2001 samples indicate that the percentage of employees working more than 50 hours per week has increased from 11 per cent in 1991 to 26 per cent in 2001. The percentage of employees working between 35 and 39 hours per week declined during this same time period from 48 per cent to 27 per cent.

Examination of the data in Table 6.5 also indicate that the number of employees taking work home to complete in the evening (i.e. SWAH) has increased over the course of the decade – from one in three respondents in 1991 to just over half of all employees in 2001. These data are consistent with our observations with respect to role overload and suggest that it has become more difficult for Canadian employees to complete their work during regular office hours.

To get a better appreciation of how time in work changed over the decade we did two additional comparisons (i.e. gender by job type and gender by dependent care status). These data (see Table 6.5) suggest that the increase in time in work and SWAH over the decade has been systemic with no group emerging unscathed. In 2001, male and female respondents (with and without dependent care, professionals and non-professionals alike) were less likely to work 35 to 39 hours per week and more likely to work 50 or more hours and to perform SWAH.

The trends observed from these data with respect to time in work and overtime work suggest that it has become more difficult over the past decade for Canadian employees (especially those working in managerial and professional positions) to meet work expectations during regular hours. It would appear that employees who work for larger organisations have attempted to cope with these increased demands by working longer hours and taking work home. Further research is needed to determine why work demands have increased over the decade. Competing explanations drawn from analysis of the 2001 data set (see Higgins and Duxbury, 2002) include:

- organisational anorexia (downsizing – especially of middle managers – has meant that there are not enough employees to do the work and managers to plan and prioritise),
- corporate culture (if you don't work long hours and take work home you will not advance in your career or not keep your job during downsizing),
- increased use of technology (the use of office technology such as e-mail has increased the number of tasks employees are expected to perform as well as magnified expectations with respect to response time and availability),
- global competition (work hours have been extended to allow work across time zones, increased competition and a desire to keep costs down has limited the number of employees it is deemed feasible to hire),
- the speed of change has increased to the point that many organisations have lost their ability to plan and prioritise (workloads often increase when organisations practise crisis management),
- employees are worried about the consequences of 'not being seen to be a contributor' (non-professionals may fear that they will lose their jobs if they do not work overtime while professionals may worry that their career will stagnate if they do not work overtime).

Non-work demands

The third objective of this study was to examine how much time Canadians devoted to non-work-related activities (home chores, childcare, eldercare) in 2001 and to estimate how non-work demands have changed over the past decade. Data on non-work demands are shown in Table 6.6 (means and standard deviations for 2001 data) and Table 6.7 (means and standard deviations for 1991 and 2001 samples).

The employees who answered our 2001 survey devoted significantly fewer hours per week to non-work activities than they did to paid employment. While virtually all respondents spent time each week in home chores

Table 6.6 Non-work demands: 2001

	Professionals		Non-professionals	
	Men	Women	Men	Women
Hours per week in childcare	10.5	11.5	10.2	10.7
Hours per week in eldercare	2.8	2.4	2.6	3.0
Hours per week in home chores	9.8	12	10.1	12.4
Hours per week in leisure	9.4	8.3	9.8	8.7

	Dependent care		No dependent care	
	Men	Women	Men	Women
Hours per week in childcare	10.5	11.1	0	0
Hours per week in eldercare	4.9	5.6	0	0
Hours per week in home chores	10.9	13.3	9.7	11
Hours per week in leisure	8.6	7.2	11.4	10.1

Table 6.7 Time spent in non-work demands: 1991 versus 2001

	Men		Women	
	1991	2001	1991	2001
Hours per week in childcare	14.7	10.5	16.4	11
Hours per week in home chores	13.6	10.9	16.6	13.3
Hours per week in leisure	14.1	8.6	12.5	7.2

Note: The 1991 and 2001 samples are not directly comparable as slightly different questions were used in the two time periods. The 1991 survey asked respondents to estimate the time spent the previous week day and previous weekend while the 2001 survey asked for time estimates over the previous week.

(99 per cent) and leisure (91 per cent), only 56 per cent spent time in childcare and 30 per cent spent time in eldercare. On average respondents spent 11 hours a week in home chores, ten hours in childcare (parents only), five hours in eldercare (providers only) and nine hours in leisure.

Change in time in non-work activities over time

While the data are not completely comparable, a comparison of who did what with respect to time in childcare, home chores and leisure is instructive. Examination of the data in Table 6.7 indicate that the men and women in the 2001 sample with dependent care activities spent less time per week in childcare, home chores and leisure than their counterparts in 1991. This finding suggests that Canadians are sacrificing time for themselves and time with their families to meet greater demands at work. Such a strategy may not be effective over the long run. Nor may this sacrifice be one that Canadian employees are willing to make indefinitely.

The link between demands and work-life conflict

A fourth objective of this research was to investigate the link between work demands, family demands and the various forms of work-life conflict. Results from the regression analysis undertaken to address this objective are shown in Tables 6.8 and 6.9.

The data are unequivocal – one is significantly able to predict two of the three forms of work-life conflict (i.e. role overload and work interferes with family) if one knows the demands employees face at work. Work demands predict:

- 13 per cent of the variation in role overload and 21 per cent of the variation in work interferes with family for men, and
- nine per cent of the variation in role overload and 20 per cent of the variation in work interferes with family for women.

While work demands are also a significant predictor of family interferes with work, the relationship cannot be considered substantive (i.e. it explains only one per cent of the variance in this construct).

On the other hand, only one form of work-life conflict, family interferes with work, can be predicted using our conceptualisation of non-work demands. While the relationships between non-work demands and role overload and work interferes with family were also significant, the amount of variation in these two forms of work-life conflict explained by their non-work demands was not substantive. Further details on the substantive relationships are given below.

Table 6.8 Summary of regression results: Work and non-work demands

	Men		Women	
	F	R^2	F	R^2
Work Demands				
Role Overload	F = 35.24, a = .000	0.134	F = 17.41, a = .000	0.09
Work Interferes with Family	F = 58.85, a = .000	0.206	F = 45.41, a = .000	0.196
Family Interferes with Work	F = 2.20, a = .008	0.01	F = 2.53, a = .002	0.01
Non-Work Demands				
Role Overload	F = 6.36, a = .000	0.04	F = 7.51, a = .000	0.04
Work Interferes with Family	F = 6.48, a = .000	0.04	F = 4.86, a = .000	0.03
Family Interferes with Work	F = 11.65, a = .000	0.06	F = 14.05, a = .000	0.08

Table 6.9   Summary of regression results: Key predictors of work-life conflict

Men		
Role overload	**Work interferes with family**	**Family interferes with work**
Impact of Non-Work Demands		
$R^2 = .038$	$R^2 = .038$	$R^2 = .064$ Resp. for childcare (1) Hrs/wk childcare (2) Hrs/wk leisure (3) Hrs/wk eldercare (4)
Impact of work Demands		
$R^2 = .134$ Unpaid OT/month (1) Hrs in work/week (2) Supervise others (3) Hrs/wk SWAH (4)	$R^2 = .206$ Unpaid OT/month (1) Weekend nights/month away on business (2) Hrs in work/week (3) Hrs/wk SWAH (4) Week nights/month away on business (5)	$R^2 = .01$
Women		
Role overload	**Work interferes with family**	**Family interferes with work**
Impact of Non-Work Demands		
$R^2 = .041$	$R^2 = .027$	$R^2 = .078$ Hrs/wk childcare (1) Hrs/wk leisure (2) Hrs/wk eldercare (3) Responsibility for childcare (4)
Impact of work demands		
$R^2 = .085$ Unpaid OT/month (1) Hrs commuting/wk (2) Weekend nights/month away on business (3) Hrs in work/week (4) Week nights/month away on business (5)	$R^2 = .196$ Unpaid OT/month (1) Weekend nights/month away on business (2) Week nights/month away on business (3) Hrs/wk SWAH (4) Hrs in work/week (5)	$R^2 = .013$

Note: Numbers in parentheses indicate relative importance as determined using Pratt's Coefficient

Work demands as a predictor of role overload

The key predictor of role overload for both men and women was the amount of time spent in unpaid overtime a month. There was only one other predictor of role overload that was important for both men and women – the total number of hours spent in work per week (second most important predictor of overload for men, fourth most important predictor for women).

These findings suggest that overload is not just a function of the amount of time spent working at the office per week, but also of work demands and expectations that must be fulfilled outside of regular work hours. This seems to be particularly true for the men where the number of hours spent in SWAH was the fourth most important predictor of role overload.

For men, holding a supervisory position was the third most important predictor of high levels of role overload. This suggests that there is a strong association between being a manager, and engaging in the types of behaviour (e.g. working long hours, the performance of unpaid overtime, performing SWAH) that lead to role overload. It is hard to determine the direction of causality of these data. Do they indicate that the workloads and the work expectations associated with being a manager encourage men to engage in the types of behaviours that contribute to role overload? Alternatively, do they indicate that men who work long hours and unpaid overtime are more likely to be promoted into management positions within their organisation? In either case, the data from this research supports the following conclusion: men who work longer hours will pay the price in terms of increased levels of role overload.

For women, on the other hand, three out of five of the most important predictors of role overload (i.e. time spent commuting to work, weekday and weekend nights away from home on business-related travel) pertained to job-related travel. The fact that none of these work demands were significant predictors of overload in men suggest that the etiology of role overload varies by gender. It would appear that for men, role overload appears to be a function of being a manager and engaging in work extension activities, while for women this form of work-life conflict is linked to being away from home on business-related travel.

What is it about business-related travel that contributes to role overload for women? Again, we can only speculate as to why this strong relationship exists. It may be that women who do a lot of business-related travel try and get things ready at home before they leave so that their absence will cause fewer problems for their family. Alternatively, it may be that women who travel on business spend a lot of their time on the road engaged in work-related activities rather than relaxing. Finally, it may also be that the activities associated with travel itself (i.e. packing, getting things ready at work and at home, travel itself, catching up when one gets back) are more problematic for women than men, perhaps because they have fewer people to help them cope with these extra demands (i.e. support staff at work, spouse at home).

The link between time spent commuting to work and role overload for women (but not for men) is also interesting. Again, it is difficult to know with certainty why this relationship exists. It may be that women, more than men, are expected to combine family chores with the commute to and from work (i.e. pick children up, drop children off). Alternatively it may be that women make different use of public transit than men or that women have less access to flexible work arrangements than men and hence are more likely to have to commute during the rush hour. Future research should focus on determining the causal mechanisms behind this finding.

Work demands as a predictor of work interferes with family

The key predictor of work interferes with family for both men and women was the amount of time spent in unpaid overtime a month – the same type of behaviour associated with high role overload. While the key predictors of role overload were associated with the gender of the employee, no such differences were observed with respect to the predictors of work interferes with family. The results show that employees who spend more time in job-related travel, perform SWAH, work unpaid overtime and work more hours per week, are more likely to report high levels of work interferes with family, regardless of their gender. This is not surprising as there are only so many hours in the day, and hours devoted to work are, by necessity, not available for other activities.

The strong association between job-related travel and this form of work-life conflict is not surprising as these individuals are more likely to be unavailable for family activities that are scheduled on week nights and on the weekend. The link between SWAH and work interferes with family is also interesting though in this case it is difficult to determine the direction of causality. It could be that people with heavier work demands are more likely to bring work home in an attempt to balance competing demands and that their levels of work interferes with family would be even higher if they could not engage in such behaviour. Alternatively, it may be that people who bring work into their home feel guilty about their work intruding on their family life.

Several strong conclusions can be drawn from these data regardless of the direction of causality. The first is that job-related travel is a strong predictor of work interferes with family. The second is that employees who put in more hours (particularly overtime hours at home) are more likely to report this form of conflict. Third, it is important to note that this form of work-life conflict is not just a function of workload but rather work demands that either physically remove the employee from their family domain, or take time that is typically reserved for the family. Finally, it is important to note that the key predictors of this form of work-life conflict are the same for both men and women.

Non-work demands as a predictor of family interferes with work

Non-work demands explained six per cent of the variation in family interferes with work for men and eight per cent for women. For both men and women this form of conflict was associated with greater responsibility for childcare, more time in both childcare and eldercare, and fewer hours in leisure. The fact that responsibility for eldercare was a significant predictor of family interferes with work for women but not men, suggests that multi-generational care-giving situations are more problematic for women. Time in home chores, education and volunteer work were not significant predictors of family interferes with work for either gender.

Impact of gender on work-life conflict

The data reviewed in this study are unequivocal – women are significantly more likely to report high levels of role overload than men. This gender difference in role overload occurred regardless of job type or dependent care status. This suggests that the gender difference in role overload can be partly attributed to the fact that society expects different things from women than from men.

It is important to note that there are no gender differences in work interferes with family or family interferes with work when dependent care status and job type are taken into account. In other words, these forms of work-life conflict are more a function of where one works and the type of work and non-work demands one assumes rather than gender.

The data presented in this paper also support the idea that men have heavier work demands than women. Men (regardless of job type or dependent care status) spent more hours per week in paid employment than women (44.1 hours versus 40.6), were more likely to work paid overtime (34 per cent versus 28 per cent), unpaid overtime (55 per cent versus 45 per cent) and SWAH (58 per cent versus 43 per cent). They also spent more hours per month, on average, in paid overtime (12 hours versus 10 hours) and unpaid overtime (20 hours per month versus 14). Men also had heavier travel demands (more likely to have to spend weekday and weekends away on business). These findings imply that there are still gender differences with respect to what companies expect from their employees and the demands employees place on themselves.

Another key finding from this research is that the role of 'caregiver' is not as strongly associated with gender as it was in the past. Traditionally, research in this area has determined that women spend more time in childcare than men. Such was not the case in this study as mothers and fathers who engaged in childcare spent essentially the same amount of time each week in childcare-related activities (the typical mother in the sample spent approximately 11.1 hours per week in childcare while the typical father spent approximately 10.5 hours). Similarly, the men and the women in the sample with eldercare responsibilities spent approximately the same amount of time per week in eldercare activities (the typical man with elder-care responsibilities spent 4.6 hours per week in care while the typical woman spent approximately 5.2 hours).

These data suggest that women's entry into the paid labour force has had a measurable impact on the division of family labour within the home. The fact that we did not observe large gender differences with respect to the amount of time devoted to childcare may be attributed to the fact that time for family-related activities has declined as time in work has increased. A comparison of the 1991 and 2001 data sets supports this interpretation. These data indicate that while both genders are now spending less time in family activities than previously, the decline in time spent in childcare has been more precipitous for women (dropped by 33 per cent over the decade) than for men (dropped 25 per cent). This finding is consistent with reports by Statistics Canada suggesting that in the 1980s and 90s men (particularly husbands and lone fathers) spent more time in unpaid work activities such as child and eldercare than was the case earlier in the decade (Vanier Institute, 2000). They are also consistent with Bianchi's (2000) observations from American time use data. She attributes the decline in maternal time in childcare and the lack of gender differences in time spent in childcare to the following factors: (1) the reallocation of mothers' time to market work outside the home, (2) overestimations of maternal time with children in the past (it was assumed that time at home was all invested in childcare when in reality a large amount was given to home chores), (3) smaller families has reduced the number of years with very young children, (4) more pre-school children spend time outside the home in school-like settings regardless of their mothers' employment status, (5) women's reallocation of their time has changed men's domestic roles and facilitated the increase in men's involvement in child rearing, and (6) technology (i.e. cell phones, beepers) has made it possible for parents to be 'on call' without being physically present in the home. In other words, the gender difference in time spent in childcare has diminished as women spend less time in childcare, men spend more, and the need to spend high amounts of time in childcare is reduced.

Finally, it should also be noted that this 'enlightened' attitude with respect to the distribution of 'family labour' does not extend to home chores. The women respondents spent substantially more time in home chores per week than the men, regardless of job type or dependent care status. This finding would suggest that in many Canadian families home chores are still perceived to be 'women's work.'

Impact of job type on work-life conflict

A number of important conclusions can also be drawn with respect to the link between job type, work and family demands and work-life conflict. First, the data show that managers and professionals of both genders had markedly higher work demands. They spent more time per week in work, had heavier travel demands and dedicated more time to unpaid overtime and SWAH. Male managers and professionals had particularly heavy workloads. Given these heavier work demands it was not surprising to find that both the male and female managers and professionals reported higher levels of role overload and work interferes with family than those in 'other' jobs. The higher levels of interference are also consistent with the fact that those in managerial and professional positions were more likely to engage in work-related activities which make it harder to tend to events outside of work.

It is interesting to note that when job type is taken into account and when work-life conflict is broken into its component parts, many of the gender differences in work-life conflict referred to in the research literature are no longer significant. This suggests that many of these differences are due more to the fact that women are typically compressed into a different set of jobs than men.

There was, however, one interesting finding from this study that could be linked to both gender and job type. The female managers and professionals were the only group of women in our sample to spend more time in childcare per week (11.5 hours) than their male counterparts (10.5 hours). This group of women also spent significantly more time in childcare than their female counterparts in non-professional positions (10.7 hours per week). These findings are interesting as they support the myth of 'supermom' – the professional woman who thinks that she has to (and can) 'do it all.' They also suggest that some of the additional burdens faced by professional women may be self-imposed.

Impact of dependent care status on work-life conflict

Who has more problems balancing work and family responsibilities? The evidence from this study supports the following conclusion: employed Canadians with dependent care responsibilities. The employees in this sample with dependent care responsibilities reported greater levels of work-life conflict than those without such responsibilities regardless of how work-life conflict was assessed or the gender of the respondent. The fact that those with childcare and/or eldercare responsibilities report greater conflict can be attributed to the fact that this group has:

- more demands on their time: while they spent more than twice as much time in non-work activities as those without dependent care (23 hours versus ten hours and approximately three hours less per week in leisure) the amount of time spent in work each week is not associated with dependent care status, and
- fewer degrees of freedom to deal with work issues (i.e. less control over their time).

It is also interesting to note that employees with dependent care responsibilities are more likely to perform SWAH. Future analysis of the data will determine if this strategy is an effective way for parents and those with eldercare to cope with increased work demands or if it is associated with increased work-life conflict.

A number of the associations between dependent care and the work and family constructs examined in this study depend on both gender and job type. For example, while time in work per week is not associated with dependent care status when the comparison is done within gender (i.e. mothers spent same time in work per week as women without children; fathers spent the same amount of time in work per week as men without children), men with dependent care responsibilities have greater work demands than their female counterparts. They invest more time in paid work per week and spend more week nights away from home than women with dependent care. This greater investment in work may give men an advantage with respect to career advancement. Similarly, while the women with dependent care responsibilities spent more time in home chores each week than their counterparts without dependent care (13.3 hours versus 11.0 hours), no such association was observed for men (men with dependent care spent 10.5 hours in home chores per week versus 9.7 for those without dependent care). This finding provides additional support for our contention that home chores are seen as 'women's work.'

Discussion and implications

The data examined in this paper support the following conclusions with respect to role overload:

- high levels of role overload have become systemic within the population of employees working for Canada's largest employers,
- the percentage of the workforce with high role overload has increased over the past decade,
- employees with higher family demands (i.e. dependent care responsibilities) and higher work demands (i.e. managers and professionals) are more likely to experience high levels of role overload,
- women are more likely than men to report high levels of role overload,
- role overload is a function of work demands first, and family demands second,
- the amount of time spent in unpaid overtime a month and the total number of hours spent in work per week are key predictors of role overload for both men and women,
- the amount of time spent in unpaid overtime per week is the most important predictor of role overload,

- for male employees role overload is a function of being a manager and engaging in work extension activities. For women, role overload is a function of being away from home on business and business-related travel.

Taken together these findings indicate that the relationship between role overload and work demands has a slightly different etiology for men than women. They also indicate that if one knows how much time an employee spends per week in unpaid overtime then they will be able to predict with a fair degree of confidence the amount of role overload they will experience.

The data reviewed in this report support the following conclusions with respect to work interferes with family:

- work interferes with family remains a real problem for one in four Canadians,
- the greater the number of responsibilities outside of work, the more likely an employee is to experience high work interferes with family,
- work interferes with family is a function of work rather than non-work demands,
- employees who spend more time in job-related travel, SWAH, unpaid overtime, and work per week are more likely to report high levels of work interferes with family, regardless of their gender.

It would appear that this form of work-life conflict is not so much a function of workload but rather of work demands that either physically remove the employee from their family domain or take time that is typically reserved for the family.

The following key observations can be drawn regarding family interferes with work:

- family interferes with work is not prevalent in Canada at this time,
- three times as many Canadians give priority to work at the expense of their family as do the reverse (i.e. give priority to their family),
- the percentage of working Canadians who give priority to family rather than work has more than doubled over the past decade,
- family interferes with work is largely a function of the demands an employee faces within the family domain rather than demands at work,
- for both men and women, this form of conflict is associated with greater responsibility for childcare, more time in both childcare and eldercare and fewer hours in leisure.

The data reviewed in this chapter support the following conclusions with respect to work and non-work demands:

- work demands have increased for all employee groups over the past decade and many Canadian employees cannot complete their work during regular work hours,
- work requirements (especially with respect to job-related travel and overtime) do not support work-life balance,
- Canadians spend less time in family demands today than they did a decade ago,
- Canadians devote considerably more time per week to paid employment than to their non-work roles.

The data with respect to work demands suggest that many of Canada's largest employers still believe in the 'myth of separate worlds.' The expectation that an employee will spend both weekday and weekend nights away from home if required by their job appears to be quite prevalent, and many employees donate a substantial proportion of their personal time to their employer.

There is 'no one size fits all solution' to the issue of work-life balance. The data from this study show quite clearly that different policies, practices and strategies will be needed to reduce each of the three components of work-life conflict. That being said, the data would indicate that there are a number of strategies and approaches that the various stakeholders can use to reduce work-life conflict.

To reduce work-life conflict employers need to focus their efforts on making work demands and work expectations more realistic. Work demands, rather than demands from outside of work, are the key predictors of role overload and work interferes with family, the two most common forms of work-life conflict in Canada at this point in time. While employers often point with pride to the many 'programs' available in their organisation to help employees meet family obligations, these programs do not diminish the fact that most people simply have more work to do than can be accomplished in a standard work week. As such employers and governments need to recognise that the issue of work-life conflict cannot be addressed without addressing the issue of workloads.

Employers can help employees deal with heavy work demands by introducing initiatives which increase an employee's sense of control. The research in this area (see for example, work by Karasek, 1979) is quite clear – employees can cope with greater demands if they have a greater sense of control. The literature suggests a number of mechanisms which should be investigated including increased autonomy and empowerment at the individual employee level, the increased use of self-directed work teams, increased employee participation in decision-making, increased communication and information sharing, time management training, training on how to plan and prioritise, and increased use of flexible work arrangements. Organisations should consider all of these mechanisms to reduce role overload and work interferes with family within their workforces.

What else can the employer do? The data from this study indicate that employers would benefit if they examined workloads within their organisations and started recording the true costs of understaffing and overwork (i.e. greater absenteeism, higher prescription drug costs, greater EAP use, increased turnover, hiring costs), so that they could make informed decisions with respect to this issue. If they find that certain employees within their organisation are consistently spending long hours at work (i.e. 50+ hours per week), they need to determine why this is the case (i.e. work expectations are unbalanced and unrealistic, poor planning, too many priorities, employees do not have the tools and/or training to do the job efficiently, poor management, culture focused on hours not output). Once they have determined the causal factors, they need to determine how workloads can be made more reasonable.

Employers also need to identify ways to reduce the amount of time employees (especially women) spend in job-related travel (i.e. increase their use of virtual teams, teleconferencing technology). In particular they need to reduce their expectations that employees will travel on personal time and spend weekends away from home to reduce the organisation's travel costs.

Employees themselves have a role to play with respect to the reduction of role overload. Accordingly we recommend that employees try to say 'no' to overtime hours if work expectations are unreasonable, reduce the amount of time they spend in job-related travel and to limit the amount of work they take home to complete in the evenings. If they do bring work home they should make every effort to separate time in work from family time (i.e. do work after the children go to bed, have a home office).

References

Bianchi, S. (2000) 'Maternal Employment and Time With Children: Dramatic Change or Surprising Continuity?' *Demography*, 37: 401–14.

BNA (1997) *Employers and Elder-Care: A New Benefit Coming of Age*, Washington, D.C.: The Bureau of National Affairs.

CCSD (1996). *Family Security in Insecure Times: Volumes 2 and 3*, Ottawa: Canadian Council on Social Development.

Duxbury, L., Higgins, C., Lee, C. and Mills, S. (1991) *Balancing Work and Family: A Study of the Canadian Public Sector*, Prepared for The Department of Health and Welfare Canada (NHRDP), Ottawa, Ontario.

Duxbury, L. and Higgins, C. (1994) 'Families in the Economy', in Baker, M. (ed.) *Family Policy*, Ottawa: Vanier Institute of the family, 29–40.

Duxbury, L. and Higgins, C. (2001) *Work-Life Balance In the New Millennium: Where Are We? Where do We Need to Go?* Ottawa: CPRN. Can be found at: http://www.cprn.org/cprn.html

Duxbury, L. and Higgins, C. (2003) *Work-Life Conflict in Canada in the New Millennium: A Status Report (Report Two)*, Ottawa: Health Canada. Can be found at: http://www.hc-sc.gc.ca/pphb-dgspsp/publicat/work-travail/report2/index.html

Fast, J. and de Pont, M. (1997) 'Changes in Women's Work Continuity', *Canadian Social Trends*, 46, Autumn.

Foot, D. (1996) *Boom, Bust & Echo. How to Profit From the Coming Demographic Shift*, Toronto: Macfarlane Walter and Ross.

Guerts, S. and Demerouti, E. (2003) 'Work/Non-work Interface: A Review of Theories and Findings', in Schabracq, M. Winnubst, J. and Cooper, C. (eds) *The Handbook of Work and Health Psychology*, Chichester: Wiley, 279–312.

Hammer, L., Colton, C., Caubert, S. and Brockwood, K. (2002) 'The Unbalanced Life: Work and Family Conflict', in Thomas, J. and Hersen, M. (eds) *Handbook of Mental Health*, Thousand Oaks CA: Sage 83–102.

Haas, L. (1995) 'Structural Dimensions of the Work-Family Interface', in Bowen, G. and Pittman, J. (eds) *The Work and Family Interface*, Families in Focus Series: National Council on Family Relations, 113–21.

Higgins, C. and Duxbury, L. (2002) *The 2001 National Work-Life Conflict Study: Report One*, Ottawa: Health Canada. Can be found at: http://www.hc-sc.gc.ca/pphb-dgspsp/publicat/work-travail/index.html

Hochschild, A. (1989) *The Second Shift*, New York: Viking Penguin.

Jick, T. and Mitz, L. (1985) 'Sex differences in work stress', *Academy of Management Review*, 10: 408–20.

Johnson, K., Lero, D. and Rooney, J. (2001) *Work-Life Compendium 2001*, HRDC, Women's Bureau, Ottawa, Catalogue SP-184-08-01E.

Kanter, R. (1977) *Work and family in the United States: A critical review and agenda for research and policy*, New York: Sage.

Karasek, R. (1979) 'Job Demands, Job Decision Latitude, and Mental Drain: Implications for Job Redesign', *Administrative Science Quarterly*, 29: 285–308.

Lowe, G. and Schellenberg, G. (1999) *Changing Employment Relationships: Implications for Workers, Employers and Public Policy*, Ottawa: Canadian Policy Research Network.

Lowe, G. (2000) *The Quality of Work: A People Centred Agenda*, Toronto: Oxford University Press.

Milkie, M. and Peltola, P. (1999) 'Playing all the Roles: Gender and the Work-Family Balancing Act', *Journal of Marriage and the Family*, 61: 476–90.

Quick, J., Nelson, D. and Hurrell, J. Jr. (1997) *Preventive stress management in organizations*, Washington, D.C.: American Psychological Association.

Scott, K. (2000) *Work Family and Community: Key Issues and Directions for Future Research*, Labour Bureau, HRDC, Ottawa. (also see http://labour.hrdc-drhc/gc/ca/doc/wlb-ctp/ccsd-ccds/c1-en.html)

Statistics Canada (1997a) *Characteristics of Dual-earner Families*, Ottawa: Statistics Canada, Catalogue 13-215-XPB.

Statistics Canada (1997b) '1996 Census: Marital Status, Common-law Unions and Families', *The Daily*, Tuesday, October 14.

Statistics Canada (1997c) *Labour Force Update: Hours of work*, Ottawa: Statistics Canada, Catalogue 71-005-XPB.

Statistics Canada (1999) Labour Force Update: An Overview of the Labour Market 1998, *The Daily*, January 27, Ottawa: Statistics Canada.

Statistics Canada (2000) *Women in Canada 2000: A Gender Based Statistical Report*, Ottawa: Statistics Canada, Catalogue 89-503-XPE.

Stone, T. and Meltz, N. (1993) *Human Resource Management in Canada*, Toronto: Dryden Press.

Thomas, D.R., Hughes, E. and Zumbo, B.D. (1998) 'On Variable Importance in Linear Regression', *Social Indicators Research*, 45: 253–75.

Vanderkolk, B. and Young, A. (1991) *The Work and Family Revolution: How Companies Can Keep Employees Happy and Business Profitable*, New York: Facts on File, Inc.

Vanier Institute (1997) *From the Kitchen Table to the Boardroom Table: The Canadian Family and the Workplace*, Ottawa: Vanier Institute of the Family.

Vanier Institute (2000) *Profiling Canada's Families II*, Ottawa: Vanier Institute of the Family.

7

Work-Life Balance and Flexible Working Hours – The German Experience

Rainer Trinczek

Introduction

The Anglicism 'work-life balance' has become a very fashionable term in both public and academic circles in Germany for some years now. 'Work-Life Balance Gets Boost in Germany' was the headline of a radio program of Deutsche Welle in early April 2005, and it was a typical headline for many programs and articles in the German media in the recent past. The red-green coalition government has also discovered work-life balance. To encourage the family-friendly company movement, the Ministry for Family Affairs launched a competition to name the nation's top employers for parents. If you search the internet using the phrase 'work-life balance', there are some 80,000 German internet sites containing that phrase, with the number of websites continuing to increase over the last few months.

One can also find statements on work-life balance on the websites of most large German organisations. For examples, the Siemens website states:

'You are willing to work hard to achieve you career goals. At the same time you are striving for a balanced personal life. We also understand that work is only one part of your life. That's why Siemens actively supports the fact that employees also need time for their private life. We are convinced that employees who have found that balance are not only dedicated and enjoy making the most of their creativity, they are also more successful at their jobs and better prepared to go that extra mile when it's needed' (Siemens, 2005).

The debate in Germany about work-life balance typically involves arguments about flexible working hours, particularly when it comes to strategies for promoting work-life balance. It is not purely accidental that the above quotation from the Siemens web-page continues as follows:

'We offer a variety of options for organizing worktime to give our employees the independence they need in order to balance their work and personal life. At many locations around the world, we have flex-itime arrangements in place – in some cases, trust-based and annualized – as well as part-time working models with different numbers of work hours and fixed or flexible attendance requirements. We also support job-sharing, variable shift models, sabbaticals and phased retirement schemes' (Siemens, 2005).

This chapter concentrates on the question of how flexible working hours can advance work-life balance in Germany. First, it will be argued that the so-called 'compatibility problem' for women is the core issue of this debate in Germany. For this reason, the paper will focus on this issue when analysing whether flexible working hours help women to ease their situation. Trust-based flexitime (*Vertrauensarbeitszeit*) is the working time model that will be used as an example in this chapter, as it offers maximum discretion on the structure of working time to employees. On the basis of an empirical research project that studied the implementation of this working time model in several German companies, it will be argued that it is not so much the working time model in itself that promotes or hinders work-life balance, but the working hours culture that prevails within the organisation.

The work-life balance debate in Germany

The work-life balance discussion in Germany is, for the most part, simply misleading rhetoric. Whilst the notion of work-life balance is taken seriously in academic discussions (cf. Eberling et al, 2004), the debate has not been legitimised in political life. The increasing use of the Anglicism of work-life balance in political circles and more practice-related contexts is merely a semantic face-lift for an old debate on the compatibility of family and paid work, which is still also to a large extent seen 'only' as an issue for women. This entails a loss of the fundamentally innovative content of the new debate, which opens up the broader issues of how men and women (both individually and within a family context) can strike the right balance between their work and private life, with private life signifying not just family and children but also leisure activities, commitments as citizens, friends, spare time and contemplation.

The backdrop to this broader perspective lies to a great extent in three sociological findings. The first relates to the slow disintegration of the bourgeois view of gender, based on clearly defined gender roles. This involves more than women simply breaking out of the socially determined concentration on the family and household sphere. Men increasingly appear to be acknowledging that there is life beyond work, and that the typical male fixation on career and the professional world at the same time also leads to one-sided experience and a lopsided development of one's personality, which can hardly be reconciled with the paradigm of a balanced life (for a summary of changing family structures in Germany, cf. Peuckert, 2002)

The second finding concerns the growing number of women in employment, particularly women with children under 18 years of age. The employment rate of these women has risen significantly during the last decades. In 2003, 31.9 per cent of women with their youngest child being under three years of age were working in Germany, with the employment rate increasing with the age of the youngest child – 65.3 per cent when the child is between six and ten; and 74.9 per cent when it is between 15 and 18 (Statistisches Bundesamt, 2004). The growing employment of women (and mothers in particular) undermines the traditional gender-specific solution of the 'work-life balance' problem. As women increasingly participate on an equal basis in professional life, the old solution whereby the man was in charge of dealing with 'work' and the woman was responsible for organising 'life' becomes less relevant.

The final finding relates to the phenomenon of increasing working hours. Average hours of work per week are increasing, particularly in highly qualified jobs, at a time when employees are becoming ever more aware of time issues (Bauer et al, 2004). On the one hand, longer working hours per se limit the time available to successfully balance the various spheres of life and interests. However, this phenomenon encounters an altered structure of employee preferences. Time takes on an increasingly important part in the subjective scale of preferences, and here it should be noted that the more highly qualified an individual, the greater their desire to have shorter working hours.

The academic debate in Germany has been driven by this apparent contradictory situation – the need for a change of balance between the various spheres of life, coupled with the inherent difficulties of putting such ideas into practice. However this debate, as described above, suffers from being conducted primarily in academic circles or by intellectual avant-garde thinkers in the political sphere, whist in political practice the label 'work-life balance' is predominantly a slightly modernised variant of traditional policy on 'family and work' compatibility.

A fairly frequent phenomenon in this context is illustrated, for example, by the way the Ministry for Family translates 'work-life balance' into German as simply 'balance between family and the world of work' (cf. in the flyer of the Ministry 'Balance von Familie und Arbeitswelt', BMFSFJ, 2003). Given that this is the case, one is not surprised to find that one of the Ministry's central projects, initiated in conjunction with the renowned Bertelsmann Foundation, is the 'Alliance for the Family', which mainly concentrates on taking action (cf. BMFSFJ/Bertelsmann Stiftung, 2003). Nor is one surprised to see the approach adopted by the 'Work-life balance as a driving force for economic growth and social stability' programme launched jointly by the Ministry and the Employers' Associations. This

Association researches the impact of organising work and human resources in a way that emphasises the balance between private life and work on companies, the economy and society. To quote a press release 'The study drawn up in 2003 on "economic effects of family-friendly schemes" as the starting point for the project' (BMFSFJ, 2004).

The Federal Ministry of Economic Affairs and Labour has adopted a similar stance. In the context of strategy to support small and medium-sized enterprises, a Ministry document states:

'Families benefit above all from an improved work-life balance – and this pays off threefold in economic and commercial terms: families – and here primarily women – are relieved of the burden of coordinating professional and family life; greater female participation in work means higher tax revenues for the state; through a family-oriented staff policy, companies gain competitive advantages and location advantages, in addition to cutting costs. Family-oriented measures are well worthwhile, particularly for small and medium-sized enterprises' (BMWA, 2005).

This use of the term 'work-life balance', reduced mainly to the compatibility of family and work, also increasingly guides company policy. For example, IBM writes, under the heading '*Diversity – Work/Life Balance*':

'A precondition for successful, committed and motivated work is that staff are well-balanced. We support them in striking a balance between work, family and leisure. Support with childcare, together with our well-being and leisure schemes, helps us to achieve this. You don't have to decide between a career and a family if you work for us!' (IBM, 2005).

In all of these (entirely typical) examples, 'life' is equated with 'family'.

This raises the question of why these problems predominate in the political and practical sphere, to such an extent that they more or less threaten to stifle the broader perspective of the 'work-life balance' debate. Several factors are responsible for this, including the traditional high – and indeed ideology-driven – status of the family in political debate in Germany. These factors relate to the economics of education as well as to the changed behaviour of women in professional life. However, at the core of this nexus lies the pivotal issue, namely demographic change in Germany. This chapter will outline the most relevant and important arguments to ensure that the specific narrowing of the topic of 'work-life balance' in the German debate becomes at least partly comprehensible. The central arguments are as follows:

Evolution of the population   Like most highly developed industrial nations, Germany also has a 'demographic problem'. The German population will shrink considerably in the foreseeable future as a result of the dramatic drop in the birth rate since the mid-sixties to a value far below replacement levels. Current forecasts assume that the German population will drop from 82 million in 2000 to between 65 and 73 million in 2050. At the same time, the age structure of the population is also shifting. There will be more people aged over 60, with the commensurate fall in the proportion of younger people. The average age for men and women in 2000 was 41.1 years, and this will rise continually to an estimated 48.2 years in 2045 and will then probably stabilise at this level (Deutscher Bundestag, 2002).

Labour supply   After 2020, there will be a pronounced fall in labour supply as a result of the natural decline in population, as workers from the age-group with the highest birth rates (i.e. the 1950s and early 1960s) will be retiring, whilst only workers from years with low birth rates will be entering the labour market. Model calculations assume that the number of employed persons will fall from 40.8 million to 27.3 million between 2010 and 2050 (Deutscher Bundestag, 2002), with the economic consequences of this remaining unclear.

Economics of education   The education reforms of the 1960s and 1970s within the broader context of the debate on equal rights for women has led to women in the Federal Republic of Germany almost pulling level with, and in some cases overtaking, men in terms of formal qualifications. More girls than boys already take the *Abitur* or university-entrance exam. There are more women than men amongst first-semester students. However, male students still dominate when it comes to degrees. In terms of the economics of education, the shortcomings in the use of the qualifications obtained by women is analysed as a bad economic investment. Too much of the investment in education is held not to give an adequate return, due to the high rate of female part-time work and/or as a result of women stopping work, sometimes temporarily, after pregnancies. It would therefore be rational to either reduce the percentage of women acquiring higher-level and expensive qualifications (which is, however, neither desirable nor practicable politically) or to ensure greater use of the productivity potential of females in the workforce.

The accumulation of these facts has resulted in an intensified social and political 'observation' of female behaviour in respect of child-bearing and professional life over the past few years. Optimising both of these simultaneously could make a significant contribution to resolving the problem depicted. The relevant steps are rooted in a broad set of political measures, which are rarely perceived by the public as a consistent strategy, although there is an inner cohesion to them. However, it is relatively easy to describe the political goals and the associated strategies to achieve them:

Slowing down and/or reversing negative demographic trends   Besides a changed immigration policy aimed at establishing Germany as a major immigration country, the political system is trying to improve the low fertility rate of women in Germany which is, at present, as low as 1.3. It is hoped that by improving the compatibility of family and work, women in Germany will change their behaviour and have larger families. This is particularly relevant for highly qualified women, as a large percentage of these women do not have any children. Currently more than 40 per cent of 40 year-old female graduates do not have children, and the trend for this figure is set to increase.

Increasing the labour supply by mobilising 'employment reserves'   One of the key factors that constrains the scope for Germany to flourish sustainably as a business location is the future fall in the supply of labour, coupled with the problems associated with financing the social security system. Various measures are being employed at present by the German Government, all of which aim to cushion the impact of aggregate population decline on the labour market. In addition to other strategies such as reducing the number of school years and stopping early retirement schemes, attempts are also being made to mobilise additional total hours worked by increasing women's participation in working life and at the same time reducing their widespread concentration in part-time employment. To this end, more all-day schools are to be set up in Germany, crèches are to be created for small children up to three years and longer nursery-school hours are to be introduced. Over and above this, family and work (where possible, full-time) should be made generally more compatible, for example by implementing more flexible working hours systems.

An important component of this long-term political strategy involves persuading women to make sustainable changes to their behaviour in respect of fertility and at the same time to play a more active part in the world of work. In this context, it should be noted that the new slogan for women, 'more children and more work' (*Mehr Kinder + Mehr Arbeit*), has in the past always been held politically to be making paradoxical demands and has hence been considered to be impossible to implement. This is because the existing empirical studies always emphasise that the converse would apply – more children equals less (paid) work and/or more work amounts to fewer children.

Therefore, via the circuitous route of the current demographic debate, the traditional women's issue of compatibility of family and work has suddenly gained increased political attention. Even if in terms of gender politics it has taken on a more modern slant, stressing that nowadays family issues are relevant to men too, or should be. It is scarcely surprising, given the political system's insatiable appetite for innovative-sounding concepts, that the emerging 'work-life balance' debate was rapidly appropriated semantically – without any further note being taken of the whole context of this discussion, which is actually much broader.

Issues relating to working hours play a central part in this constrained work-life balance discussion. All the relevant research agrees that the most frequent reply by employees when asked what measures a firm should take to be considered 'family-friendly' is that the company should introduce flexible working hours, allowing employees a certain degree of autonomy in terms of working time. Employees feel that this would make it simpler to combine family and work.

Work-life balance is almost automatically associated with innovative and flexible working hours. The call for applications for the BestPersAward, the major award in Germany for excellent and integrated HR policies in medium-sized companies ('Mittelstand'), can be taken as a typical example of this. The call for applications states:

'Work-life balance is becoming increasingly important, even in a difficult economic situation, and all the more so in small and medium-sized enterprises. The goal is to maintain this and put it into practice in each specific company context. Imagination is called for here. Offering scope for part-time or teleworking is one way to provide the basis for work-life balance, as is the option of working flexible hours' (BestPersAward, 2005).

In the section that follows the question of whether it is justified to hope that implementing flexible working hours models will make a valuable contribution to guaranteeing work-life balance is addressed, by concentrating on the most innovative working time model: Trust-based flexitime (*Vertrauensarbeitszeit*).

Trust-Based flexitime and the compatibility problem

The system of trust-based flexitime is polarising the current policy debate on working hours in the Federal Republic of Germany more than perhaps any other model of working hours. Trust-based flexitime describes a model of corporate organisation of working time in which the company renounces control of employee working hours and it is up to staff to determine where and when their work will be done, in agreement with their colleagues and superiors. A typical characteristic of the trust-based system is the abolition of formal time-keeping by company bodies.[1] Trust-based flexitime has spread considerably amongst German companies during the last few years. Despite the fact that there is no representative survey on the overall dissemination of this working time model, there are several smaller studies mainly concentrating on certain branches or companies of certain sizes (e.g. Brasse, 2003; IFO, 2002; Janßen, 2003; Pletke and Wieczoreck-Haubus, 2003). According to these studies, the percentage of companies using trust-based working hours is reported to be between 20 per cent and about 40 per cent of all companies in Germany. This does not necessarily mean that all employees of these companies work in this working time arrangement; all research shows that white collar workers (*Angestellte*) are more likely to have trust-based working hours than blue collar workers (*Arbeiter*). Irrespective of the exact percentage of organisations employing trust-based flexitime, two points may be made: First, trust-based flexitime seems to be a popular strategy amongst German companies, and second, this model seems to fit into the long-term strategy of German companies to generally increase the flexibility around working time arrangements.

It seems fair to say that the polarising effect of trust-based flexitime is primarily connected to the considerable promises to, and unreasonable demands on, employees that may be associated with this model for working hours. The promises in this context are primarily a new 'freedom in working hours', as employees move beyond the dictate of 'clocking on and off', core working hours and an obligation to be present in the work-place. The system entails relatively few formal provisions that employees would have to comply with – in the 'worst' case scenario, one would have to coordinate with one's colleagues. In contrast, critics argue there are unreasonable demands placed on workers in the shift to trust-based flexitime, from a time-oriented to a task-oriented approach. Employees are now expected to be flexible in adapting the actual hours worked to the specific time required to carry out their work activities. That means that if there is a lot of work, staff working hours would tend to be extended and when there is little work to be done, working hours would be reduced. There is also a fear that the implementation of trust-based flexitime could cause a general increase of working hours, due to the endless supply of work (by way of example, see IG Metall, 1999; and Pickshaus, 2000) coupled with the disappearance of strict recording of working time and the associated rules.

It is easy to see that the impact of the two scenarios on the 'compatibility problem' of combining work and the interests of one's life-world would be diametrically opposed. While the new freedom in working hours promises to significantly facilitate efforts to coordinate various different individual time interests, the unreasonable demands scenario would, on the contrary, directly generate a more problematic framework in which to conduct one's life-world. This paper will present results from a recent research project[2] on the unresolved question of how trust-based flexitime impinges on the chances of combining work and life.

In addressing these issues, the focus is on the case of employees with children that require care because the difficulties experienced by these employees in balancing work and family life feature prominently in the literature.

The potential of the trust-based system in shaping family time schedules

The evidence from research on family sociology reveals the high degree of pluralisation and differentiation in the lives and practical everyday arrangements of working parents. This means that it is now more difficult than ever to assume uniform patterns of 'parent-typical' working hours arrangements or requirements for certain working hours. Rather, we are confronted with a considerable degree of differentiation, arising from the age and number of children, material resources, social networks and the institutional childcare facilities available (see for example, Ludwig and Schlevogt, 2002). In this context, the general framework determined by material, social and institutional conditions is in essence 'translated' into either a successful or generally problematic balance between professional and family demands on the parents' time, as a function of the arrangements that couples choose. Current studies reveal a broad spectrum of different choices. These range from a traditional gender-specific division of labour, with the 'male breadwinner' constellation, to egalitarian forms of division of labour within the family.

In this context, the evaluation of 'pro-family corporate concepts' in large-scale industry (e.g. Gemeinützige Hertie-Stiftung, 1998) has again provided an exemplary demonstration that flexible working hours models are an essential precondition for combining a job and a family, although not the sole prerequisite. Parents' time arrangements rely on flexible working hours, partly due to frequently complex childcare arrangements, but also to allow them to respond to 'disruptions' in these generally fragile networks, such as if a child or carer falls ill. Given the aforementioned pluralisation, arrangements enabling a 'tailor-made' organisation of working hours, allowing for highly individual shaping of working time, are primarily held to provide support for parents.

The central elements of this type of 'tailor-made' model encompass flexibility of starting and finishing time, individual control over how extra hours can be accrued and used up in a time-budget, together with no rigid obligations to be present in the workplace at particular times. All these features are in essence compatible with various childcare arrangements.

Prima facie, one might contend that a system of trust-based flexitime, encompassing the potential for complete openness to individual options in shaping working options, is highly compatible with these differentiated time needs. One might say that the trust-based system's complete liberation of when and where working hours are effected makes it, theoretically, a virtually ideal option to implement time arrangements modulated to fit individual needs. As the system of trust-based flexitime offers all employees a broader repertoire of working hours structures that the company could envisage and consider legitimate, one could also argue that employees with children could thus free themselves from the stigma of limited efficiency which has previously regularly been associated with unconventional working hours arrangements (or wishes).

Furthermore, the image of staff conveyed by the trust-based model means this system does more than simply offer open options to shape work structures, actually fostering this openness – in a sense as a new structural quality in the company in question. A trust-based flexitime system is introduced as a symbol of an innovative work culture, which management – at least on a rhetorical, visionary level – associates with a corresponding ideal image of a self-motivated and self-directed staff member. This positive presumption of an employee type that acts with a relative degree of autonomy rather than on the basis of instructions, is manifested in particular in management's explicit decision not to control how employees shape their working hours. Rather than merely enabling individual and creative time management responsive to the vicissitudes of the work process, on the contrary, there is an attempt, or even a requirement, to establish this as a new norm. Employees who continue to cling to marked routines and rigid time patterns will tend to find themselves under pressure if management pursues this goal vigorously and integrates it into the evaluation criteria for 'good work' or 'great efficiency'. This type of behaviour is then held not only to demonstrate a lack of time flexibility, but interpreted much more broadly as a 'traditional' 'employee' attitude (or worse still, a 'civil servant' attitude), which is increasingly stigmatised in the 'new' work culture, tarred with the assumption that this tends to indicate a propensity to resist calls for greater productivity.

Applying this logic, employees with children could become protagonists of this 'new' concept. On the one hand, they have a genuine interest in unconventional working hours due to their lifestyle structure and therefore must develop a 'creative' way of dealing with working hours, whilst on the other hand the constant need to organise and coordinate professional and private demands means they have already acquired the appropriate self-management skills.

Conversely, employees with children are not simply keen to have unconventional working hours, but equally have an interest in longer-term stability and scope to plan their working hours, as well as within certain limits on the overall number of hours worked. In organising childcare, parents often find themselves in complex dependency relationships with external 'time dictators' i.e. individuals and institutions with specific temporal rhythms such as the school or childcare centre. These arrangements are thus often described as a 'balancing act'. It becomes much clearer against the backdrop of increased professional ad hoc demands requiring flexible time-keeping just how precarious and volatile these childcare arrangements are. At the same time, the volume of work taken on by employees with children is also necessarily subject to certain limitations, due to the need, or rather the wish, to create shared family time. Often morning and evening rituals are central to family life, not to mention spending the weekend together, and these times cannot be restricted arbitrarily without negative consequences. Last but not least, the energy used up in work-related activities must also be limited, for part of a parent's resources is 'exhausted' by work in the family.

From management's perspective however, the autonomy to shape one's working hours thus propagated must of course be oriented to respect corporate-economic demands and needs i.e. fluctuations in the amount of work, customer wishes or in-house requirements for coopera-tion. It is furthermore also linked to claims on employees' full commit-ment and energies – 'corporate thinking and action'. Critics therefore point out that, given the 'primacy of economics' and contrary to the positive interpretation of the trust-based system, it will, in the most extreme scenario, become impossible to combine work and a family. Whilst companies do indeed promise a little less control and a little more freedom, at the same time they intensify pressure on other parame-ters pertaining to the work situation. In other words, companies indi-rectly increase pressure to perform by cutting (labour) resources, setting ever-higher goals, exposing employees more directly to customers' wishes and in several other ways. According to this thesis, companies thus succeed through these strategies of indirect control in shifting more economic pressure and entrepreneurial risk onto individual employees. This enables firms to mobilise the entire staff to show greater commit-ment to work, whilst at the same time suggesting to them that this is linked to a greater degree of individual time-keeping autonomy. As a consequence of these mechanisms we see unlimited expenditure of energy in work and employees thus mobilised being willing to expose themselves to being constantly available to work more hours (on this point, see for example, IG Metall, 1999; Glißmann and Peters, 2001; and Geramanis, 2002). For parents with children requiring childcare, the time demands associated with these exactions may, to a much greater extent than for employees with fewer life-world commitments, simply be asking too much and defeat attempts to combine professional and family commitments.

Working time culture – the decisive parameter

In the contradictory scenarios outlined so far, it has been assumed that the concept of a trust-based system for working hours has unambiguously posi-tive or negative potential when it comes to combining work and family. A differentiated and empirically grounded analysis of the impacts of this trust-based system will now examine the specific conditions in which this potential 'unfolds' in each scenario.

Looking in comparative terms at the companies studied, the findings suggest that no single uniform pattern has emerged for use of trust-based working hours systems. This however cannot be attributed, as one might have expected, to the individuality of time interests or to the structuring influence of recognised parameters such as work organisation or the degree of formal structuring of working hours. Instead, the specific form employees give to working hours, which are now to a large extent deregulated, with all controls potentially lifted, depends essentially on the working time culture prevailing in the company. Working time culture in this context is defined as a set of implicit norms and standards relating to how time is dealt with in the company. In the companies studied, this emerged as the decisive factor in guiding how working hours are structured and the extent to which new informal and collective regulation was compelled within these organisations. The norms of the working time culture are embedded in the super-ordinate context i.e. in the corresponding understanding of performance and leadership as central dimensions of the organisational culture.

'Culture' here does not refer, as is usually assumed in management literature, to a strategic concept employed consciously and used 'from above' (for example in 'guideline development' procedures) for management control. Rather, the term 'culture' is used here to refer to the fundamental theoretical consideration that people in organisations do not only act against the backdrop of their individual (professional) biographical experiences, but always too, against the backdrop of notions of values, norms and interpretations held collectively in the organisation. These are on the whole accessible to members of the organisation in the form of implicit knowledge – that is, knowledge about what one may or may not do, which behaviour is linked to a positive response and which provokes negative reactions and so on. According to this definition, 'culture' describes a shared pattern of interpretation, which characterises an organisation and makes it possible to distinguish it from others; its members take this organisation as a framework in interpreting their experience and regulating their actions.

Even in conventional systems governing working hours, implementation of formal provisions on working hours thus occurs in and through concepts comprised in the organisational culture (and which are to a large extent implicit) as to what is 'appropriate' behaviour in respect of time worked. In the case of trust-based working hours, the cultural control of how one behaves time-wise at work does take on a new quality, for the corporate time-keeping culture is virtually the only yardstick in determining one's own actions in respect of time, given the far-reaching disappearance of formal provisions. That is a further reason why employees have to activate their implicit cultural knowledge in the trust-based system – and the way in which employees carry out the requisite reorientation is directed by, and refers to, the shared cultural framework.

Accordingly, we can only answer questions about the potential and constraints of the trust-based working hours system in combining family and profession by considering the specific culturally-determined practical implementation of this trust-based system.[3] Our study demonstrates that whether, and to what extent, a parent claims the right to use the possibilities that are formally present (such as parental leave or part-time work) – and is then actually able to make use of these schemes – depends on whether and to what extent self-directed working time is employed in the spirit of the demands and needs of their life-world. Above all, it is determined by the 'price' parents 'pay' for this, both in their life-world and in the professional context. This depends on the decisive question of the prevailing time-culture in a particular company or indeed in a particular team.

Compatibility arrangements in the context of different organisational cultures – two cases from an empirical study

The considerations on the relevance of various working hours cultures in shaping arrangements to combine work and a family outlined above will be examined below in more concrete terms by looking at the example of two 'cases' of highly qualified female employees, both working in knowledge-based service sector companies, with work cultures very comparable to those in the New Economy. They thus represent one of the employee groups primarily affected by the trust-based system of working hours. Furthermore, highly qualified women specifically constitute a growing employee type due to greater educational opportunities and an increasing focus on professional life and careers.

Concentrating on women's situation takes into account evidence showing that gender asymmetry has essentially been preserved in modern couples – albeit to a different degree and in a different form (Koppetsch and Burkart, 1999). In almost all the cases we studied, the female partner shoulders responsibility for childcare and coordination. These arrangements are 'modernised' by a growing tendency for men, particularly if they are highly qualified, to take on more responsibility for their children. In looking at the key term of 'co-parenting' (Hess-Diebäcker and Stein-Hilbers, 1991) about half of the fathers interviewed ascribed great importance to regular close contact with their children. However, with the exception of a few cases, this commitment remained optional, with the 'emphasis on pleasure', making it thus on the whole irrelevant to everyday issues of caring for and providing for the needs of the children ('dads for fun'). Accordingly, for fathers the demands of the family do not have to be reflected in working hours explicitly shaped to manage compatibility issues. In contrast, for women with children, the question of limiting how much they work and dealing with the flexibility that companies demand, almost never appears as an option but is almost always perceived as something they are compelled to do.

In the two cases presented below, women who have a toddler under three returned to their original positions after brief parental leave. The desire to go back to their previous positions is substantiated by the typically high degree of identification with the content of their work and/or with the company's goals, which tends to be part of highly qualified employees' understanding of being professional. However, neither of the companies concerned aims to enable women with children to return to work. For example, there is great scepticism about part-time work; both women nonetheless succeeded in making their family and professional commitments compatible. Both of the women managed to negotiate 'tailor-made' arrangements on their working hours individually with their superiors.

However, that is more or less all they have in common. Ms. Albrecht and Ms. Boettcher are embedded in different organisational cultural contexts in their working time behaviour. In the first case, we see a time culture oriented to increase productivity and emphasising delimitation of working hours, whilst the time culture in the second case recognises the diversity and difference of individual structuring of working hours to a much greater extent and considers 'limitation' as a professional skill.

The compatibility problem in the context of an increased productivity culture

Ms. Albrecht works in a company ('Committed-AG'), in which constantly being prepared to make time available and to be reachable is equated with competence and efficiency, and where constant productivity increases are expected. Committed-AG is part of the software-industry. The plant where Ms. Albrecht works is the German headquarters of a multinational, foreign-owned company. Ms. Albrecht is 38 years old, has a two year-old child, is a university graduate and has been working at Committed-AG for nine years. She works in Communication and Marketing, and is responsible for large advertising campaigns.

Scope for flexibility in the hours worked is a genuine component of the concept elaborated in the company culture of Committed-AG. The typical statement by this company 'Working hours do not play a role' refers, on the one hand, to an express decision to abstain from formal regulations and, on the other hand, to the notion that hours worked are not held to be an explicit topic or up for negotiation, either in relations between employees or in relations between staff and their superiors. Theoretically, this could open up immense scope to devise individual practices as to time worked, particularly as a high degree of personal autonomy and a self-directed approach in structuring both work content and processes play a constitutive part in the employees' self-image as 'professionals' in this company. The corporate structure here, however, functions in terms of a constantly effective, comprehensive and highly institutionalised reorganisation dynamic, implying a demand for permanent productivity increases. In this view, time reserves gained by more efficient work should and must be reinvested in new increases in productivity. The permanent demand for delimitation in the spirit of expending one's full energy corresponds to the demand for employees not to place limits on the hours worked.

An essential point in this system is the need to show a willingness to increase productivity through a particular way of dealing with time. The desired indicators or symbols for the 'right' way of dealing with working hours are being present[4] in the company during an extended informal core working day, flexibility and spontaneity in respect of the hours worked, seen almost exclusively in terms of company needs, and a willingness 'not to watch the clock'. Generally speaking, more hours are worked per week than stipulated by contract. The way in which individual working hours are structured is regulated and given a clearer shape by the demand to be present over an extended period and reachable by customers and colleagues. Ad hoc meetings and the expectation that queries will be answered immediately place extreme limitations on the extent to which an individual can control and plan the work to be done and the hours that must be worked. A constant high level of pressure to perform thus develops for all employees, but in particular for those who can no longer fully meet these demands as a priority due to life-world constraints.

In Ms. Albrecht's case the restrictions arising from her life-world are reflected in her decision to limit the number of hours she works to a nominal 30 hours a week, which she puts in over four days. In addition, her specific childcare arrangements, made up of institutionalised and family forms of care means that she has to adhere to fairly rigid times for starting and ending work. Ms. Albrecht interprets the fact that the discrepancy between this 'restrictive' individual model and the dominant 'unlimited' company culture is tolerated as recognition of the professional capacity to work efficiently which she has demonstrated in the past. 'I am one of two out of a thousand staff members allowed to work part-time, I'm grateful for that, so I don't care about overtime and extra work'.

A potentially ambivalent status as a 'special individual case' is thus constituted for her. On the one hand this status conveys the certainty, felt to be positive, that she is particularly 'valuable' to the company. On the other hand this status constantly refers to the notion that, compared with her colleagues and with earlier phases in her own career biography, she only expends her energies on work to a limited extent, or, to put it more precisely, can only to a limited extent demonstrate her willingness to increase productivity. A contributory factor is that the mere fact of having children signals a lack of flexibility in the spirit of the collective professional self-image and the culture of unlimited working hours.

In order to counteract this negative stigma of an (assumed) 'productivity limitation', she makes considerable efforts to compensate. These can be grouped together into two main strategies:

- *Compressing work* by rationalising one's working time, which means doing without breaks, consistently planning work to eliminate 'spare' time and increasing the speed at which one works;
- A willingness to do *extra work* on an ad hoc basis or during particular phases for no additional pay or for compensation through additional free time. However this extra work is done at home when the child is asleep and is thus 'invisible' to the company environment.

For Ms. Albrecht these strategies result in an overall significantly greater burden, when compared with her colleagues whom we interviewed, who are not subject to restrictions arising from their life-worlds, and thus are not exposed to the presumption of a deficit in their work input within the specific demands arising due to the culture of the organisation. This greater workload arises as, when one takes a closer look, the work culture depicted here is nonetheless very much focused on the process of doing one's work and thus on a particular form of dealing with time (presence and unlimited hours) although this culture does adopt a results-oriented approach as its key emphasis on a rhetorical-normative level. For that reason Ms. Albrecht's chosen mode of working, by compressing work into less time and limiting the time she is present in the company, is held to represent a 'shortcoming', although she generally attains goals set by herself or agreed with others. Despite all her efforts she will therefore remain in a psychologically worrying 'no-win situation' for as long as the restrictions arising from life-world commitments exist. Her skills in planning, structuring and limiting her working hours can only to a limited extent be fed into implicit and explicit negotiation processes within the company.

This specific work dynamic is exacerbated still further by the contours of her professional identity. In the interview she repeatedly underscored her highly developed skills of structuring and limiting working time, which she draws on within her compatibility arrangement. At the same time it becomes clear that in the light of her own conception of work performance and professionalism, which on the whole coincides with the dominant culture, she definitely experiences her own situation as being highly precarious and subject to attacks, which she seeks in turn to compensate for by greater productivity.

The potential problems of the trust-based system as outlined above become clear if one considers the de facto constraints inherent in the scope for a self-directed approach in the trust-based working hours system and thus the determination of one single possible way of dealing with the time worked, namely by placing no limits on the number of hours worked, as well as Ms. Albrecht's own internalised conception of work performance.

The problem of compatability in the context of a time culture respecting the diversity and limitation of time worked

Ms. Boettcher is working at 'Diversity-GmbH', a well-known publishing house. Specialising in high quality travel literature and art books, Diversity-GmbH belongs to the premium sector of book publishers in Germany. Like Ms. Albrecht, Ms. Boettcher is a university graduate and is working in the Communication and Marketing Department, focusing on advertising and press campaigns. Ms. Boettcher is in her mid-30s and is living together with her partner and has one child.

Comparing the New Economy culture of the 'professionals' in Committed-AG with the second company Diversity-GmbH, one finds similar expectations that employees will be autonomous and free to make their own decisions in substantive, organisational and, above all, time-related matters. Whilst in Committed-AG there is a scarcely perceptible difference between individual and company identity, at Diversity-GmbH, the employees' understanding of professionalism is much more oriented to the content of activities and the professional standards derived from this. It transpires that the company and performance culture are shaped by this specific understanding of professionalism. Instead of the work climate being characterised by increased productivity and a permanent willingness to work, a result-oriented approach prevails, which is grounded in management's confidence that staff are capable of performing the work required.

A high degree of recognition of individual staff members' professional competence is the foundation stone and company-oriented flexibility is not asserted as an absolute priority. Rather, life-world demands may be reflected to a considerably higher degree in diverse individual approaches to structuring time worked. There is more of a focus on processes of coordination and cooperation, rather than simply a call for employees to be constantly present in the workplace. The times when one is present and the areas where cooperation is needed are agreed upon long-term, both to avoid reduced efficiency through friction and to enable different profiles for presence at work. Unlike Committed-AG neither internal nor external communication and cooperation relationships are understood here as indirect instruments of control to standardise working hours but are instead always viewed as factors that can be shaped and controlled.

Correspondingly, reorganisation is not employed as a driving force to increase productivity. Instead, reorganisation is carried out on an ad hoc basis and is at the discretion of individual departments or employees.

Introducing trust-based working hours is not seen as the first step towards a 'new' dynamic understanding of work performance, but is held instead to be a meaningful innovation, which tallies to a high degree with how the company and employees understand self-directed work and limitation of the hours worked.

In keeping with this, in Diversity-GmbH individualised organisation of working hours in the trust-based system is linked to the introduction of a traffic light account.[5] If this is to be used meaningfully, it presupposes to a certain extent that individuals will document the time worked. This form of regulation signals companies' desire to control and limit working time. Given the preconditions described, a working time culture develops, characterised precisely by recognition of colleagues' individual organisation of their working hours. This attitude is the product of a collective discourse within which there is explicit discussion of different positions on links between individual ways of structuring working time and criteria for evaluating work performance.

In this context Ms. Boettcher is employed full-time and distributes her work over four days when she is present in the company and one day working from home. Her childcare arrangements mean that the times at which she starts and ends work are more or less as rigidly fixed as is the case for Ms. Albrecht. Similarly too, she feels that her individually negotiated working hours model testifies to a recognition of her great ability.

The decisive difference between the two cases presented here is that in this case the predominant cultural context does not equate time worked so directly with performance. To a much greater extent than in Committed-AG, employees use their own individual self-direction and professional competence to determine how they will structure the process by which they perform their work. This signifies more openness to different modes of organising the work process and a clearer focus on results.

As mentioned above, Diversity-GmbH has not so far had a policy on the compatibility of family and work, and parenthood is also understood here as a potential restriction on performance. Nonetheless, the introduction of trust-based flexitime has removed the stigma concerning restricting time worked in response to life-world needs. As this does not primarily or exclusively concern employees with children, their 'special' status can be very much set in perspective.

Ms. Boettcher's time strategies for combining work and a family correspond to a high degree with those adopted by Ms. Albrecht. Here however, in contrast to 'Committed-AG', time gained by compressing work processes (structuring, intermeshing and accelerating) can be individually 'appropriated'. Attempting to limit working hours, which of course all employees in the company will not manage to do to the same extent, is thus not seen as a shortcoming, but is instead recognised as an integral part of professional competence in the sense of a self-directed attitude. One might sum up by noting that trust-based flexitime's potential for self-direction is taken much more 'seriously' in this culture and can thus tend to develop a positive effect.

Conclusion

This chapter started with some remarks on the work-life balance discussion in Germany and its typical concentration on the 'family-work' compatibility problem. Then we turned to the question: 'Does trust-based flexitime solve the compatibility problem?' After discussion of the empirical case studies, we must note that the question does not actually include a sufficient degree of complexity for, quite obviously, it is not primarily the formal regulations of working time systems that make it possible to resolve the problem of compatibility or render this more difficult. In this context it is much more the dominant working time culture in a company that is decisive. Ms. Albrecht and Ms. Boettcher are both highly qualified employees in flourishing 'modern' companies, and are both integrated into comparable working time models, yet their everyday working practice is very different despite these similarities. Both are indubitably confronted with very different degrees of leeway in managing the compatibility problem.

Whilst Ms. Albrecht is 'harnessed' to a company and working time culture characterised by a more restrictive general framework for individual structuring of working time, Ms. Boettcher benefits in her attempts to successfully integrate work and life from a working time culture based on an acceptance of more diverse individual time preferences and on an established discourse on limiting (excessive) working hours. Hence, our thesis will scarcely be surprising. In the light of current evaluation of the empirical material, when considering the failed assertion of individual time interests, the respective culture of working hours, which functions as the decisive mechanism, de facto regulating employees' working hours' behaviour, is just as relevant as 'hard' framework business conditions (such as the company's economic situation).

To an extent, the working time model 'trust-based flexitime' (*Vertrauensarbeitszeit*) does generally offer a lot of leeway for possible ways to solve the compatibility problem. However, it is the norms and rules of work time action as reflected in the respective work time culture that will 'decide' whether these options prove to be something employees can actually use. Thus in a 'liberal' working time culture, employees may have a much greater degree of temporal freedom, even in the case of restrictive time models, than would be the case in a trust-based flexitime scheme, which formally is much more open but is however embedded in a rather restrictive work time culture. However, in considering these matters it is important to avoid throwing the baby out with the bath water, so to speak, and prematurely conclude that formal work time provisions are irrelevant. For trust-based flexitime is certainly a more favourable precondition for solving the compatibility problem than, for example, a rigid 'nine to five' working day.

Therefore, a 'work culture perspective' does not deny the significance of formal work time models in addressing the compatibility of family and work, although it does put them in perspective. Above all, however, looking at things from this point of view poses questions that go beyond those examined in studies to date on corporate time action, such as the genesis of different work time cultures in comparable firms or the question of 'elective affinities' between particular work time cultures and factors shaping the business context. We believe that it would be much more promising to explore this when considering the compatibility of work and life than to simply concentrate on the question of whether a particular work time model provides a better solution than another model to the compatibility problem.

Notes

1. The concept of the trust-based system of working hours is often associated with the working hours consultancy practice, Dr. Hoff, Weidinger & Partner (Berlin), who promoted this both in their corporate consultancy work and in public debate (cf. Hoff, 2002).
2. This is a research project organised from March 2001 to February 2003 with funding from the Hans-Böckler Foundation with the title 'Trust-based flexitime: a new working hours model from the perspective of employees, works councils, trade unions and companies' (Böhm et al, 2004). In the context of this study the compatibility problem was only one of several thematic focal points. The project was designed to encompass discussions with experts and open interviews focused on guidelines with employees in around ten companies in the 'old' and 'new' economies. The study focused on three thematic groups of issues: processes of negotiation and implementation of the system of working hours based on trust, current practice of the trust-based systems and work and life situation, together with the issue of the need for regulation at the corporate level and in collective wage agreements. This chapter refers to a specific analysis of the empirical material (cf. Böhm et al, 2002).
3. Increasing reference is made not just to formal rules but also to the great importance of the prevailing time-culture in the company (Höpflinger, 2002; Gemeinützige Hertie-Stiftung, 1998) when current research on the compatibility of work and family calls for a 'corporate family policy' to be introduced or given a new slant.
4. Presence at agreed concurrent times also guarantees an individual's visibility and hence in this culture also the perception of his or her willingness to work by others. Work that is done in a non-visible manner – for example at home – tends to be devalued.
5. The term 'traffic-light account' is used for schemes in which accumulating various levels of credit or debt balances on a working time account triggers 'interventionist measures' of varying degrees of severity. In the 'green phase' of reducing a relatively small balance, responsibility lies exclusively with employees. If a higher balance has accumulated, i.e. in the 'amber phase', it is generally recommended that employees and their superiors seek to establish ways to reduce the level as soon as possible. Finally, in the red phase, the high balance has to be returned to the green level with the help of a binding reduction plan.

References

Bauer, F., Groß, H., Lehmann, K. and Munz, E. (2004) *Arbeitszeit 2003. Arbeitszeitgestaltung, Arbeitsorganisation und Tätigkeitsprofile*, Köln: ISO.

BestPersAward (2005) *Work Life Balance*, (http://www.bestpersaward.de/worklifebalance.php). Sourced on 07/06/05.

BMFSFJ – Bundesministerium für Familie, Senioren, Frauen und Jugend (2003) *Balance von Familie und Arbeitswelt. Allianz für die Familie*, Berlin: BMFSFJ.

BMFSFJ – Bundesministerium für Familie, Senioren, Frauen und Jugend/Bertelsmann Stiftung (2003) *Allianz für die Familie. Balance von Familie und Arbeitswelt. Grundlagenpapier der Impulsgruppe*, Berlin/Gütersloh: BMFSFJ/Bertelsmann Stiftung.

BMFSFJ – Bundesministerium für Familie, Senioren, Frauen und Jugend (2004) *Wirtschaft und Politik gemeinsam für eine familienfreundliche Unternehmenskultur. Bundesministerin Renate Schmidt zu Gast beim Präsidium des BDI* (press release from 08/03/2004), Berlin: BMFSFJ.

BMWA – Bundesministerium für Wirtschaft und Arbeit (2005) *Work Life Balance*, Berlin: BMWA, (http://www.bmwa.bund.de/Navigation/Wirtschaft/mittelstandspolitik,did=60472.html).

Böhm, S., Herrmann, C. and Trinczek, R. (2002) 'Löst Vertrauensarbeitszeit das Problem der Vereinbarkeit von Familie und Beruf?' *WSI-Mitteilungen*, 55: 435–41.

Böhm, S., Herrmann, C. and Trinczek, R. (2004*) Herausforderung Vertrauensarbeitszeit. Kultur und Praxis eines neuen Arbeitszeitmodells*, Berlin: Sigma.

Brasse, C. (2003) *Junge Branchen, alte Muster. Vom Arbeiten und Leben in den Neuen Medien. Daten und Analysen zur Arbeitssituation der Beschäftigten in der Multimediabranche*, Hannover: Prospektiv/AG BIB/connexx.de.

Deutscher Bundestag (ed.) (2002) *Enquete-Kommission Demographischer Wandel. Herausforderungen unserer älter werdenden Gesellschaft an den Einzelnen und die Politik*, Berlin: Deutscher Bundestag/Referat Öffentlichkeitsarbeit.

Gemeinützige Hertie-Stiftung (ed.) (1998) *Mit Familie zum Unternehmenserfolg. Impulse für eine zukunftsfähige Personalpolitik*, Köln: Hertie-Stiftung.

Geramanis, O. (2002) 'Vertrauensarbeitszeit – die verpasste Chance?' *WSI-Mitteilungen*, 55: 347–52.

Glißmann, W. and Peters, K. (2001) *Mehr Druck durch mehr Freiheit: die neue Autonomie in der Arbeit und ihre paradoxen Folgen*, Hamburg: VSA.

Hess-Diebäcker, D. and Stein-Hilbers, M. (1991) 'Geteilte Elternschaft: Modell für die Gleichverteilung von Haus und Erwerbsarbeit berufstätiger Eltern', in Teichert, V. (ed.) *Junge Familien in der Bundesrepublik*, Opladen: Westdeutscher Verlag, 119–36.

Hoff, A. (2002) *Vertrauensarbeitszeit: einfach flexibel arbeiten*. Wiesbaden: Gabler.

Höpflinger, F. (2002) *Beruf und Familie – zwei Lebensbereiche, ein Leben*, (www.mypage.bluewin.ch/hoepf/fhtop/fhfamil1f.html). Sourced on 07/06/05.

IBM (2005) *Diversity – Work/Life Balance* (http://www-05.ibm.com/employment/de/diversity/balance.html). Sourced on 07/06/05.

IFO – Institut für Wirtschaftsforschung (2002) *Arbeitszeit in der Metall und Elektroindustrie. Ergebnisse einer Umfrage im Auftrag von Gesamtmetall*, Köln: Gesamtmetall.

IG Metall (ed.) (1999) *Meine Zeit ist mein Leben. Neue betriebspolitische Erfahrungen zur Arbeitszeit, Denkanstöße – Dokumentation*, Frankfurt, Germany: IGM.

Janßen, P. (2003) 'Investive Arbeitszeitpolitik. Mehr Weiterbildung durch Arbeitszeitflexibilisierung', *iw-trends*, 30(2).

Koppetsch, C. and Burkart, G. (1999) *Die Illusion der Emanzipation. Zur Wirksamkeit latenter Geschlechtsnormen im Milieuvergleich*, Konstanz: UVK.

Ludwig, I. and Schlevogt, V. (2002) 'Bessere Zeiten für erwerbstätige Mütter?' *WSI-Mitteilungen*, 55: 133–8.

Peuckert, R. (2002) *Familienformen im sozialen Wandel*, 4th edition, Opladen: Leske and Budrich.

Pickshaus, K. (2000) 'Das Phänomen des "Arbeitens ohne Ende". Eine Herausforderung für eine gewerkschaftliche Arbeitspolitik', in Pickshaus, K., Peters, K. and Glißmann, W. (ed.) *'Der Arbeit wieder ein Maß geben'. Neue Managementkonzepte und Anforderungen an eine gewerkschaftliche Arbeitspolitik*, Supplement der Zeitschrift Sozialismus 2/2000, 1–19.

Pletke, M. and Wieczoreck-Haubus, M. (2003) *Arbeitszeit ohne Kontrolle*, Personalwirtschaft No. 4/03: 59–63.

Siemens (2005) *Work/Life Balance*. (http://www.siemens.com/index.jsp?sdc_p=t4cs6uo1133076d1138598pn1133066flm). Sourced on 07/06/05.

Statistisches Bundesamt (2004) *Leben und Arbeiten in Deutschland. Ergebnisse des Mikrozensus 2003*, Wiesbaden: Statistisches Bundesamt.

8
Should Mothers Work? An International Comparison of the Effect of Religion on Women's Work and Family Roles

Ken Reed and Betsy Blunsdon

Introduction

A key theme in the work-life debate is the extent to which lifestyles reflect value-oriented choices or social and structural constraints. There is widespread agreement that women in affluent countries have more freedom now than in the past to choose how they allocate time to market and domestic work. Hakim's work is a leading example of the argument that differences in women's employment status largely reflects differences in the relative value they place on involvement in work, family life or other domains (see for example, Hakim, 1991, 2000). This argument has been taken up by labour economists (e.g. Wooden and Loundes, 2002) who argue that the main policy implication flowing from this is the need to ensure the availability of opportunities for non-standard working hours for women.

In this view, there is an implicit model of choice that defines the 'problem' of work-life balance in terms of social changes that have simultaneously reduced barriers to employment for women, and increased the desire for careers. The arguments of Hakim (2000) and Inglehart and Norris (2003) in particular, focus on delineating changes in the structure of opportunities and constraints that have reduced the desirability and feasibility of careers for women in the past, and condition their choices currently. The key theme in this body of work is the claim that modernisation leads to increased choice in the allocation of time devoted to paid employment and family.

In contrast, other perspectives emphasise the extent to which various factors constrain choice, particularly for mothers of young children. There are a set of constraints on voluntaristic choice usually referred to as structural (e.g. Crompton, 1998; McCrae, 2003) such as the availability of jobs, access to transport and markets and the availability of affordable childcare.

These are constraining to the extent that they limit opportunities to choose the amount and type of employment undertaken.

McCrae also suggests that women are subject to normative constraints, in that social expectations of gender roles are internalised to form part of women's identities and, through the attitudes of those around them, are a persistent component of the social environment. Such attitudes may themselves reflect institutionalised constraints: Sundstrom, for example, analyses attitudes to women in paid employment in Germany, Sweden and Italy, arguing that 'normative expectations, expressed in attitudes towards the gender division of labour, to a certain degree reflect ... national policies' (1999: 195). Such institutional pressures or social expectations generally constrain choice through normative control based on sanctions such as punishment, approval or censure, as exemplified in the requirement that certain people go to school; the expectation that some categories of people should work while others should not; that the responsibility for childcare and housework is gender-based; or taken-for-granted moral positions like the belief that laziness is a vice and diligence a virtue.

Normative constraints differ from structural constraints in that normative control depends on the internalisation of norms, and the effectiveness of sanctions. These, in turn, depend on the strength of relationships within social and cultural milieux. Within societies, communities and groups characterised by dense social ties, consensus and support for norms will be stronger, and values more homogeneous, and these will be sustained and reproduced through agents of socialisation – families, schools and religious organisations. Thus the power of normative constraints lies in the individual's identification with the cultural values of a social group or society, and the relative power of the group or society to impose or withhold sanctions. For example, an important aspect of the social norms of gender and of sexual values is the influence of religious authorities. As Inglehart and Norris suggest, 'The influence of religious authorities has often served to limit the opportunities for women outside the home, in education, at work, and in positions of authority' (2003: 70).

Gender roles exemplify normative constraint. They reflect core beliefs, deeply ingrained through socialisation, and are institutionalised expectations about behaviour appropriate for the genders. They link central features of people's personality and character with the culture of social groups, and so tend to be a key mechanism of social integration, and link people's lives to the broader institutional context. Sundstrom, for example, argues that international differences due to welfare policies are important in structuring employment possibilities and opportunities '... assuming that the origins of social and political structures largely depend on interests and identities represented by varying social groups, the ways gender issues are expressed vary under the specific historical features of the country' (1999: 194).

The focus of this chapter is on the role of religion in shaping views about the appropriateness of mothers participating in the labour market, and the effect of such norms and roles on women's employment status. Inglehart and Norris argue that religion has had a major influence on sex roles and gender equality, and that '...religion has functioned as one of the most important agencies of socialization determining social norms and moral values with regard to gender equality in all societies, and influencing support for feminism and attitudes toward the second-wave women's movement' (2003: 50). Their analysis of data from the World Values Survey establishes that religiosity continues to exert a strong influence on social norms around the household division of labour and gender roles, though this is particularly the case for agrarian societies. The influence of religion on attitudes to women's gender roles is well documented in the social science literature including a number of studies that investigate fundamentalism, gender roles and family structure (see for example, Bartkowski, 1999; Bartkowski and Read, 2003; Read, 2003). And there is good evidence that religious institutions provide individuals and families with norms of relationships, marriage and child-rearing (see for example, Booth et al, 1995; Lehrer, 1995).

Berger (1967, 1970, 1992) has argued that religious beliefs are socially constructed and must have a social base (for example, a community of believers) to survive as fundamental assumptions. A community of believers constitutes part of a network social structure where belief and values are discussed, confirmed and reinforced or disconfirmed. Such community processes determine the strength of the beliefs and to a large degree determine whether or not beliefs are sustained. Petersen and Donnenwerth (1998) examined traditional beliefs about gender roles and homosexual rights to test Berger's argument that beliefs that are not falsifiable do need high levels of group support to be maintained. They argue that unfalsifiable beliefs can be sustained through the confirmation of group members even when objective changes in society call the belief into question – for example, when improved job opportunities and wages for women make it difficult to sustain the belief that women should not engage in paid employment. They conclude that 'In the absence of strong support from others in one's social networks, beliefs of this type may be highly susceptible to erosion' (Petersen and Donnenwerth, 1998: 368). By corollary, high levels of group support may maintain beliefs and norms even when societal changes might call these into question.

Religious participation tends to reinforce traditional gender views and reduces support for feminism (Bolzendahl and Myers, 2004; Peek, Lowe and Williams, 1991). Inglehart and Norris (2003) find that the type of religion influences attitudes to gender roles, although strength of religiosity has no significant effect. Their analysis shows 'the strongest contrast in attitudes toward the appropriate division of sex roles among women and men is that between Western Christian and non-denominational populations living in affluent post-industrial societies, who adhere to the most egalitarian beliefs about the family, workforce, politics, and Muslims living in poorer, agrarian nations, who are by far the most traditional group in their attitudes to gender equality.' (2003: 68). Different religious traditions have different positions in regards to gender roles (see Davis and Robinson, 1999; Greely, 1989; Hoffman and Miller, 1997, 1998), and Bolzendahl and Myers' findings '... indicate that conservative Protestants are the least supportive of non-traditional gender roles and Jews are the most supportive, with Catholics and mainline Protestants falling somewhere in between.' (2004: 766). They found that Catholic men are less supportive of liberal public gender roles than mainline Protestants, and in particular '...men belonging to [fundamentalist] denominational grouping are more conservative across all domains...' (2004: 779). But overall, the results of their analysis of attitudinal change over the period 1974–1998 show that '...support for gender equality is experiencing continual diffusion across many societal strata and that the gains of feminism are not limited to particular social categories' (2004: 781).

Similarly, Inglehart and Norris propose that if traditional beliefs and values are eroding, and society is becoming more secular, this could explain the increasing support for gender equality in post-industrial societies. 'This is a plausible proposition that deserves analysis; but so far, little systematic cross national survey data has been available to examine how religious beliefs and practices vary around the globe, or how they may ebb and flow in response to the processes of societal modernization and broader shifts in the cultural zeitgeist' (2003: 51).

Hakim is not so sure. She argues that although broad beliefs and attitudes (such as what people think is best for society) has little effect on behaviour, there is a much stronger relationship between beliefs specific to oneself (such as personal preferences) and one's behaviour. She claims that 'Attitudes can have important short-term and long-term impacts, even if their influence disappears among social structural factors in many studies, like water in sand. Beliefs and values may be intangible, but people act on them' (2000: 75).

In this chapter we examine the impact that religion has on conceptions of women's roles, particularly beliefs about the appropriateness of mothers engaging in employment outside the home, and whether such conceptions are translated into behaviour – that is, whether different views about women's work-family roles lead to different employment outcomes. To answer these questions we use data from a set of international surveys, the International Social Survey Programme (ISSP).

The ISSP is a collaboration of social scientists that coordinates the collection of common survey questions across a large number of studies. We draw data from the 2002 round, which focused on the theme of 'Family

Table 8.1 Sample sizes by country

Country	Original	Complete cases	Country	Original	Complete cases
Australia	1352	1224	Latvia	1000	994
Austria	2047	2032	Mexico	1495	1253
Brazil	2000	1789	Netherlands	1249	1244
Bulgaria	1003	974	New Zealand	1025	944
Cyprus	1004	1004	Northern Ireland	987	955
Czech Republic	1289	1198	Norway	1475	1409
Denmark	1379	1245	Philippines	1200	1195
Finland	1353	1158	Poland	1252	1235
Flanders	1360	1341	Portugal	1092	1079
France	1903	1755	Republic of Chile	1505	1487
Germany East	431	421	Russia	1798	1706
Germany West	936	920	Slovak Republic	1133	1129
Great Britain	1960	1943	Spain	2471	2371
Hungary	1023	1008	Sweden	1080	1037
Ireland	1240	1163	Switzerland	1008	967
Israel	1209	1174	Taiwan	1983	1979
Japan	1132	1052	United States	1171	1161

Note: The five eastern federal states of Germany were deliberately over-sampled to enable comparisons between the former East and West Germanies.

and Gender Roles'. We use data from 34 countries, but the country samples do not constitute a systematic random sample of countries, as participation in the Programme depends on the ability of members to fund participation. However, a major advantage of this data source is that it provides a sufficiently large sample to estimate the specific effects of religion on attitudes to gender roles.

Sample

There are 46,638 respondents in the ISSP surveys, of whom 43,546 provide complete data. Table 8.1 shows sample sizes by country, comparing the original data with the samples of complete cases used in the analysis.

'Women's work-family roles' attitude scale

The ISSP survey includes a number of questions measuring attitudes to family and gender roles. These are five category agreement items (e.g. 'A man's job is to earn money; a woman's job is to look after the home and family' – Strongly agree; Agree; Neither agree nor disagree; Disagree; Strongly disagree) or three category ordinal responses (e.g. 'Do you think that women should work outside the home full-time, part-time or not at all under the following circumstances? After marrying and before there are children' – Work full-time; Work part-time; Stay at home).

The first stage of analysis is to construct a scale that reflects the main underlying variation in respondents' attitudes to women working. Preliminary analyses suggested nine items concerned with attitudes to women working. These were recoded to combine 'strongly agree' with 'agree' and 'strongly disagree' with 'disagree', so that all items were three category ordinal variables. We use the first principal axis of a correspondence to identify quantifications of the ordinal categories that best summarise the main dimension of variability in the data (Greenacre, 1993). This method is known as optimal scaling or categorical principal components analysis.

The outcomes of this method are (1) quantifications of the original ordinal categories and (2) a set of object (respondent) scores on the first principal axis, which constitute their scores on the attitude scale. Table 8.2 shows the quantifications for each category of each item, allocating a numerical score to the original ordinal categories based on the pattern of similarities and differences between respondents' response profiles. Note that a positive value is associated with more traditional attitudes to women's work-family roles, so that, for example, responding 'stay at home' to the item 'Should women work: after marriage, before kids' indicates a strongly traditional view, whereas saying a mother should work full-time when there is a child under school age strongly indicates modern attitudes.

The first principal axis – the scale – is equivalent to respondents' average scores of the quantifications of the original ordinal categories

Table 8.2   Quantifications of the original ordinal categories

	Stay at home	Part-time	Full-time
Should women work: after marriage, before kids	1.69	0.70	–0.24
Should women work: child under school age	0.78	–0.30	–1.04
Should women work: youngest kid at school	1.42	0.11	–0.87
Should women work: when kids left home	1.41	0.62	–0.29

	Agree	Neither	Disagree
Working woman: family life suffers	0.70	–0.15	–0.87
What women really want is home & kids	0.53	–0.06	–0.72
Men's job is work, women's job household	0.87	0.17	–0.61
Working mother: warm relation child OK	–0.37	0.29	0.86
Working mother: pre-school child suffers	0.64	–0.24	–0.89

Table 8.3 Loading of nine items measuring attitudes to women working on the first principal axis of a correspondence analysis

Questionnaire item	Loading
Working woman: family life suffers	0.70
Should women work: youngest kid at school	–0.70
Working mom: pre-school child suffers	0.69
Men's job is work, women's job household	0.65
Should women work: child under school age	–0.63
What women really want is home & kids	0.54
Working mom: warm relation child OK	–0.52
Should women work: after marriage, before kids	–0.51
Should women work: when kids have left home	–0.50

across the nine items. The association between the quantified items and the axis can be shown as a table of loadings or correlations, as in principal components or factor analysis. Table 8.3 shows each quantified item's loading on this first axis. The scale of the principal axis is arbitrary, so the scores on the original principal axis are rescaled to have a range of 0–100 to facilitate interpretation of the results presented from Table 8.5 onwards.

The analysis focuses on two basic questions: does one's religion affect one's attitudes to work-family roles (specifically, the appropriateness of women working); and, if so, are these attitudes translated into behaviour, in the sense that women with traditional attitudes, or the wives of men with traditional attitudes, are less likely to work.

We begin by testing an ANOVA model with the 'women's work-family roles' attitudes scale as the dependent variable, and country of respondent, their religion, gender, age and marital status as independent variables. The ANOVA is based on type III sum of squares, so the effect of each variable is independent of the others. This is particularly important for country effects, as there are strong associations between country and religion in some cases – for example, 84 per cent of the Israeli respondents are Jewish, whereas 90 per cent of the Danish respondents are Protestant.

The reference category for the ANOVA is:

- Norwegian,
- Of no religion,
- Female,
- Aged 15–24, and
- Single (never married).

Table 8.4 Tests of between-subjects effects

Source	Type III Sum of squares	df	Mean square	F	p
Corrected Model	2,998,376	55	54,515.92	227.82	0.00
Intercept	1,505,852	1	1,505,852.46	6,292.89	0.00
Country	1,427,892	33	43,269.46	180.82	0.00
Religion	127,549.2	11	11,595.39	48.46	0.00
Gender	106,742.6	1	106,742.59	446.07	0.00
Age	519,617.1	6	86,602.85	361.91	0.00
Marital status	21,251.62	4	5,312.90	22.20	0.00
Error	10,537,321	44,035	239.29		
Total	83,232,138	44,091			
Corrected Total	13,535,696	44,090			

Adjusted R^2 = .22

Table 8.4 shows that the effects of each independent variable are statistically significant.

Country differences

The results show substantial differences between countries. Table 8.5 shows Norway as the reference category, and countries are ordered according the size of the difference between it and Norway in the mean score on the work-family roles scale (as estimated by the ANOVA and presented as the B value).

Care must be taken not to impute too much about differences between country per se from this result – as indicated earlier, 'country' also includes effects associated with differences between the actual surveys. Even so, the well-documented gender egalitarianism of the Scandinavian counties is evident, as is the more gendered orientations of Brazil, Mexico and Chile (plus the Philippines). Generally, the former Soviet bloc countries display more traditional attitudes, particularly Russia and Latvia, though eastern Germany is a notable exception. An interesting contrast is that between eastern and western Germany with western Germany averaging nearly ten percentage points higher (i.e. more traditional) than eastern Germany.

Religion differences

Table 8.6 displays the differences in means for the main categories of religion. Four of these (preceded by an asterisk in the table) are residual categories comprising minor denominations and religions not covered by the major categories, or responses that could not be classified accurately.

Table 8.5   Country differences in attitudes to women's work-family roles

Parameter	B	Std. Error	t	p
Intercept	20.81	0.52	40.02	0.00
Denmark	−2.68	0.60	−4.49	0.00
Germany eastern	−2.55	0.87	−2.93	0.00
Sweden	−1.87	0.63	−2.97	0.00
Norway	0.00			
Cyprus	1.89	0.86	2.20	0.03
Finland	2.47	0.59	4.18	0.00
Ireland	4.68	0.65	7.19	0.00
Netherlands	5.62	0.63	8.96	0.00
Great Britain	6.02	0.55	10.95	0.00
France	6.12	0.59	10.41	0.00
United States	6.29	0.62	10.22	0.00
Flanders	6.97	0.63	11.05	0.00
Australia	7.34	0.61	12.05	0.00
New Zealand	7.35	0.65	11.34	0.00
Germany western	7.36	0.66	11.12	0.00
N. Ireland	7.42	0.65	11.34	0.00
Spain	8.43	0.56	14.94	0.00
Taiwan	8.98	0.70	12.78	0.00
Japan	9.63	0.69	13.96	0.00
Israel	10.10	1.14	8.83	0.00
Switzerland	10.13	0.65	15.57	0.00
Austria	10.25	0.57	17.83	0.00
Poland	10.50	0.65	16.26	0.00
Hungary	10.94	0.66	16.50	0.00
Bulgaria	11.51	0.81	14.14	0.00
Portugal	11.96	0.66	17.99	0.00
Czech	12.12	0.64	18.98	0.00
Slovakia	13.25	0.65	20.45	0.00
Russia	14.34	0.70	20.40	0.00
Latvia	15.22	0.66	22.96	0.00
Brazil	19.97	0.58	34.29	0.00
Philippines	20.87	0.65	32.22	0.00
Mexico	23.95	0.63	37.89	0.00
Chile	24.04	0.61	39.56	0.00

Two things stand out in these results. First, there is a contrast between Jews and Muslims, with Jews displaying the most modern attitudes, while Muslims are the most traditional. Second, Muslims are much more traditional than the other religious groups. Hindus, for example, score 3.8 percentage points higher than those who state 'no religion' whereas Muslims are 11.7 percentage points higher.

The attitudinal difference between Muslims and Jews can be shown more concretely by comparing their responses on one of the variables used to

Table 8.6 Differences between main religious groups

Parameter	B	SE	t	p
Jewish	–2.68	1.12	–2.39	0.02
No religion	0.00			
Buddhism	1.88	0.65	2.88	0.00
*Other Eastern Religions	2.25	0.74	3.02	0.00
Christian Orthodox	3.28	0.56	5.83	0.00
Protestant	3.51	0.28	12.60	0.00
Roman Catholic	3.77	0.25	15.03	0.00
Hinduism	3.80	2.21	1.72	0.09
*Other Christian Religions	4.21	0.54	7.84	0.00
*Other Religions	4.69	0.79	5.90	0.00
Islam	11.74	0.76	15.49	0.00
*Other non-Christian Religions	16.43	5.50	2.99	0.00

*See explanation of page 142.

Table 8.7 Comparison between two religious groups and two countries on whether women should work when the youngest child is at school (row percentages)

		Should women work when: youngest child at school			Total
		Stay at home	Part-time	Full-time	
Religion	Jewish	7	51	42	100
	Islam	24	54	22	100
Country	Denmark	3	59	38	100
	Chile	33	54	13	100

construct the women's work-family roles scale. A comparison of the two most different countries, Denmark and Chile, are also shown, in order to give an idea of how differences between the religious groups compares with differences between the two most dissimilar countries.

Among Muslims, 24 per cent say mothers should not work at all, compared with only seven per cent of Jews. Jews are nearly twice as likely as Muslims to believe that mothers should work full-time once all their children have started school. The country effect is stronger: only three per cent of Danes believe that mothers should not be working, compared with a third of the Chileans, and Danes are almost three times as likely as Chileans to think mothers should work full-time. Part-time work is generally most favoured.

Age and gender differences

There is a strong association between age and attitudes to women's work-family roles – predictably, from the 25–34 year-old age group, each older group is more traditional. With cross-sectional surveys there is typically a problem of inferring whether age-related attitudinal effects imply aggregate change (the group changes because new cohorts with different attitudes replace older cohorts) or individual change (people's attitudes change as they get older, regardless of when they were born). In this case, this conflation of possible causation is of no great concern – it is certainly the case that younger cohorts have more modern attitudes than older cohorts, and probably the case that, currently, people's attitudes are becoming more modern over the life course.

Males average about three percentage points higher than females on the women's work-family roles scale. This is quite a small difference, but implies that men have more traditional views of women's work-family roles than do women themselves. We tested for interaction effects between gender and the other independent variables to see whether the gender difference varied by country, religion and so on, and the results (not shown) were not statistically significant. This implies that the difference is fairly consistent across different social and cultural conditions.

This gender difference implies that women may be subjected to two forms of normative constraint. First, normative constraints operate internally through self-definitions of identity, in that they are constraining to the extent that behaviour is influenced by the desire to act according to an image of what is appropriate for a particular role or status. But, secondly, normative constraints act through the approval of others. The strength of such external constraints is largely a function of how much the approval of others is valued, and the ability of others to impose their definitions of identity or role. Thus, gender differences with regard to women's work-family roles matter to the extent that men impose their definitions on women.

Table 8.8 Gender and age differences on attitudes to women's work-family roles

		B	p
Gender	Female	0.00	
	Male	3.21	0.00
Age	15–24	0.00	
	25–34	0.15	0.61
	35–44	1.57	0.00
	45–54	3.54	0.00
	55–64	6.67	0.00
	65–74	10.69	0.00
	75+	14.15	0.00

Table 8.9   Gender differences in two countries (row percentages)

Country		Should women work when: youngest child at school			Total
		Stay at home	Part-time	Full-time	
Chile	Male	35	51	14	100
	Female	30	57	13	100
Denmark	Male	4	54	42	100
	Female	2	63	35	100

However, there is an important gender difference that the scale obscures, and that is a greater tendency for women than men to prefer that women work part-time rather than full-time. We compare males' and females' responses to whether women should work, even when the youngest child has started school, in the most modern and traditional countries (Denmark and Chile, respectively). As Table 8.9 shows, men are more likely than women to think mothers should not work. But those who believe mothers should work tend to favour part-time work rather than full-time, and this tendency is stronger among women than men. This suggests an alternative interpretation of 'preferences' to that proposed by Hakim – if most people believe that mothers should work part-time, then it suggests a normatively-constrained, rather than a voluntaristic, basis for choice.

Marital status differences

The last attribute we include in the model is marital status. Table 8.10 shows no statistically significant difference between single and divorced people, and only small differences between singles on one hand and separated, widowed and married people on the other.

Table 8.10   Effect of marital status on attitudes to women's work-family roles

Parameter	B	SE	t	p
Single, never married	0.00			
Divorced	0.58	0.36	1.60	0.11
Separated, but married	1.04	0.53	1.96	0.05
Widowed	1.78	0.37	4.80	0.00
Married, living as married	1.94	0.22	8.77	0.00

Do attitudes affect behaviour?

Hakim argues that there is only a weak link between personal preferences and choices, and the 'generalized abstract values' measured by surveys such as the ISSP (Hakim, 2000). We examine whether women's work-family roles attitudes are translated into behaviour by posing the question of whether differences in scale scores lead to differences in women's employment status, for female respondents, or the employment status of their wives, for male respondents. Technically, this should be analysed using discriminant analysis or multinomial logistic regression. These techniques are consistent with the posited causal direction – attitudes lead to behaviour. However, these are notoriously difficult to interpret and communicate and for that reason, and for consistency with the preceding presentation, we use a comparison of means here.

We hypothesise that women with more traditional attitudes, as measured by the women's work-family roles scale, will be less likely to work. Conversely, women who are not employed outside the home will have more traditional attitudes than women who do work in paid jobs – it is this form of the proposition that we test. Similarly, men with more traditional attitudes will tend to be married to spouses who do not hold paid jobs. Again, we test the proposition that men whose spouses are employed in home duties will have more traditional women's work-family roles attitudes.

We test this using the residuals of the general linear model presented above. We use country, religion, age, gender and marital status to predict the respondent's score on the women's work-family roles scale. These predicted scores are subtracted from the actual scores to give residuals that represent variation that is independent of the variables included in the model. This can be thought of as measuring attitudes to women's work-family roles, when country, religion, age, gender and marital status have been controlled for. We then compare the means for three categories of employment status: working full-time, working part-time and home duties. We do this separately for married and single female respondents, and spouses for male respondents. These means are presented in Table 8.11, and provide strong evidence that one's beliefs about women working are translated into decisions about work.

Table 8.11 The relationship between attitudes to women's work-family roles and employment status

Employment status of ...	Employment status		
	Full-time	**Part-time**	**Home**
Male's spouse	−4.71	−0.44	5.74
Married female	−3.44	0.27	5.68
Single female	−1.74	−1.30	9.17

Conclusion

This chapter addresses the issues of whether one's religion affects one's attitudes to work-family roles, and then whether these attitudes lead people to make different choices about employment. It is clear from the evidence of the ISSP data that religion does affect such attitudes – Jews tend to have more modern attitudes than do those reporting no religious affiliation, whereas Christians tend to be a bit more traditional, and Muslims a lot more traditional. The data also show that these attitudes do affect behaviour, with more traditional attitudes associated with a tendency for women not to engage in outside employment.

We focused on religion in order to study normative constraints on choice. Our argument is that beliefs and values constrain through the desire to conform to norms or to beliefs that are supported within one's community. But what this means for the future is unclear. On one hand, there is clear evidence of generational change – our results, consistent with previous research, show that the older one is, the more traditional are one's attitudes to women's work-family roles, and it is probable that younger people will continue to hold more egalitarian attitudes as they grow older. This implies a general tendency, at the level of a society, towards more modern attitudes over time. On the other hand, though, the countries with a strong Judaeo-Christian heritage (which are also the most secularised countries) are also increasingly multicultural. This suggests that it is important to view affluent societies as comprising multiple ethnic and religious communities that will produce a diversity of norms and favoured expressions of identity.

Finally, our analysis suggests that the relationship between constraint and preference is not as clear-cut as it might seem. Normative constraints are, in a very real sense, also preferences. Normative constraints, as exemplified through religious constructions of gender identities, affect choice in two ways: they shape one's evaluation of the desirability of certain courses of action, and thus are tightly connected to the values that underlie preferences. Second, they limit the feasibility of particular courses of action that depend on the approval of those with the power to provide or restrict opportunities.

References

Bartkowski, J.P. (1999) 'One Step Forward, One Step Back: "Progressive Traditionalism" And The Negotiation Of Domestic Labor Within Evangelical Families', *Gender Issues*, 17: 40–64.

Bartkowski, J.P. and Read, J.G. (2003) 'Veiled Submission: Gender, Power And Identity Among Evangelical And Muslim Women In The United States', *Qualitative Sociology*, 26(1): 71–92.

Berger, P.L. (1967) *The sacred canopy: Elements of a sociological theory of religion*, Garden City, NY: Doubleday.

Berger, P.L. (1970) *A rumor of angels: Modern society and the rediscovery of the supernatural*, Garden City, NY: Doubleday.

Berger, P.L. (1992) *A far glory: The quest for faith in an age of credulity*, New York: Doubleday.

Bolzendahl, C.I. and Myers, D.J. (2004) Feminist Attitudes and Support for Gender Equality: Opinion Change in Women and Men, 1974–1998, *Social Forces*, 83: 759–90.

Booth, A.D.R., Johnson, A., Branaman, A. and Sica, A. (1995) Beliefs and behavior: Does religion matter in today's marriage? *Journal of Marriage and Family*, 57: 661–71.

Crompton, R. (1998) *Women and Work in Modern Britain*, Oxford: Oxford University Press.

Davis, N. and Robinson, R. (1999) 'Religious Cosmologies, Individualism, And Politics In Italy', *Journal for the Scientific Study of Religion*, 38(3): 339–53.

Greely, A.M. (1989) *Religious Change in America*, Cambridge, Mass: Harvard University Press.

Greenacre, M.J. (1993) *Correspondence Analysis in Practice*, London: Academic Press.

Hakim, C. (1991) 'Grateful Slaves And Self-Made Women: Fact and Fantasy In Women's Work Orientations', *European Sociological Review*, 7: 101–21.

Hakim, C. (2000) *Work-Lifestyle Choices In The 21st Century: Preference Theory*, Oxford: Oxford University Press.

Hoffman, J.P. and Miller, A.S. (1997) Social and Political Attitudes among Religious Groups: Convergence and Divergence Over Time, *Journal for the Scientific Study of Religion*, 36: 528–46.

Hoffman, J.P. and Miller, A.S. (1998) Denominational Influences on Socially Divisive Issues: Polarization or Continuity? *Journal for the Scientific Study of Religion*, 37: 528–46.

Inglehart, R. and Norris, P. (2003) *Rising Tide, Gender Equality and Cultural Change Around the World*, Cambridge, UK: Cambridge University Press.

International Social Survey Programme (ISSP) 2002 'Family And Changing Gender Roles III'. Computer file and codebook, Koeln, Germany: Zentralarchiv Fuer Empirische Sozialforschung.

Lehrer, E.L. (1995) The effects of religion on the labor supply of married women, *Social Science Research*, 24: 281–301.

McCrae, S. (2003) Constraints and choices in mothers' employment careers: a consideration of Hakim's Preference Theory, *British Journal of Sociology*, 54: 317–38.

Peek, C.W., Lowe, G.D. and Williams, L.S. (1991) Gender and God's Word: Another Look at Religious Fundamentalism and Sexism, *Social Forces*, 69: 1205–21.

Petersen, L.R. and Donnenwerth, G.V. (1998) Religion and Declining Support for Traditional Beliefs About Gender Roles and Homosexual Rights, *Sociology of Religion*, 59: 353–71.

Read, J.G. (2003) 'The Sources Of Gender Role Attitudes Among Christian And Muslim Arab-American Women', *Sociology of Religion*, 64: 207–22.

Sundstrom, E. (1999) Should mothers work? Age and Attitudes in Germany, Italy and Sweden, *International Journal of Social Welfare*, 8: 193–205.

Wooden, M. and Loundes, J. (2002) 'How Unreasonable Are Long Working Hours', *Melbourne University Melbourne Institute Working Paper Series*, No. 1/02.

9
The Childless Working Life

Brita Bungum

Introduction

Time is an important aspect in understanding the organisation of modern family life. As such, working life is the main regulator of adult time in our society and because of this the working lives of adults have a great impact on children's time as well as on their lives. Parents have to deal with competitive time demands when combining care for children and working life. Children have to deal with parents' time practices connected to different time cultures in working life. The aim of this chapter is to discuss how children are understood in sociological research about working time and family life. The purpose is to try to develop a sociological perspective that may capture children's experience of the adult working life. The framework for this is gender studies and the sociology of work, but the aim is to develop a new approach to the study of how Norwegian children interact with the adult work life, and how they negotiate with their parents in regard to time practices connected to work.[1]

In Western society, working life is an adult arena, while schools and kindergarten are places for children, and this division is also reflected in research agendas. Studies of the 'workplace' and studies of 'family life' have been characterised by separate research traditions (Deven et al, 1997). This chapter will begin by identifying the lack of a child perspective in studies of Norwegian and Western working life. Children are usually not included in studies about work and family life but if they are included they are most often regarded as passive appendages to the adults or as their parents' property, usually their mothers'. Two questions are central to this chapter: To what extent are children perceived of as a passive appendage or their parents' property? And are children perceived as 'the others' without an independent 'voice' in studies of work and family life? Based on these questions this chapter examines how and why a child perspective needs to be developed in this research field. Following this, it focuses on parallels between gender perspectives and child perspectives and argues that feminist writings can point to ways to include a child perspective in working life research. In particular, the similarities between children's and women's positions as 'the others', as 'victims' or a 'social problem' without an independent voice in research on working life, are highlighted. Development of a child perspective will contribute new knowledge to our understanding of work and family life.

The agency perspective is offered as a means to establish a sociological understanding of children in studies of work and family life. This includes a presentation and discussion of three different studies within the field of working and family lives which in different ways have employed an agency perspective. Finally, important questions for future research on the balance between work and life through the lens of a child perspective, are discussed.

The adult working life

In sociological research concerning work and family life, children have been virtually ignored as independent and active participants. How the variable 'children' or 'dependents' is distributed is often regarded as relevant when searching for reasons for stress and illness among employees (Lee, 1998; Mastekaasa and Dale-Olsen, 1998). For example, questions concerning gender differences in sickness absence makes children visible as a variable. In Norwegian studies on working conditions, children are included as one of many possible variables that may explain why women in Norway are more absent due to sickness than men are (Statistics Norway, 2004). In research about part-time work, children also appear as a variable used to investigate why a higher proportion of women work part-time than men. In this way, especially in survey research, children are most often treated as a characteristic or quality of employees. The category 'children' is defined or characterised as an appendage to adults and employees (McKee, Mauther and Galilee, 2003).

On the other hand, when children are included as an independent variable, this can be a *supplement* to research on children's life with working parents and in this way contribute to make children's situation more *visible*. One important goal for research about children has been to include them as citizens of the society and as a social category in research (Qvortrup, 1997).

Work in social policy has begun to search for 'children's voices' (Hallett and Prout, 2003) and so too is the need to include 'children's voices' in policy concerning working life. For example, in Norway, the government in 2005, is introducing a new Working Environment Act containing a liberalisation of working time regulations in the Norwegian work force (Ot.prpnr 49, 2004–2005). This new regulation will make it easier for Norwegian employers to allow their employees to legally work more overtime than has previously been allowed. The consequences of a deregulation in working time regulations are of great importance as to how much time children can spend with their working parents. Asking what implications new work time practices have on children's everyday life is important for working life researchers and policy-makers. To include a child perspective in working life research can contribute to making children more 'visible' and to allow their 'voices' to be heard in the shaping of policy for families, households and future work life.

Children as gendered burdens?

It is not surprising that there is a lack of children's 'voices' in mainstream working life research. As I have argued, in this research tradition human beings have been understood as abstract and gender neutral. The main focus has been on workers and the time they spend at work, and not on how they combine this with their private life. In this understanding, children belong to people's private life and are not understood as relevant for the approaches that are being used. The issue may be more clearly understood by searching for a child perspective in the areas of working life and family life.

Research on work and family life has generally included children as 'victims' of working life regulations and as a source of demands on mothers and fathers: for example, the child as a 'care receiver', a 'burden' and a 'strain' to working parents, especially working mothers. In contrast, there is also a perspective that emphasises children as a 'resource' for working parents with children conceived of as a positive and qualifying factor for both mothers and fathers. A study of female civil engineers and their families shows that these women gain benefits from having children. Things they emphasise in connection to this are that their children have taught them to collaborate more effectively and to 'read' other people's verbal and non-verbal signals (Kvande and Rasmussen, 1990).

Previous work has investigated the time working mothers and fathers take to care for small children (Bungum and Kvande, 2002; Bungum, Brandth and Kvande, 2001). Scandinavian research about work and family life and welfare state arrangements have mainly focused on how adults can manage to get enough time to take care of their kids (Bekkengen, 2002; Bungum, Brandth and Kvande, 2001; Gjerstad and Kvande, 1998). The question of equal opportunities between mothers and fathers in caretaking has been, and continues to be, important to the research field and in policy work in this area.

However, less attention has been given to children themselves and how they interact with their parents' working lives. To date, the focus has been on the adult experience of attempting to combine working life and family life, and not on the children's experience of having parents who are engaged in paid work. This need for including a children's perspective does not diminish the fact that documenting the gender division in the labour market and understanding the differences between men and women's lives, is an important feminist project, in the critical tradition of sociology. However, the aim of the present work is to explore the possibilities of including a 'child perspective' and to what knowledge and insight this brings to understanding work-life issues. Viewed from a feminist perspective, it is important to study how mothers and fathers divide time between work and family. A child perspective will demand that we turn our eyes to the child, for example to observe the consequences of the parents' time practices on the child.

A Norwegian survey on *Fleksible fedre* ('Flexible fathers') shows that only five per cent of Norwegian fathers work part-time while 41 per cent of the Norwegian mothers are part-time workers (Brandth and Kvande, 2003a). One-third of fathers with small children work more than 40 hours a week.[2] Viewed from a feminist perspective of equal opportunities, this division of labour between fathers and mothers is unfortunate because it maintains a gendered labour market that gives women a weaker position in terms of their access to money and influence in society. The same survey also shows that some Norwegian mothers are working more than normal working hours with their partners who also work long hours (Brandth and Kvande, 2003a). From an equal opportunity perspective these couples are the most equal, the ones that have managed to succeed in their 'equality project'. However, this is not the case from a child's perspective in that these parents simply have very little time to spend with their children (Kvande, 2004). By shifting the view from the parents to the children, something else is revealed about time practices which will not be gleaned from focusing solely on parents' experiences.

Employing a child perspective can be done in different ways and often involves different research methods such as empirical research with children as the subjects for interviews, observation or case studies. At the same time it is also possible to read old data with 'new glasses' by adopting a child perspective. As part of the national evaluation of cash support in Norway, which is a care arrangement for parents with small children, a study was conducted to understand the consequences cash support would have for equal opportunities in work and family life (Bungum, Brandth and Kvande, 2001). Data collection consisted of interviews with fathers and mothers with children between one and three years, since this is the particular age group for the cash support arrangement. Later, this same data was analysed to consider parents' reflections on what they thought was the best solution for their children and then on the consequences the parents' different time practices have for *children's time* with their parents. Results show that the children with mothers who reduce their working hours to spend more time at home, do not necessarily get more time with the whole family, although this was one of the main intensions from the Norwegian Government that introduced the cash support (St.prp 53.1997). In these families it is common for the fathers to increase their working hours, while mothers' part-time work is often done on weekends or in evenings. In this way, many of the 'cash support children' are mainly spending time alone with their mothers, they get little time with their fathers, and they seldom enjoy the company of the whole family together (Bungum, 2005). A child perspective with a main focus on children's time with their parents can make a difference, and previous research reveals that it can establish new findings from data that adopt a child perspective initially (Brandth and Kvande, 2003b; Bungum, 2005).

Lessond from feminist writing

The pursuit of making children visible as active participants in research on work, shares some similar features with the early feminist projects making women's lives and work visible. The parallels are drawn by recent writers such as Strandell (2001) who has been working in both these research fields. She refers to methodological knowledge from women's studies as useful for the research about children and points out how both women and children have been conceptually marginalised as belonging to 'the others', being 'different from' women in relation to men, children in relation to adults (Strandell, 2001). Oakley (1994) also discusses similarities and differences between research on children and women with regard to questions relating to justice. She shows, for example, how women's rights have been and still are limited in many countries, and that children's rights are similarly underdeveloped. Seen from the perspective of history, women's rights are a relatively new and western phenomenon. Oakley reminds us that children were not included in the United Nations Human Rights Convention from 1948; human rights were reserved for adults (Oakley, 1994).

It has been an important feminist aim to give women a voice in research and at the same time describe the world and analyse data through an alternative women's perspective. According to this, concepts and theory have their basis in women's lives and experience. The value neutrality of mainstream research has been criticised from a feminist point of view (Berg, 1977; Smith, 1988; Wærnes, 1990). In the same way, child research provides the opportunity to search for a children's voice and to explore perspectives based on children's lives and experience. Instead of just viewing children as objects, child researchers have argued that we need to understand children as subjects and pay more attention to their everyday life here and now (Tiller, 1989).

Critical feminist perspectives discuss value neutrality by focusing on who are being understood as 'the others'. They argue that women have different understandings and, in this way, experience the world differently. Therefore, development of knowledge must take place in women's material reality (Smith, 1988). In the same way, the child perspective represents a critical view of adult-centered research, where children are conceptualised as passive appendages without any agency (Kjørholt, 2001).

An assumption of gender neutrality dominates mainstream research on working life. The abstract, bodiless and universal human is characteristic of research about work and organisations (Acker, 1990). An abstract understanding of the human being is central to the growth of the modern image of the human being in our culture (Ryan and Gordon, 1994). Acker (1990) maintains that the image of the abstract worker contributes to the reproduction of underlying gender relations. So too, the absence of children in research also contributes to this reproduction. One underlying gender relation is found in the idea of a working life based on the traditional masculine breadwinner model where the concern about children mainly deals with provision and not care responsibility. In contrast, research about modern Norwegian fatherhood shows that fathers not only experience responsibility to provide but also a care responsibility for their children (Brandth and Kvande, 2003a).

Oakley (1994) sees similarities in the understanding of children and women as social minorities in a culture dominated by masculine power. The tight alliance between women and children may have many different cultural appearances. Women give birth to children and women take care of children, whether we talk about paid or unpaid work of a caring nature, regardless of whether we choose to use the gender-neutral concept 'parents' to describe who is taking care of the children. Oakley also reminds us that it is not the fathers' achievements that have made it possible for mothers to enter working life but rather the supply of different care arrangements and society's demands for compulsory school attendance for children (Oakley, 1994).

The critical feminist perspective seeks to conduct research on women's terms by seeing and interpreting the world through 'the image of women' (Holter, 1982); in the same way we can find a corresponding ambition to see the world through 'children's eyes' in child research (Hagbard and Esping, 1992). There has been an exposition from understanding gender as a noun, to understanding gender within social constructivism as a verb. Gender is not what we *are* but what we *do*. The main question is how is gender shaped, and not what gender is. Using the concept 'doing gender' allows for variation over time and in different contexts (Kvande, 2003). Child research may receive a similar criticism to that lodged against conceiving 'women' as a universal concept; there is likewise no universal experience of childhood (Kjørholt, 2001; Lee, 1998; Oakley, 1994). 'There is nothing "natural" with childhood or what it means to be a child', Katz (2002: 250) claims when discussing children's position in relation to globalisation and social reproduction. For example, to be an eight year-old girl in Norway today is of course something quite different from being an eight year-old girl in Afghanistan five years ago, 50 years ago or today, for that matter.

There are several similarities between the feminist project to include women as actors in work and organisation theory and to include children as actors in the same field. The most important similarity is in understanding 'the worker'. Like feminist perspectives, a child perspective can challenge the abstract and universal understanding of human beings in working life research.

The agency perspective

The rather new field of child research has criticised and challenged the narrow understanding of children as an appendage to adults (Corsaro, 2005; Hallett and Prout, 2003; James and Prout, 1997; Lee, 2001). Today we recognise the construction of the child as a subject with democratic rights and discussions about children's participation and presence in society (Kjørholt, 2003). Children have been reconceived as a resource that should be listened to and understood as participating subjects rather than as victims. Children's rights and demands have developed from a criticism carried out by adults both in child research and in politics. One example is the Norwegian commissioner for children. This position was introduced in 1981 and was the world's first commissioner for children. The main task for the Norwegian commissioner for children is to secure children rights and speak on behalf of children's interest in public and private areas in society (The Ministry of Foreign Affairs, 1998).

Corsaro (2005) discusses why children and childhood has been ignored in sociological research. He refers to Qvortrup (1997) who argues that children have not so much been ignored as they have been marginalised. Children are marginalised in sociology because of their subordinate position in societies and in theoretical conceptualisations of childhood and socialisation. This is very similar to the feminist critic concerning women's position and marginalisation in society and in sociological research. However, Corsaro also points to another reason for ignoring children. Adults (including sociologists) he claims, most often view children in a forward looking way, with an eye to what they will become as future adults, and rarely what they are, children with ongoing lives. The strong influence from the traditional socialisation theories can also explain why children have not been understood as active participants in society. Socialisation theories have given children a passive role where the notion is that children are shaped by forces external to themselves in order to adapt to society (Corsaro, 2005).

This criticism of traditional sociological approaches by child researchers has lead to a development of an agency perspective. An *'agency perspective' involves an understanding of children as active and acting subjects and instead of focusing on what they will become when they finally grow up, the focus is on what they are today.* This implies a shift from viewing the child as *human becoming*, to viewing the child as a *human being*. This shift in the understanding of children can be understood in relation to the growing attention to children's rights in society. I will argue that the approach to children as human beings also need to be explored and reflected in research agendas around work and family.

Children as both dependent and independent

The adult working life is an important context for many children in how they can live their everyday life, yet this has not been an important subject in child research. There is a tendency to study children as if they were totally disconnected from family, local society and their parents' working life (McKee, Mauther and Galilee, 2003).

Anne Trine Kjørholt (2003) argues that research on childhood and children's everyday lives must include the mutual relations between children's lives in the surrounding society and their cultural contexts. Kjørholt refers to a criticism of ethnographic research which often focuses on children as social acting subjects belonging to particular age groups, constructing their own cultures in playgrounds, schools and streets. Studies of children have only included to a small degree adult working life as an important context in children's life. These studies have focused on children as active individuals. The agency perspective is common in studies about how children participate in particular age groups in playgrounds, schools and streets, but they have rarely focused on how these practices are connected to a larger social context. The emphasis on processes at the micro level often prevents us from recognising the significance of macro structures. 'Children's voices' are voices from a particular subject in a particular discourse (Kjørholt, 2003).

In recent child research studies there is a growing attention and concern for children's possibilities or lack of opportunities for freedom to play and live without adult control and organising. Parents in western countries are more and more afraid for their children's safety in public spaces and children's lives seem to be more controlled and limited to special areas with organised activities by adults (James, Jenks and Prout, 1998; Prout, 2003). This evidence suggests that children's and adult's lives are less separate and it provides even more reasons to include a child perspective in the work-life research agenda. If children's lives are more controlled by adults than before it is even more timely to consider how the adult world influences childhood experiences and how children's experiences influence the adult world.

In his criticism of the agency perspective in ethnographic children research, Lee (2001) points out that agency to a stronger degree must be

connected to context and relations. The eagerness in understanding children as participating subjects has made us overlook that children are
always moving between being 'dependent' and 'independent'. Children's
statements cannot be read only as 'children's voices', because children's
voices are always situated and placed within a context and in relationships. Human beings, children or adults, are rarely able to act as sover-
eign actors, independent of context or relationships. Lee proposes that we
can ask other questions related to the agency perspective: 'So with this
approach to agency, instead of asking whether children, like adults,
possess agency or not, we can ask how agency is built or may be built for
them by examining the extensions and supplements that are available to
them' (2001: 131).

This approach can be useful in the case of trying to include children
as social actors in relation to adult time practices in working life. Even
though adults practically always have more power or influence as compared to children, an agency perspective offers the opportunity to
search for a breach in this power relation. Despite adult working lives
heavily affecting parents' time practices, the agency perspective gives
us a chance to question whether children may influence how
their parents divide their time between work and family. The agency
perspective can be placed within an ethnomethodological tradition,
and it is possible to derive various approaches from this perspective as
found in Kvande (2003) in her discussion of the perspective 'doing
gender'.

Three approaches are useful to understanding children as social actors
in research on work and family. First, the *interactional approach* that
involves a main focus on how children become active participants
through interaction with adults, and how they can influence the shaping
of the adults' everyday lives. Second, the *practices approach* provides an
opportunity to study how practice shapes social relations (see Smith,
1988). This approach could, for instance, shed light on children's experience of, and influence on, their parents' time practices in regards to work
and family. Finally, the *negotiation approach* provides an opportunity to
study if and how children negotiate as participants with adults. This
approach is based on the fact that as participants we may have different
interests and that we negotiate, cooperate, or fight for our interests. In
an agency perspective children may also be participants in negotiations
on, for instance, adults' time management.

In the following section, three different studies conducted within the
fields of work and family that have included a child perspective are examined according to the interactional, practices and negotiation approaches.
These studies are examples of how an agency perspective can be employed
and contribute in different ways to new knowledge in research on working
hours and family life.

Babies as social actors

An example from Norwegian research on fathers and childcare highlights that it is possible to include a child perspective in research on the combination of work and care responsibilities. Norwegian parental leave arrangements allow a total of 42 weeks leave of absence with 100 per cent salary or 52 weeks with 80 per cent salary in the first year of the child's life. Mothers and fathers may share the leave as they like, but the first six weeks after birth are reserved for mothers and four weeks in the parental leave period are reserved for fathers. However, the parental leave arrangement is mainly being used by Norwegian mothers. The politics behind the four week 'father's quota' (*fedrekvote*) has therefore been to encourage fathers to be more involved in the caring for their children. If a father chooses not to use his four weeks 'father quota', the parents lose these four weeks of their parental leave period. The father's quota has been a success in Norway, an arrangement that 85 per cent of fathers use (Brandth and Kvande, 2003a). There is, however, different ways of practicing this father quota period among parents. Some fathers choose to spend the father quota period together with their partner, because it is quite common for many mothers to take their holiday in the same period. Other fathers spend their father quota at home alone with their child, while the mothers are back at work.

Brandth and Kvande (2003b) ask how small children influence their father's care practices and how fathers learn to 'read' their children's needs. They claim that the difference between spending time alone with the child or not is important for the father's possibilities of learning from their children. Their approach concerns fathers using their father's quota, but the perspective is that of the children, and not the parents. The child is an explicit subject in the cases where the fathers are spending time alone with the child, without the mother present. The narratives from the fathers indicate that fathers who get the possibly to spend their leave alone with their child do not have to ask their wives or cohabiters what they think the child needs. These fathers have acquired skills to read their children's needs when staying home with the child without any help from their partner (Brandth and Kvande, 2003b).

When picturing children as social participants, most often it is of children old enough to communicate through language. However, Brandth and Kvande's study reveals that it is possible to understand babies as active participants in interaction with their fathers. Methodologically, Brandth and Kvande use interviews with the fathers, making the children's perspective only indirectly represented through the father's narratives of their interaction with their children. This study is also an example of an analysis employing an *interactional approach*, focusing on how these babies can influence their fathers' care practices. In corresponding studies of young children, observation could be an appropriate method to capture the children's perspective. This study demonstrates that the father's quota is not only a matter of sharing the benefits between mothers and fathers, it may also be used to understand a children's discourse in family policy.

Working time practice and the consequences for children

An example of a study that focuses on what parents' working lives mean to children's lives is an exploration of work conditions in the oil and gas industry in Scotland (McKee, Mauther and Galilee, 2003). The children in this study were between eight and 12 years old and had at least one parent working in this industry. In most cases, this would be the father since this is a male-dominated sector. The children were asked how they perceived their parents' working life. One of the findings was that the children displayed a high degree of sensitivity and knowledge about the positive and negative effects and consequences of their parents' working lives both to their parents and to themselves. The children could, for example, identify their parents' contradictory and contemporary feelings towards work as 'happy and strained' or 'angry and tensed'. The children were able to see the effects of different working cultures and flexible working practices on their parents.

At the same time, this study found that the children were very pragmatic towards their parents' work situation and demonstrated a high degree of ability to adjust to changes involving themselves. Several of these children had to move a lot and to different countries in the world because of their father's job. McKee, Mauther and Galilee (2003) found that the children rarely spoke about challenging their parents' division of labour or their balance between work and family life. On the contrary, they generally found an uncritical acceptance among the children towards their parents' solutions. This, the authors argue, opens up several interpretations and they suggest that it may be the children's initial experience that they have no right to decide which of the parents goes to work, how much they work and where in the world they are going to live at any time. The children had doubts about the degree to which they could influence their parents' working life. They were aware of the financial realities that influenced their parents' decisions, and they claimed that work was especially important for their fathers. Several of the children expressed great empathy with their parents, especially with their fathers who often complained about the company's greediness and missed the children when they had to spend much time away from home (McKee, Mauther and Galilee, 2003).

In McKee et al's study we see an approach slightly different from the interactional one found in Brandth and Kvande (2003b). McKee and colleagues mainly focus on the consequences for the children of the parents' practice related to working life and family life. As the children in this study are somewhat older than the children in Brandth and Kvande, it was possible to conduct separate interviews with the children where they could reflect upon their parents' working lives.

McKee et al employ an agency perspective when investigating whether the children feel they can influence their parents' time management and balance between working life and family life. Their approach is associated with a *practices approach* where the main focus is on which and how the consequences of the parents' actions or lack of actions affect their relations with their children. The study shows how the children, to a greater extent than expected, realised the realities of the adult working life. These children could not escape the negative effects of their parents' greedy working life. The study shows how a focus on children's experience of working life can provide new knowledge of how working life affects family life. This knowledge could lead to new ways of thinking and new approaches to how working life ought to be shaped and organised in the future.

Children in negotiations

Another example of a study which focuses on children with parents who work long hours is Hochschild (1997). This book became a bestseller and a frequently-cited work. The continuous discussion of Hochschild's findings among work researchers, however, makes it even stranger that this book, to only a very little degree, has received attention for using a child perspective and for including children's experience and negotiations with parents about time and time practices. Through observations of the children at the daycare center, Hochschild introduces us to 'The Waving Window' where the children say goodbye to their parents in the morning. Some of the kids protest against their parents leaving, while others seem to accept the fact. This extensive and repeated waving is not further analysed by Hochschild in her book. Nevertheless, one is left with the impression that this 'waving ritual' has an important symbolic function both to the parents and their child; maybe this has something to do with care in this situation of leaving and being left?

As a result of the working time culture in the company 'Americo', the children spend long days at the daycare center. Hochschild describes how the daycare center works on 'child time'. 'Its rhythms are child paced and mainly slow' (Hochschild, 1997: 5). This slow 'child time' provides a powerful contrast to the hectic lives their parents are living at home and at work. Hochschild also visits and observes these children and parents at home, giving insight into how everyday life is both experienced by adults and children. Hochschild's inclusion of the child as a social participant in her study gives us a fundamental and more complete knowledge of the consequences of participating in long working hours in dominant and pervasive companies.

In an earlier work Hochschild (1995) highlights children's negotiations with their parents about time and time practices. A central story is about four year-old Sarah. After spending nine hours at the daycare center, Sarah is picked up by her babysitter. The babysitter takes Sarah and her older sister out for dinner. They arrive at home at 7:00 p.m. to meet with their parents and two guests. Hochschild describes how Sarah is asked to go in to another room to play with a gift during dinner, and that the babysitter takes her outside into the garden to the swings. But after a quick swing Sarah returns and stands next to her mother. At this point she announces that she wants to dance, and her father puts on her favorite dance music. Everyone looks at Sarah and her dancing, a few twirls and then she stops in a refusal to go on. Her mum tries carefully to make her go on, but Sarah stands still without moving. The babysitter says 'I think Sarah is tired'. Hochschild's story about Sarah ends with her mother carrying her to bed with loud protests from the child.

Hochschild uses several approaches when she analyses this story about Sarah and her unfinished dance. One involves Sarah as a participant towards her parents. Hochschild suggests that Sarah's refusal to finish the dance can be understood as a hidden bargain with her mother; 'If you won't give me time and attention', she might be saying, 'I will withhold my time from you and I won't be your showcase child'. In this way Sarah can be understood as a participant in relation to her mother's time practice. Hochschild also asks how often people in relationships try to see each other. How well ensured and guarded is their time? Do people avoid different types of time damage? She introduces the concept of 'time work' which means work to avoid time damage, like turning off the answering machine or the cell phone. She then asks how much 'time work' Sarah's parents are doing for their daughter. In this way she seeks to discuss the patterns of time and social relationships (Hochschild, 1995).

Hochschild's discussion of Sarah's unfinished dance is an illustration of how it is possible to understand children both as 'dependent' and 'independent' in relation to the adult world. Methodologically, Hochschild employs observation; she did not interview Sarah or her older sister. The observation method gives Hochschild the opportunity to catch the very negotiating situation like Sarah's refusal to continue her dance. Sarah is four years old and she probably would not be able to reflect verbally upon this episode later, as an older child could, which is why the observation method is appropriate in this situation. In Hochschild's analysis, Sarah becomes an active and acting participant, negotiating with her parents. *The negotiation approach* is employed here where Sarah's unfinished dance becomes her negotiating move against her parents' time practice, which she dislikes. The strength of the negotiation approach lies in the differences in interests and power in human relations. Children and adults may often have different interests related to how the time between the adult working life and family life is balanced. A negotiation approach as employed by Hochschild, makes it possible to explore how children try to influence adults' time practice.

Conclusion

Working life in Norway, as in other Western countries, is mainly an adult arena. Many of the different approaches to problems in working life are not especially important or relevant to children's everyday life and experience. It is not difficult at all to find explanations for the lack of 'children's voices' in work research; it is a field principally understood from an adult perspective. The question is: why should children's perspectives and perspectives on childhood be of any interest to working life researchers?

Although children in most Western societies do not, in the main, participate in paid working life, the adult working world has great implications for their everyday life. This is reason enough to study how children experience working life. Deregulation and reorganisation of adult working time can have a major impact on children's lives and the opportunity to spend time with their working parents. Working life researchers could explore what these consequences would look like in children's everyday life in order to contribute to a more complex view of the 'worker'. Using the traditional and limited approach of 'the abstract worker' in work research can be a safe and often convenient solution, perhaps because it gives an impression of scientific objectiveness. However, this 'abstract' understanding needs to be challenged. The 'abstract worker' still characterises much of the literature in this field and this understanding contributes to politics in the working life area. Behind the illusion of the abstract worker we find 'the rational man'. This job-oriented individual has no worries about reaching the daycare center or school in time after work and no problems with long hours or a lot of travel days at work.

Working life research has the potential to produce new knowledge on the consequences of adults' working lives on children's lives. The experience from feminist studies demonstrates how new perspectives can contribute new insights, and it demonstrates how children can be viewed as social actors related to the adult working life. In research on work and family life, the main focus has been on parents' time with children or on the parents' 'equality project'. Sometimes it can be useful to move the focus from the parents to the children. Studies about family life are often disconnected to studies about working life, although people in real life participate in both areas. Research on relations between work and family are in this way exceeding traditional research spheres. This gives great opportunities to study social processes and phenomena in connection, on both the micro and structural levels.

For example, in Norwegian welfare politics, there has recently been several political parties claiming that today's children should spend more time with their working parents. This is mainly the reason why the Norwegian Government introduced the 'cash support' scheme in 1998, to be used by adults to reduce working hours. If increasing children's time with their parents is an important political goal, than it cannot be enough to think narrowly about welfare policy and reforms such as cash support or parental leave arrangements. Related to this, it becomes a paradox that the new Working Environment Act in Norway that regulates adult working time, probably will have a greater impact on children's possibilities for spending time with their parents than all these family reforms together. To include a child perspective in research on work and family could contribute to understanding the connections between adult use of time for work and the consequences this can have for children's everyday lives.

Future research on working hours and family life may benefit from including children as participants. By including children in the research agenda the image of the 'combination problem' of work and family may be sharpened and new aspects and approaches may be added. Even though assumptions exist of how children experience their lives, there is little empirical evidence of children's experience of the adult working life. Employment and welfare policies provide a framework for how children's and adults' everyday lives can be lived and the opportunities and constraints to make choices about this. The 'voice' of the children also needs to be heard in these forums. Introducing a child perspective in the broad sociological research field and, more specifically, in the areas of work and family life, will potentially improve the lives of children and working parents through enhanced understanding and more targeted policies.

Notes

1. *Time negotiation between children and the adult working life*, Phd project, Department of Political Science and Sociology, Norwegian University of Science and Technology.
2. In Norway a normal work hour per week is 37.5 hours.

References

Acker, J. (1990) 'Hierachies, Jobs, Bodies: A Theory of Gendered Organizations', *Gender & Society*, 4(2): 139–58.

Bekkengen, L. (2002) *Man får valja, Om foreldraskap och foreldraledighet i arbetsliv og familjeliv* [One has to choose, Parenthood and parental leave in work life and family life], Malmø, Sweden: Liber.

Berg, A.M. (1977) *I kvinners bilde* [In women's image], Oslo: Pax.

Brandth, B. and Kvande, E. (2003a) *Fleksible fedre* [Flexible fathers], Oslo: Universitetsforlaget.

Brandth, B. and Kvande, E. (2003b) 'Fathers Presence in Childcare', in Jensen, A.M. and McKee, L. (eds) *Children and the Changing Family*, London: Routledge, 61–75.

Bungum, B., Brandth, B. and Kvande, E. (2001) *Ulik praksis – ulike konsekvenser: En evaluering av kontantstøttens konsekvenser for likestilling i arbeidsliv og familieliv* [Different practice – different consequences: An evaluation of the consequences of cash benefits for gender equality in working life and family life], Trondheim: SINTEF Teknologiledelse IFIM og NTNU Institutt for Sosiologi og Statsvitenskap.

Bungum, B. and Kvande, E. (2002) 'Tid til barn' [Time for children] in Forseth, U. and Rasmussen, B. (eds) *Arbeid for live* [Work for life], Gyldendal Norsk Forlag, Oslo: Gyldendal Akademisk, 145–57.

Bungum, B. (2005) 'Å velge det beste for barna' [Making the best choice for the children] in Bungum, B., Brandth, B. and Kvande, E. (eds) *Valgfrihetens tid* [Time of the Freedom of Choice], in press 2005, Oslo: Gyldendal Norsk Forlag.

Corsaro, W.A. (2005) *The sociology of childhood*, London: Pine Forge Press.

Deven, F., Inglis, S., Moss, P. and Petrie, P. (1997) *State of the Art Review on the Reconciliation of Work and Family Life for Men and Women and The Quality of Care Service*, Final Report, Brussels: European Commission Equal Opportunities Unit (DGV).

Gjerstad, B. and Kvande, E. (1998) 'Fedre mellom arbeid og permisjon' [Fathers between work and leave], *Notat* 98/5, Trondheim: Allforsk/NTNU.

Hagbard, S. and Esping, U. (1992) *Med barns ogon* [In the eyes of children], Stockholm: Allmanna Barnhuset.

Hallett, C. and Prout, A. (2003) *Hearing the voices of children. Social policy for a new century*, London: Routledge.

Hochschild, A.R. (1995) *Work, Family and Time as the Locus of Symbolic Interaction.* William Aubert Memorial Lecture 1995, ISF report 96, 6(22): 5–22.

Hochschild, A.R. (1997) *The Time Bind. When Work Becomes Home, and Home Becomes Work*, New York: Metropolitan Books.

Holter, H. (1982) *Kvinner i felleskap. Kvinners levekår og livsløp* [Women together. Women's living conditions and lives], Oslo: Universitetsforlaget.

James, A., Jenks, C. and Prout, A. (1998) *Theorizing Childhood*, London: Polity Press.

James, A. and Prout, A. (eds) (1997) *Constructing and Reconstructing Childhood*, London: Routledge.

Katz, C. (2002) 'Stuck in a place: Children and the globalization of social reproduction', in Johnston, R.J., Taylor, P.J. and Watts, M.J. (eds) *Geographies of Global Change: Remapping the World*, Oxford: Blackwell, 248–60.

Kjørholt, A.T. (2001) 'The participating Child – A vital pillar in this century?' *Nordic Educational Research*, 21(2): 65–81.

Kjørholt, A.T. (2003) 'Creating a Place to Belong. Girls and boys hut-building as a site for understanding discourses on childhood and generational relations in a Norwegian community', *Children's Geographies*, 1(2): 261–79.

Kvande, E. and Rasmussen, B. (1990) *Nye kvinneliv. Kvinner i menns organisasjoner* [New female lives. Women in men's organisations], Oslo: ad Notam Arbeidslivsbiblioteket.

Kvande, E. (2003) 'Doing Gender in Organizations – Theoretical Possibilities and Limitations' in Gunnarson, E., Andersson, S., Rosell, A.V, Letho, A. and Salminen-Karsson, M. (eds) *Where Have All the Structures Gone? Doing Gender in Organizations, Examples from Finland, Norway and Sweden*, Stockholm: Center for Women's Studies, Stokholm University, 15–45.

Kvande, E. (2004) *Foreldre i det fleksible arbeidslivet* [Parents and the flexible working life], Lecture at the Norwegian Sociology Association Winter Seminar, January.

Lee, C. (1998) *Women's health. Psychological and Social Perspectives*, London: Sage.

Lee, N. (2001) *Childhood and society. Growing up in an age of uncertainty*, Buckingham: Open University Press.

Mastekaasa, A. and Dale-Olsen, H. (1998) *Kjønnsulikheter i helse* [Gender differences in health], Rapport 98:9, Oslo: Institutt for Samfunnsforskning.

McKee, L., Mauther, M. and Galilee, J. (2003) 'Children's perspective on middle-class work family arrangements', in Jensen, A.M. and McKee, L. (eds) *Children and the Changing Family Between Transformation and Negotiation*, London: Routledge, 27–45.

The Ministry of Foreign Affairs (1998) Nytt fra Norge [News from Norway], Commissioner for Children in Norway, http://odin.dep.no/odinarkiv/norsk/dep/ud/1999/publ/032005-990429/dok-bu.html

Oakley, A. (1994) 'Women and Children First and Last: Parallels and Differences between Children's and Women's Studies', in Mayall, B. (ed.) *Children's Childhood Observed and Experienced*, London: Falmer Press, 13–33.

Ot.prpnr 49 (2004–2005) *Om lov om arbeidsmiljø, arbeidstid og stillingsvern mv* [Proposal for the Working environment act, working time, employment protection etc], (arbeidsmiljøloven) Tilråding fra Arbeids og sosialdepartementet av 25 february 2005, godkjent i statsråd samme dag, (Regjeringen Bondevik II).

Prout, A. (2003) 'Participation, policy and the changing conditions of childhood', in Hallet, C. and Prout, A. (eds) *Hearing the Voices of Children*, London: Routledge, 11–25.

Qvortrup, J. (1997) 'A voice for children in statistical and social accounting; A plea for children's right to be heard', in James, A. and Prout, A. (eds) *Constructing and Reconstructing Childhood: Contemporary Issues in the Sociological Study of Childhood*, London: Routledge, 85–103.

Ryan, M. and Gordon, A. (1994) *Body Politics Disease, Desire and the Family*, London: Westview Press.

Smith, D. (1988) *The Everyday World as Problematic*, Milton Keynes: Open University Press.

Strandell, H. (2001) *Identitet eller interaktion – perspektiv på inneborder av kon* i Haavind, H. (ed.) *Kjønn og fortolkende metode. Metodiske muligheter i kvalitativ forskning* [Identity or interaction – perspectives on gender borders in Haavind, H. (ed.) Gender and the interpretive method. Methodological opportunities in qualitative research], Gyldendal Norsk Forlag.

Statistics Norway (2004) *Statistical Yearbook of Norway*. http://www.ssb.no

Tiller, P.O. (1989) *Hverandre. En bok om barneforskning* [Each other. A book on child research], Oslo: Gyldendal Norsk Forlag.

Wærnes, K. (1990) 'Informal and formal care in old age. What is wrong with the new ideology in Scandinavia today?' in Ungerson, C. (ed.) *Gender and caring. Work and Welfare in Britain and Scandinavia*, London: Harvester Wheatsheaf, 110–32.

10

Adult Working Students and Time Use in Taiwan: The Moderating Effects of Credentialism, Job Stress and Family Stress

Heh Jason Huang

Introduction

The amount of time spent in paid work inevitably affects the time available for non-work activities. From the German experience, Trinczek (2004) noticed that working hours are on average growing longer and limit the time available to successfully balance the various spheres of life. For people in Taiwan, this is an even more agonising job-stress problem as Taiwan is ranked first worldwide in terms of working hours. Working hours is used by the Switzerland-based IMD as one of the 20 labour-market criteria for business efficiency in measuring a country's international competitiveness. According to the 2003 IMD survey, Taiwan had the most hard-working workers with an average number of 2,282 work hours per year.

However, it is widely observed that despite being afflicted with certain level of job stress, a growing percentage of working students in Taiwan have decided to return to school seeking a higher degree. At the same time, many universities in recent years have scheduled their class times into evenings and weekends to fit the needs of those working students who are mostly middle-aged and married. Statistics showed that the number of graduate students in Taiwan is more than 100,000, which is four times as many as ten years ago. More importantly, 30 per cent of them are working students who attend classes in evenings or weekends (Yang, 2002).

While there may be economic and social explanations for the rapid increase of working students in Taiwan, two cultural factors deserve our close attention. First, people in Taiwan are still obsessed with a traditional credentialism that people always take pride in a higher academic degree from famous institutions. Secondly, in a collectivistic culture people in Taiwan may find it easier to obtain support from their family members who tend to have a sense of obligation to support, assist, and respect the family. As emphasised by Fuligni and Zhang (2004), this sense of family obligation is generally associated with a higher level of academic motivation among Chinese adolescents. Taken together, in their use of time those adult working students are conceivably affected by forces from three sources: self-motivation (e.g. credentialism), the job (in the form of training needs or job stress), and the family (in the form of family support or family stress). These three kinds of forces would have driven those working students back to school in the first place and later on may also influence the students in their time allocations for different activities. Specifically, this study investigated time allocations in study, exercise, sleep, and housework. By treating the time for work and the time for school as the two independent variables and examining the moderating effects of credentialism, job stress, and family stress, this study can provide an overall description about how Taiwanese working students strike a balance of their time demands between work, family and school.

Theory and hypotheses

Time for work

Time for work, or working hours, is one of the most widely studied structural aspects of employment in the work-life literature (Barnett et al, 1999). When time is a limited resource, workplace, family, and school systems traditionally have had competing interests (Googins, 1991). However, in most workplaces, the definition of commitment remains rooted in a traditional concept of the ideal worker as someone for whom work is primary, and the demands of family, community, and personal life are secondary (Rapoport, Bailyn, Fletcher and Pruitt, 2002). The norms of the working-time culture are embedded in the superordinate context as central dimensions of the organisational culture (Trinczek, 2004). It is generally agreed that the number of work hours contributes to the experience of job demands, a major workplace stressor (Barnett et al, 1999). Consequently, a higher requirement for work time will bring about less available time for study, exercise, sleep, and housework. Stated formally:

Hypothesis 1: *The amount of time for work will negatively affect the adult working students' allocated time for study, exercise, sleep, and housework.*

Time for school

Time for school includes the time for classes and the time needed for commuting to the school. Time for school represents another major time requirement of adult working students. While the time for study logically should have a positive relationship with the time for school if the students wish to maintain quality of study, the time for other activities (e.g. time for exercise, time for sleep, and time for housework) would be negatively affected by the amount of time for school. Thus, the following hypothesis can be proposed:

Hypothesis 2: *The amount of time for school will negatively affect the adult working students' allocated time for exercise, sleep, and housework, but will be positively related with allocated time for study.*

Credentialism

Credentialism refers to an undue emphasis on the importance of academic degrees from famous institutions. Chinese people are renowned for their enthusiastic pursuit of diplomas and academic degrees. This credentialism might be traced to the civil examinations in the empire era when the examination system promised those in the lower echelons of society a chance to become the nobility (Huang, Eveleth and Huo, 2000; Sue and Okazaki, 1990). Credentialism was invented by schools and is enforced mostly by institutions. People in Taiwan traditionally consider education and credentials as an effective way for upward mobility. People with credentialism may consistently want to spend more time in pursuing a higher degree at the expense of time for other spheres of life. For example, they may want to draw on the supportive system of their family members (spouses and parents, etc.) so that they usually don't have to spend much time for housework. Therefore, credentialism can be considered as a moderator for time use:

Hypothesis 3a: *Credentialism moderates the effect of time for work on the adult working students' allocated time for study, exercise, sleep, and housework.*

Hypothesis 3b: *Credentialism moderates the effect of time for school on the adult working students' allocated time for study, exercise, sleep, and housework.*

Job stress

All jobs come with some degree of stress. Although stress is not necessarily a bad thing to have, it is a problem when demands get so great that a person's normal level of coping is no longer able to handle the amount of stress. Current research suggests that work-related stress should be studied as a multifaceted problem involving the personal characteristics of the individual, situational factors, and the organizational and cultural context (Schaie and Willis, 1996). A number of personal characteristics associated with an individual's being particularly vulnerable to high levels of stress have been identified: being too idealistic; setting unrealistic goals for self and clients; over-identifying with others; high need for self-affirmation; and high work orientation. The level of job stress is arguably an important moderator on students' decision-making over time use.

Hypothesis 4a: *Job stress moderates the effect of time for work on the adult working students' allocated time for study, exercise, sleep, and housework.*

Hypothesis 4b: *Job stress moderates the effect of time for school on the adult working students' allocated time for study, exercise, sleep, and housework.*

Family stress

Family stress results from the current system because families are traditionally expected to adjust, adapt, and bear the burden of the changing social and economic scene. Family stress can be defined as a real or imagined imbalance between the demands on the family and the family's ability to meet those demands (Boss, 1986; McCubbin and Patterson, 1981). In Taiwan, not only parents under strain from working long hours but also children are overloaded with school and extra-curricular activities. There is a lot of stress on families and not enough time to get everything done. Studies of work and occupations traditionally have focused almost exclusively on the individual only as a worker, neglecting the fact that he/she concurrently functions as a member of a family unit (Moen, 1989). Family stress at home can affect job and school performance, which in turn causes more stress. For this reason and many others, maintaining a stress-free home environment is very important. The level of family stress can be seen as an important background factor that affects the students' decisions on time allocations.

Hypothesis 5a: *Family stress moderates the effect of time for work on the adult working students' allocated time for study, exercise, sleep, and housework.*

Hypothesis 5b: *Family stress moderates the effect of time for school on the adult working students' allocated time for study, exercise, sleep, and housework.*

Methods

Sample and data collection

To investigate the hypothesised relationships, I used survey method to collect data from working students in 14 different classes at a prestigious university in southern Taiwan. This data collection was conducted from March to April in 2004. A total of 336 responses were collected. Response rate was very high (over 98 per cent) because data collections were administered in the classroom under the instructors' assistance.

Most of the working students studied were in the College of Management and College of Social Science (62 per cent and 20 per cent respectively). Sixty-seven per cent of the sample were men. The average age of the respondents was about 39 years old. With respect to job titles, 57 per cent of the respondents held various management positions. Seventy-five per cent of the sample were married. Among those married, 77 per cent of their spouses had a full-time job and 6 per cent had a part-time job. The average number of children was 1.7 for those married students.

Dependent variables

There were four dependent variables in this study: time for study, time for exercise, time for sleep, and time for housework. They were measured in terms of number of hours daily. On average, adult working students spent 1.61 hours in every day studying, 0.39 hours for exercise, 6.51 hours for sleep, and 1.08 hours for housework.

Independent variables

Time for work.   Respondents were asked to write down the average number of hours they spent on their work weekly. As a whole, the average weekly working time of the sample was 42.96 hours, which is higher than the regular working time (84 hours in two weeks) stipulated in the Taiwan's Labor Standards Law.

Time for school.   The respondents were asked which days during a week they attended classes and how much time they spent in those classes. They were also required to report the number of hours spent on the road whenever they have to come to school. All these data were aggregated to represent the time (in hours) requirement for school.

Control variables

Age.   Respondents were asked to report their age in years. The mean and standard deviation of age for the sample were 39.06 and 7.58 respectively.

Gender.   Respondents indicated their sex on the survey, and this study created a categorical variable in which females were assigned '0' and males assigned '1'.

Marriage.   Unmarried and divorced were coded as '0'. Married and coupled were coded as '1'.

Living with Parents.   '0' indicated that respondents did not live together with their parent(s) and '1' indicated a situation where the respondents still live with their parent(s).

Position.   Position was coded as '1: non manager', '2: first-line manager', '3: middle manager', and '4: top manager'.

Moderation variables

Credentialism.   Six items such as 'A person's degree is an important criteria used to measure her/his ability' were used to measure credentialism (see Appendix for detailed items). Cronbach's alpha was .79. A median of 4.00 was used to differentiate the students with higher credentialism from those students with lower credentialism.

Job stress.   Five items such as 'I become ill-tempered in the workplace' were used to measure job stress. Cronbach' alpha was .74. The median of

2.67 was used to separate the sample into two categories of high job stress and low job stress.

Family stress. Family stress was measured by eight items such as 'My family members have complained to me about the lack of time I spend with them'. Cronbach's alpha was .80. The data showed a median of 2.86 which was used to divide the sample into a high-family-stress group and a low-family-stress group.

Results

Table 10.1 presents descriptive statistics and correlations for all the variables in the study. It seems that the older students exercise more and have a happier life with less job stress and less family stress. As generally expected, job stress and family stress have a significantly positive relationship. The significant levels and the signs shown in the correlation matrix demonstrate support for Hypothesis 1 and Hypothesis 2.

Results of t-tests reported in Table 10.2 clearly show that the working students with higher level of job stress exercise less and sleep less. This phenomenon is also exhibited for those students with higher levels of family stress. Gender differences interestingly exist to show that males exercise more while females do more housework. Another interesting finding is that the students who were married exercise more.

To test the hypotheses, multiple regression analyses were performed regressing time allocations on the two predictive variables and the five control variables. The results of regression models are shown in Table 10.3 to Table 10.6. Table 10.3 shows the regression results at the time for study. Both main effects and moderating effects exist. At a significant level, working hours negatively affected the time for study, but these effects disappeared in the cases of high credentialism, high job stress, and high family stress. As predicted by Hypothesis 2, time for school demonstrated a positive effect on time for study, but this effect is only true for those with high job stress and those with high family stress.

Table 10.4 displays the regression results for the time for exercise. As predicted, both time for work and time for school had negative effects on time for exercise, but the effects did not reach a significant level. However, an examination of the moderating effects showed significant effects in the cases of high-job-stress students. This is a warning for those people with high job stress. Results in Table 10.4 also give a warning to those high-ranking managers because this study revealed that high-ranking managers obviously devoted less time to exercise, and this was more obvious for those with higher level of credentialism, high job stress, and high family stress.

Table 10.1 Correlations and descriptive statistics

Variables	Mean	s.d.	1	2	3	4	5	6	7	8	9	10
1. Time for study	1.61	.99										
2. Time for exercise	.39	.42	.29***									
3. Time for sleep	6.51	.91	-.07	.09								
4. Time for housework	1.08	.73	.11*	.16**	-.01							
5. Credentialism	3.90	.60	.04	.06	-.01	-.10^t						
6. Job stress	2.69	.68	-.04	-.22***	-.15**	-.13*	-.05					
7. Family stress	2.92	.71	-.06	-.15**	-.17**	.05	.07	.49***				
8. Age	39.06	7.58	.15**	.39***	.02	.10t	.02	-.27***	-.12*			
9. Position in organisation	2.03	1.03	.07	.08	.03	.05	.05	-.03	-.01	.46***		
10. Time for work	42.96	10.21	-.16**	-.09	-.12*	-.17**	-.06	.00	-.09	.03	.09^t	
11. Time for school	10.63	6.27	.12*	-.14**	-.12*	-.03	-.11^t	.21***	.10^t	-.20***	-.04	-.10^t

N's range from: N = 296 to N = 336
***p < .001; **p < .01; *p < .05; ^{t}p < .10

Table 10.2   t-test comparisons of time use

		N	Mean	Std. Dev.	t-value
Time for study					
Gender:	Female	109	1.532	1.076	−1.095
	Male	223	1.659	.949	
Marriage:	Single		1.691	1.168	.607
	Married	81	1.604	.929	
		248			
Credentialism:	Low	155	1.638	1.012	.249
	High	175	1.611	.975	
Job stress:	Low	168	1.637	.963	1.040
	High	157	1.529	.909	
Family stress:	Low	153	1.627	.972	.307
	High	160	1.593	.966	
Time for exercise					
Gender:	Female	111	.307	.375	−2.574**
	Male	224	.435	.447	
Marriage:	Single		.304	.383	−2.181*
	Married	81	.424	.442	
		251			
Credentialism:	Low	156	.356	.454	−1.653[t]
	High	176	.434	.406	
Job stress:	Low	170	.464	.408	3.729***
	High	157	.297	.399	
Family stress:	Low	154	.477	.451	2.871**
	High	161	.337	.411	
Time for sleep					
Gender:	Female	111	6.613	.926	1.393
	Male	224	6.464	.913	
Marriage:	Single		6.531	1.001	.144
	Married	81	6.514	.896	
		251			
Credentialism:	Low	156	6.519	.919	.078
	High	176	6.511	.925	
Job stress:	Low	170	6.635	.895	2.590**
	High	157	6.376	.916	
Family stress:	Low	154	6.636	.975	2.019*
	High	161	6.428	.849	
Time for housework					
Gender:	Female	109	1.229	.878	2.330*
	Male	218	1.009	.636	
Marriage:	Single		.925	.725	−2.320*
	Married	80	1.142	.728	
		248			
Credentialism:	Low	152	1.118	.780	.740
	High	173	1.058	.696	
Job stress:	Low	166	1.126	.740	1.583
	High	154	1.000	.686	

Table 10.2   t-test comparisons of time use – *continued*

		N	Mean	Std. Dev.	t-value
Family Stress:	Low	149	1.027	.734	–1.197
	High	160	1.125	.707	

Notes: ß is the standardised regression coefficient.
***p < .001; **p < .01; *p < .05; ᵗp < .10

Table 10.3   Regression results of time for study
Dependent variable: Time for study

Independent variables	Total sample	Credentialism		Job stress		Family stress	
		Low	High	Low	High	Low	High
Age	.217**	.357***	.137	.208*	.187ᵗ	.360**	.138
Gender	.118ᵗ	.108	.145ᵗ	.056	.178*	–.033	.214**
Marriage	–.125ᵗ	–.259*	–.052	–.094	–.069	.011	–.129
Living with parents	.022	.089	–.018	.060	–.022	.077	–.004
Position	.004	.093	–.068	–.055	.029	–.180ᵗ	.110
Time for work	–.144*	–.227**	–.095	–.087	–.232**	–.050	–.233**
Time for school	.132*	.120	.145ᵗ	.053	.193*	.087	.201*
N	293	137	155	150	140	134	144
R²	.081	.167	.063	.043	.141	.089	.183
Adj. R²	.059	.121	.018	–.004	.096	.038	.141
F	3.611***	3.683***	1.404	.909	3.11**	1.759	4.34***

Notes: ß is the standardised regression coefficient.
***p < .001; **p < .01; *p < .05; ᵗp < .10

Table 10.4   Regression results of time for exercise
Dependent variable: Time for exercise

Independent variables	Total sample	Credentialism		Job stress		Family stress	
		Low	High	Low	High	Low	High
Age	.462***	.513***	.437***	.386***	.496***	.384***	.509***
Gender	.097ᵗ	.099	.087	.182*	.018	.070	.112
Marriage	–.083	–.136	–.052	–.050	–.009	.055	–.169*
Living with parents	.033	.030	.051	.064	.023	.160ᵗ	–.116
Position	–.143*	–.100	–.189*	–.105	–.226*	–.118	–.181*
Time for work	–.093ᵗ	–.094	–.104	.033	–.217**	–.059	–.147ᵗ
Time for school	–.093ᵗ	–.026	–.147ᵗ	–.033	–.174*	–.157ᵗ	–.026
N	296	138	156	152	140	135	145
R²	.199	.193	.213	.162	.261	.180	.239
Adj. R²	.180	.150	.176	.122	.221	.135	.200
F	10.22***	4.45***	5.71***	3.98***	6.64***	3.97***	6.14***

Notes: ß is the standardised regression coefficient.
***p < .001; **p < .01; *p < .05; ᵗp < .10

Main effects and moderating effects were significantly demonstrated in Table 10.5 for sleep time, as predicted. Both time for work and time for school had negative influences, which obviously deprived the working students of their time for sleep. However, these influences disappeared in the case of low credentialism and in the case of high job stress. An interesting finding in Table 10.5 is that family stress moderated the time-for-work effect and the time-for-school effect in different directions. While the time-for-work effect disappeared in the case of high family stress, the time-for-school effect disappeared in the case of low family stress.

Table 10.5 Regression results of time for sleep
Dependent variable: Time for sleep

Independent variables	Total sample	Credentialism		Job stress		Family stress	
		Low	High	Low	High	Low	High
Age	−.023	−.023	−.015	−.166	.076	−.215^t	.029
Gender	−.065	−.039	−.086	.005	−.067	−.109	−.033
Marriage	.030	.058	.013	.011	.014	.105	.034
Living with parents	−.071	−.079	−.072	.036	−.152	−.117	−.021
Position	−.035	−.161	.050	.125	−.158	−.063	.031
Time for work	−.119*	−.046	−.174*	−.182*	−.108	−.279***	.044
Time for school	−.163**	−.130	−.187*	−.165*	−.105	−.110	−.245**
N	296	138	156	152	140	135	145
R^2	.048	.056	.064	.067	.074	.142	.074
Adj. R^2	.025	.005	.020	.021	.024	.094	.027
F	2.089*	1.096	1.446	1.470	1.496	2.993**	1.571

Notes: ß is the standardised regression coefficient.
***p < .001; **p < .01; *p < .05; ^{t}p < .10

Table 10.6 Regression results of time for housework
Dependent variable: Time for housework

Independent variables	Total sample	Credentialism		Job stress		Family stress	
		Low	High	Low	High	Low	High
Age	.063	.123	.011	.175^t	−.138	.150	.015
Gender	−.200**	−.253**	−.127	−.276**	−.099	−.155	−.259**
Marriage	.221**	.206*	.204*	.228*	.239*	.195^t	.191*
Living with parents	.022	.082	−.050	−.005	.007	.013	.041
Position	−.002	.111	−.106	−.092	.100	−.034	.026
Time for work	−.141*	−.122	−.170*	−.061	−.219*	−.173*	−.093
Time for school	−.069	−.102	−.053	−.060	−.086	−.028	−.114
N	291	135	154	149	138	132	144
R^2	.089	.139	.080	.129	.089	.107	.102
Adj. R^2	.067	.092	.036	.086	.040	.056	.056
F	3.959***	2.934**	1.822^t	2.977**	1.812^t	2.120*	2.211*

Notes: ß is the standardised regression coefficient.
***p < .001; **p < .01; *p < .05; ^{t}p < .10

Table 10.6 shows the regression results for the time for housework. They only rendered support in the part of time for work. There were no significant findings in respect to time for school. The level of work hours did negatively affect the time devoted to housework. However, its influence disappeared in the cases of low credentialism, low job stress, and high family stress.

Discussion

For adult working students the time for work and the time for school represent time demands with little flexibility. The purpose of the present research was to explore how these time demands influenced students' available time for other spheres of life. Hypothesis 1 and 2 were suggested in this regard. If influences did exist, this study intended to examine the moderating effects of the three presumably important psychological variables: credentialism, job stress and family stress, as proposed in Hypothesis 3 to Hypothesis 6. The results of data analyses strongly support all the hypotheses in time allocations for study, sleep, and housework while marginally supporting the hypotheses in time for exercise. Exercise may be arguably a kind of habit that is not so receptive to the change in time demands for other activities. An exceptional finding was the absence of significant evidence for the effect of school time on housework time. The adaptability of family support for working students may provide an explanation for this exception.

The level of credentialism did moderate the effects of working hours on time allocations for study, sleep, and housework. As a whole, time for work did have a significantly negative effect on time for study, but this negative effect disappeared among those working students with high credentialism who obviously want to keep studying hard. On the other hand, significant effects of working hours exhibited in the group of high-credentialism students have a negative impact on their time allocations for sleep and housework. In other words, the high-credentialism students, in a situation of increasing working time, tend to keep a stable level of study time, and this may be at the expense of their sleep time and housework time.

The present study provides evidence for the adverse impact of the time for work on time allocations. Adult working students who work longer hours obviously spent less time in study, sleeping, and housework (at a marginally significant level they also spent less time in doing exercise). These findings support the arguments for shorter working hours – that shorter working hours are necessary in order to protect the health of the working population (Pierce, Newstrom, Dunham and Barber, 1989). More importantly, job stress acted as a moderating variable on time allocations in all categories. This argues for the merit of job-stress reduction because the negative impacts of time for work on the allocated time in study, exercise, and housework became insignificant for those with low level of job stress. However, the fact that in the case of high-job-stress students, the non-significant effect of time for work on the time for sleep, is not a good signal. It may be that the high-job-stress persons consistently sleep less (as indicated by t-test in Table 10.2) and are unresponsive to the change of time for work.

As hypothesised, time for school showed a significantly positive effect on time for study but a significantly negative effect on time for sleep. The negative relationship between time for school and time for sleep can be interpreted from a competitive view because people spend time for school at the expense of their sleep. The positive relationship between time for school and time for study can be explained as a phenomenon of spillover. Spillover refers to the positive or negative feelings, attitudes, and behaviors that might emerge in one domain and are carried over into the other (Moen, 1989). Both 'competitive' effect and 'spillover' effect of the school time only exhibit in the group with a high level of family stress. While it is conceivable that increasing time for school of those high-family-stress students would lead to decreasing time for sleep, the reason for high-family-stress students studying longer under increasing school time is not clear. The explanation may be the other way around, that it is the increasing demand of study time resulting from increasing demand of school time that caused the working students higher family stress.

References

Barnett, R., Gareis, K. and Brennan, B. (1999) Fit as a mediator of the relationship between work hours and burnout, *Journal of Occupational Health Psychology*, 4, 307–17.

Boss, P. (1986) Family Stress, in Sussman, M. and Steinmetz, S. (eds) *Handbook on Marriage and the Family*, 695–723, New York: Plenum.

Fuligni, A.J. and Zhang, W. (2004) Attitudes toward family obligation among adolescents in contemporary urban and rural China, *Child Development*, 75(1): 180.

Googins, B.K. (1991) *Work/Family Conflicts*, New York: Auburn House.

Huang, H.J., Eveleth, D.M. and Huo, Y.P. (2000) A Chinese work-related value system, in Lau, C.M., Law, K.S., Tse, D.K. and Wong, C.S. (eds), Asian Management matters: Regional Relevance and Global Impact, Hong Kong: Asia Academy of Management.

McCubbin, H. and Patterson, J. (1981) *Family Stress, Resources and Coping*, St. Paul, Minn.: Department of Family Social Science.

Moen, P. (1989) *Working Parents: Transformations in Gender Roles and Public Policies in Sweden*, Madison, Wisconsin: The University of Wisconsin Press.

Pierce, J.L., Newstrom, J.W., Dunham, R.B. and Barber, A.E. (1989) *Alternative Work Schedules*, Boston: Allyn and Bacon, Inc.

Rapoport, R., Bailyn, L., Fletcher, J.K. and Pruitt, B.H. (2002) *Beyond Work-Family Balance*, New York: Jossey-Bass.

Schaie, K.W. and Willis, S.L. (1996) *Adult Development and Aging*, 4th Edition, New York: HarperCollins.

Sue, S. and Okazaki, S. (1990) Asian-American educational achievements: A phenomenon in search of an explanation, *American Psychologist*, 45: 913–20.

Trinczek, R. (2004) Work-life-balance and flexibilization of working hours – The German experience, Paper presented at The Work Times/Life Times Colloquium at The Management Centre, Deakin University, Victoria, Australia. Dec. 13–15.

Yang, C.S. (2002) The latest development of higher education, *National Policy Forum Research Report*, April 12.

Appendix

Scale Items
Response scales ranged from 'strongly disagree', 1, to 'strongly agree', 5. 'R' indicates reverse coding. Values on the right are scale reliabilities.

Credentialism   .79
1. A person's degree is an important criteria used to measure her/his ability.
2. The time and money spent for an advanced degree are worthwhile.
3. As long as personal circumstances and abilities allow, I will continue pursuing higher education.
4. Most people believe that the higher the education, the greater the knowledge.
5. A high level of education will help advance my career, such as higher position and higher salary.
6. A high level of education can improve one's social status and influence among colleagues.

Job Stress   .74
1. I have too many things on my mind so that I have difficulty in sleeping.
2. I'm not alert enough at work.
3. I often suffer from headaches and stomachaches.
4. My work efficiency has declined because of overloading of my work and class.
5. I become ill-tempered in the workplace.

Family Stress   .80
1. I have a lot of family responsibilities.
2. My family members have complained to me about the lack of time I spend with them.
3. My children cause me to be unable to concentrate on my schoolwork.
4. I would have to consider hiring someone to help with my housework.
5. Family responsibilities cause me to feel frustrated.
6. I feel that I don't have much time to look after my children.
7. It troubles me very much that no one helps me with my housework.
8. My family members are very considerate of my situation. (R)

11

Improving Services, Balancing Lives? A Multiple Stakeholder Perspective on the Work-Life Balance Discourse

Susanne Tietze, Gill Musson and Tracy Scurry

Introduction

The discourse of work-life balance (WLB) has gained prominence on the agendas of policy and decision-makers and has begun to inform organisational efforts to achieve and sustain product and service-related competitiveness and 'value-for-money', while safeguarding employees' morale and welfare. This discourse manifests itself in a series of flexibility initiatives, which are said to enable the organisation to remain competitive or accountable, while empowering individuals to live rich and fulfilled lives. However, the achievement of such dual objectives is beset by tensions and contradictions, which inform the relationships between different organisational and non-organisational stakeholders.

Homeworking is an increasingly popular form of flexible working. The introduction and practice of homeworking as part of overall WLB policies plays an important part in the delivery of both organisational and individual WLB objectives. Indeed, it is considered to be at the core of the WLB discourse and as such expresses both its potential to 'balance' different areas of life activity as well as the latent dilemmas inherent in achieving such precarious balance.

Starting off with an investigation of the WLB discourse, its rationale and objectives as much as its inherent contradictions and tensions, this chapter explores how the relationships between organisational stakeholders are opened up and become subject to negotiation and change in and through the introduction of home-based working. We argue that the WLB discourse requires organisational agents to frame each other in new, partly contradictory ways, so that the enactment of this discourse requires considerable organisational effort to control the disruption of established relationships and routines. The empirical work is based on an in-depth case study conducted in a Local Authority (LA) in the UK. The research interviews and observations included homeworkers themselves, their family or households if appropriate, line managers and team leaders, and senior human resource managers, as well as those co-workers of homeworkers, who remained office-based. Thus it is possible to develop a 'stakeholder' perspective on homeworking, which provides a more comprehensive picture on the consequences of introducing this form of working. The findings show that established relationships, roles and routines were changed and became more complex, because all stakeholders (including the homeworkers themselves) are continuously required to conceptualise homeworkers as simultaneously inhabiting multiple roles. This, in turn, colours the relationship held with co-workers, managers and household members. The findings of the study also demonstrate that existing imbalances between the employees of the case organisation are reinforced through the introduction of homeworking. In this regard the WLB discourse is shown to be an 'enabling tool' only for a select group of hierarchically senior employees.

The work-life balance discourse

A discourse is a set of related meanings, which provide social actors with conceptual frames to make sense of the social world, and with trajectories for action which, in turn, influence the construction of the social world (Burr, 1995; Tietze et al, 2003). The WLB discourse then provides a frame to understand, explain, define and potentially change the relationship between two major areas of social life (at least in the context of advanced industrial societies): production and reproduction, i.e. the areas of paid work, work organisation and labour markets and those of unpaid work, household and community. The logic of the WLB discourse is built on establishing a connection between its two constituent parts (work, life) and their related meaning systems. The area of (paid) 'work' is put into a binary opposition with the area of 'life' (i.e. non-paid work); they are assumed to be in potential conflict with each other, so that 'balancing them' becomes important to achieve the twofold objective of providing both business advantage in the area of 'work' as well as individual and collective well-being in the area of 'life'.

The WLB discourse has gained hold in and beyond most advanced industrial societies (see Moraes et al, 2004) and is discussed in the contexts of flexibility policies and work-life, work-family or work-leisure conflicts. It has been argued that particular parts of the WLB discourse as promoted by the Department for Employment and Education (DfEE) in the UK for example (Perrons, 2003), are little more than making the business case for flexibility by showing how it can increase productivity, reduce absenteeism, increase employee retention and morale and so on. Perrons argues that within such a perspective, flexible working is 'more concerned with accommodating life to rather demanding and unquestioned working hours than that of reorganizing work to allow time for domestic or caring responsibilities …with employers often retaining control over the parameters of flexibility' (Perrons, 2003: 69). Perrons' argument can be supported by a glance at some channels through which the WLB discourse is disseminated. Positive accounts of how WLB can be achieved through flexibility are recounted time and time again in the UK, in magazines such as the practitioner-focused *Personnel Management*, and also in the popular press (see Bryant 2000 for similar comments on the Canadian context). For example, a feature on flexibility/WLB in the financial pages of the UK newspaper, *Mail on Sunday* (2001), shows a happily united family with a supporting text outlining the advantages of flexible working from the point of view of individuals and families: achieving WLB through working flexibly is put into a causal relationship with achieving more effective household management, financial gains/savings, closer parent-child relationships and the avoidance of numbing routines: 'There is a greater emphasis on family-friendly policies and finding a work/life balance. Working at night can mean that parents see more of their children' (73). An article in *Personnel Management* (2001) points to the advantages to be gained from the organisational perspective as financial savings (reduced estate costs), improved employee loyalty and morale and an increase in productivity: 'The introduction of work-life balance polices at BT has reaped financial rewards and helped to improve staff loyalty ... productivity had improved and absenteeism had been reduced.' (Personnel Management, 2001: 11).

The language employed in such articles is optimistic, even utopian at times. Opportunities to harmonise paid work and family responsibilities are continually stressed, so that flexible work is heralded as desirable and progressive. Possible 'problems' to such progress, if discussed at all, tend to be represented as technical-rational problems, which can be overcome by management or personal effort.

Increasingly, there is an academic body of literature which critically engages with the sometimes naïve enthusiasm of such commentaries. Generally speaking, this body of work views WLB initiatives as positioned in complex contexts so that the reconciliation of production and reproduction is at best precarious, at worst counterproductive to the achievement of its proclaimed goals. More specifically, many studies have focused on the impact of WLB/flexibility policies on gender aspects (Bryant, 2000; Perrons, 2003; Sullivan, 2003a; Smithson et al, 2004), privilege and interest (Felstead et al, 2002a); career development (MacDermid et al, 2001; Rogier and Padgett, 2004); issues of autonomy, control and communication (Hardill, 2003; Musson and Tietze, 2004; Sennett, 1998; Shumate and Fulk, 2004); and effectiveness of WLB initiatives and family-friendly policies (Glass and Estes, 1997; Pillinger, 2002). These accounts provide a more complex and sceptical perspective on WLB/flexibility – most of them neither rejecting nor embracing the potential, objectives and philosophy of this discourse. Rather, within their specific research contexts they address the imbalances, setbacks and contradictions created by the WLB/flexibility discourse. Of the above studies, for example, Hardill (2003) points to both opportunities for autonomy and control in telework; Bryant (2000) sees reasons for pessimism (reinforcing gender, class and other inequalities through homework) as well as optimism (increased control over everyday life; renegotiation of the status quo); Musson and Tietze (2004) see potential for degrees of micro-emancipation at least for particular groups of homeworkers.

Balancing work and life through homeworking[1]

Sennett (1998: 59) in his critical essay on flexible or new capitalism, refers to homeworking as 'the ultimate island of the new regime' where control is exercised via the computer screen. Perhaps less critically, Felstead et al (2002b) too, see homeworking as a cornerstone of a raft of family-friendly or WLB initiatives, which they conceptualise as the heightened change for choice and autonomy with respect to establishing and crossing boundaries between work and non-work. Tietze and Musson (2005, forthcoming) too, view homeworking as linked to criss-crossing the discourses of industrial and household production, with resulting (frequently tension-ridden) adjustment processes between home and work. Thus, the two areas of the WLB discourse (work, life) can be taken to meet directly in and through homeworking. It is because of this direct and therefore observable meeting, that homeworking is considered by some researchers to be symbolic and constitutive of the objectives and dilemmas of the WLB discourse.

Considerable progress has been made in understanding the spread and depth, the trends and patterns, the social/psychological and occupational dynamics of this way of working (Felstead and Jewson, 2000; Felstead et al, 2002b). Also, in recent years research endeavour has begun to concern itself with the complexities of homeworking, how it can change the flows of power and knowledge (Brocklehurst, 2001); how surveillance and control are exercised (Hardill and Green, 2003); and colonisation and appropriation of time and space of the home (Steward, 2000). Increasingly, such studies begin to include 'the voice' of the household and empirical work is located directly in the home of homeworkers (Bryant, 2000; Moore and Crosbie, 2003; Sullivan and Lewis, 2001; Musson and Tietze, 2004). These accounts of how the arrival of paid work affects the organisation of the household have begun to provide a richer picture of the experience of homeworking from the point of view of both the homeworker and the household; how it is affected by and affective of gender and identity; household size and age; social and occupational status; and flows and exercise of power and knowledge (Ammons and Markham, 2004; Bryant, 2000; Perrons, 2003).

However, there is less understanding about how the network of work and non-work relationships in and across both work organisation and household are affected by homeworking. Bailey and Kurland (2002: 391) comment that 'interpersonal processes and outcomes at the workplace remain overlooked' and that scholars should concern themselves with more comprehensive populations including colleagues, support staff, managers and 'others'. In this chapter we develop such an approach, which is inclusive of colleagues, line managers and team leaders, homeworkers and their families, as well as the perspective of corporate human resource managers.

Based on the above exposition of the WLB discourse (and its tensions and contradictions), the chapter explores how the relationships between these different stakeholders are affected in and through homeworking. All these constituents have to change their conception of 'a colleague' to include 'colleague-as-homeworker'. A manager has to see the homeworker in a new and dual way: in addition to being a 'human resource' at their disposal, homeworkers are also legitimately private persons, embedded in a culturally different context during working hours. Similarly, a colleague of a homeworker might continue to see the homeworker as an 'office mate' and fellow employee, while also having to respect their private roles. Also, the colleague might feel degrees of resentment should it become necessary to take on some non-transportable work of the homeworker. In this instance, the conceptualisation of the former 'colleague' might begin to carry emotional connotations (homeworker-as-burden). Similarly, team leaders who are in charge of day-to-day operations might continue to see the homeworkers as team members and colleagues, but their recurrent absence requires effort to be expanded and expended in reorganising tasks and appeasing 'present' team members. Homeworkers might hold self-perceptions embedded in the world of work of themselves as 'professionals', 'office-mates', 'colleagues'; they will have to counterbalance these with perceptions formed in the private world as 'parents, family members, neighbours, friends'. Thus homeworking provides a context in which the relationships between the various stakeholders can, potentially, be changed.

The study: improving services, balancing lives

The empirical work was conducted within a LA in the UK. This authority had received European funding from the European Social Fund/Objective 1, whose aims are broadly to assist restructuring programmes and build prosperity in disadvantaged regions.[2] In receiving these moneys, the LA committed to raising awareness of WLB and promoting WLB initiatives. A WLB project group was set up. It included a project leader (a senior person seconded from corporate Human Resources Department) and two WLB officers, who were recruited for the lifetime of the project. In early 2004 an awareness raising exercise included the generation and distribution of a series of documents and brochures, a launch event and several training events for managers. More concretely, WLB initiatives also were used as a driver to supplement existing flexibility options (flexi-time; part-time; compressed hours of nine working days a fortnight) with new ones. One such initiative was a homeworking pilot, which was located in two units (Human Resources (HR); and Planning and Policy Unit (PPU)) of the Social Services Directorate. Interestingly, the possibility of a homeworking pilot was driven not so much in the first instance by employees pursuing their right to request this (cf. Employment Act 2002), but by a combination of factors such as ongoing and increasing estate problems, the arrival of external funds (and thereby the need to 'deliver' on outputs) and an affirmative attitude of one of the senior managers in the Social Services Directorate, who had positive experience of homeworking early on in her career.

The HR unit comprised 24 employees, of which eight would homework for a minimum of one day per fortnight. The PPU department comprised 15 employees, of which eight would regularly homework for one or two days per week. Importantly, these were homeworkers who would regularly (rather than permanently) work from home (Felstead and Jewson, 2000), while retaining a base in the LA offices. While there was some difference in the experience and rank of the homeworkers, they can all be described as 'professional staff' with college degrees or qualifications from their respective professional bodies.

The process of introducing homeworking was closely managed. A task group was set up consisting of one representative of each affected group (homeworkers, colleagues, team leaders, manager) plus one member of the WLB balance group and an IT expert. The group decided that the homeworkers would keep a 'log-book' to document their learning and to record potential problems. Team leaders/managers had to address the concerns of homeworkers and colleagues and establish new routines (e.g. a noticeboard or flag system on which everyone had to record their attendance) and roles (e.g. a 'duty manager' to deal with queries and phone calls and any concerns). In order to safeguard a degree of objectiveness, the pilot was to be evaluated externally (i.e. by the authors).

Methods

We had approached the LA with a view to conduct research into the implementation and management of flexibility initiatives, with particular reference to 'working from home'. Our interest coincided with the foundation of the WLB project group and 'access' was gained in return for an evaluation report on the homeworking pilot.

The current chapter is based on data from a case study approach, which comprised a variety of research tools. Document analysis (of WLB literature as produced by project groups; flexibility policies; and homeworking documentation) enabled the authors to understand the context of the homeworking pilot. In addition, a raft of meetings (project group; training events; planning events; launch event) were observed and provided important contextual information on the negotiated emergence of flexibility initiatives. An interview schedule comprised several group interviews with the WLB group, as well a series of interviews (one before and one approximately two-thirds into the six-months pilot) with those stakeholders affected by the implementation of homeworking. The first round of interviews focused on process issues, i.e. how was the homeworking pilot set up, what drove it, how was selection managed, what were the expectations, concerns and fears of the respective stakeholder groups. The second round of interviews (of which the ones with the homeworkers themselves took place in their home and included household members if available) concentrated on the experience of the pilot, how it was managed, whether fears or expectations had materialised and affected relationships and roles.

The stakeholder groups included: one senior manager of the Directorate for a general overview of the remit, tasks and structure of the Directorate as well as to have the perspective of a senior postholder; and four team leaders/line managers to understand the implications of homeworking for the operations of the work groups. The discussions with stakeholders included themes of communication, cultural cohesion, and developmental issues. We also interviewed five colleagues of homeworkers to understand their expectations about homeworking and to find out how selection of homeworkers took place. In addition, all the homeworkers were interviewed to understand the reasons why they opted for homeworking.

Generally speaking, our research apparatus was designed to explore the different stakeholder perspectives on homeworking. The overarching research objective was to examine how relationships between different stakeholders are affected in this form of flexible working, and in so doing develop a more sophisticated take on the WLB discourse.

Findings

In this section we present quotes taken mainly from the interviews, but also from observed meetings and informal conversations. We provide a brief interpretation of these examples, indicating, for example, to what extent they are typical or contextual. A fuller discussion is provided in the following section, where the findings are explored within the broader themes of this chapter and a critical interpretation of the WLB discourse.

The relationship between homeworkers and (office-bound) colleagues

From the perspective of the homeworkers, little had changed in the relationship with their colleagues – they remained *approachable, good team members, pulling their weight* (various interviews with homeworkers). Most of them were, however, aware of the potential divide between homeworkers and non-homeworkers and the privileged position associated with homeworking: *There is resentment. It rubs into a sore point between lower grades and higher grades (...) it is also associated with the excitement of laptops and not to be included is bad and sad for some people* (homeworker, Principal Officer, PPU). In one case, the homeworker who worked in close liaison with a colleague, acknowledged that for her colleagues life was likely to be more burdened by her absence: *Andrea feels more pressure when I work at home. ... people will go to her to check the adverts. Usually we share this.* (homeworker, HR Officer). In the same vein, the homeworker felt more burdened when a more senior colleague was homeworking: *When Evelyn homeworks, we all feel it ... you always know she's homeworking, because you get more things in your tray with comments 'can you deal with that'.* About half of the homeworkers reported that they found it difficult to find slots for homeworking – *I found it really difficult to find slots for homeworking. It is difficult to decline to attend a meeting or ask for it to be rearranged* (telephone conversation with homeworker, PPU, trying to organise a home visit). Cultural expectations often demanded constant availability (for attendance at meetings, for example) and it became necessary for homeworkers to learn to manage colleagues' expectations and become skilled at saying 'no'.

From the point of view of the colleagues, one of the fears identified in the pre-pilot stage was that of having to carry burdensome quantities of extra work – in particular a deluge of additional phone calls and queries were identified. On the whole, this concern did not materialise, partly due to the closely managed and monitored systems put in place. However, the issue of 'difference' and 'privilege' continued to irritate colleagues who had not been asked to participate – despite some of them attempting to claim for themselves this mode of working: *I have a mentally disabled partner, who I care for. Sometimes it would help me, to work from home.* (colleague, PPU assistant). This perceived 'injustice' exacerbated an existing 'us and them' mentality. According to these lower graded colleagues some of their tasks also lent themselves to homeworking: *I would love to homework myself, but we were told that in our jobs it wasn't feasible (...) but you know, [like] sometimes, I have been doing task[s] lending themselves to homeworking* (colleague, HR assistant). Practically, such 'injustice' became visible in office cover arrangements: the same people always covered Friday afternoons (i.e. not the homeworkers). While monitoring systems were in place (e.g. a 'notice board' for recording absence or presence on a weekly basis), one colleague in PPU pointed out that she in particular had to *nag* people into making sure they filled it in. In addition, she received emails from homeworkers asking her to email them documents, which they had either forgotten to download or could not easily access through the system. Overall, colleagues felt they would continue to support the homeworkers, but such statements resonated with feelings of being *left behind*. Finally, additional work was created for IT people, a group affected by homeworking, yet not included in discussions about impact: *The IT* [Information Technology] *people had a lot of extra work to do, more so at the beginning, but also continued support work and stuff* (colleague, PPU, Principal Officer).

Changes in the relationship between homeworkers and team leaders/ managers

In a similar vein, homeworkers did not comment on a changed relationship with team leaders or managers. They did not feel (and neither were they) more closely monitored and controlled than when they were in the office. They attributed this to their 'professional status' and the standing that they enjoyed as senior members of staff: *No, name [team leader] does not monitor and control me in any way. Once you're senior or principal officer, this no longer applies* (homeworker, PPU). Team leaders confirmed this – one commented: *We are a mature team (...) Members are able to self-manage and demonstrate integrity and responsibility. I would be against an overbearing monitoring system* (email conversation with team leader, HR).

Team leaders had to implement systems to manage homeworking, but felt that once they were in place, they were carried by a team effort: *all of us pull our weight to keep it going* (team leader, PPU). They also felt that good trust relationships had been established. Two managers commented that they had to learn to trust their staff more than before and that overall homeworking had propelled this along: *I had to learn how to trust them all and let go of control ... the idea that I need to control them.* (manager, PPU). One team leader (HR) commented in depth on how it became harder to attune herself with the emotional well-being of her staff: *You can normally tell who has got a smile on and who has got shoulders down ... you can tell who needs more support and where things are not going quite as well.* Similarly, team leaders were also more aware and concerned about the 'divide issue' and consequently some of them expended more effort to make 'the colleagues' feel accepted as equals.

Generally, the further removed – either hierarchically or functionally – the managers were from the homeworking pilot, the more they tended to frame it within a technical-rational perspective, in which problems were defined as primarily technical: *There were some technical hiccups at the beginning... they have been sorted. Otherwise it is going fine* (Manager, HR). Team leaders, by contrast, were more involved in resolving rather tricky operational, emotional and cultural issues.

Changes in the relationship between homeworkers and family members

Homeworkers tended to get slightly more involved in household and domestic tasks – doing the laundry, shopping, picking up kids, walking dogs, letting the plumber in, preparing tea [a regional expression for preparing the evening meal] were mentioned by all of the homeworkers as ways of *making life easier; making life nicer; so much more convenient* (various interviews, homeworkers). Family members on the whole welcome such presence: *It's ok for her to be around. It can be nice* (son, 13, of homeworker). However, they also expressed a degree of ambiguity in that boundaries needed to be redrawn over access to space and time: *Friday afternoon is my time. I potter around the house* (husband of homeworker); *she must not be here more than once a fortnight. I like my 'lone' time. I am in charge of the house, then* (daughter, 14, of homeworker). However, these renegotiations took the form of adjustments, rather than radical changes.

Homeworkers reported benefiting greatly from this mode of working, in terms of their performance on behalf of the employer and the service. Expressions such as *I am flying away. I do a job in 6 hours, which would take me two days in the office* (homeworker, Principal Officer, PPU); It's like *losing weight and ridding yourself of all the backlog which has accumulated* (homeworker, Senior Officer, PPU) were fairly typical. They also expressed a concomitant increase in job satisfaction and benefited in terms of what they considered to be a more relaxed lifestyle. This, they considered, led to increased health (bar one case, where the homeworker smoked more heavily) and overall quality of life: *It's nice. It's absolutely brilliant and your whole being, your well being, [changes] because of that. (…) [compare this] to being on the 10th floor of Council House – it makes you feel busy in your head before you have done anything. You know, this is where the difference lies* (homeworker, Senior Officer, PPU). Despite some drawbacks (carrying files and folders, laptop; a degree of loneliness felt by some; additional planning for homeworking days), all of them wished to continue homeworking beyond the pilot, and the majority wished to increase the number of homeworking days.

Homeworkers: issues of learning and adjustment

These homeworkers, then, perceived themselves to benefit greatly from homeworking. They all reported an increase in well-being achieved through degrees of learning and needing to adjust to homeworking: *I had to adjust in a way and learn about it* (Principal Officer, PPU). These learning processes included the acquisition of different routines, conceptual and emotional redrawing of boundaries as well as mastering technical practicalities. If there is a price to pay for this preferential way of living and working it was in their struggle to come to terms with feelings of 'guilt' (*I felt guilty a lot; I still feel guilty, but it is getting better; a slight feeling of guilt is part of it –* various interviews). These feelings of guilt were attributed mainly to reasons of being absent from the traditional office (*not being there*) rather than because homeworkers felt that they worked less hard. Therefore self-monitoring and the exercise of discipline added degrees of 'policing themselves'. Consequently, some homeworkers reported that they worked harder or longer (*I found myself in the 'head down' mode, without getting my head up. So my eyes were sore, my back ached; I worked until 7pm occasionally – I would never do this in the office; I worked my way through an illness – I would not have done this if it weren't for home working* – various interviews) than they would have at the office or through a state of illness.

Discussion

Within the more academic literature the WLB discourse is often critiqued for fashioning clichés, with promises of achieving the 'perfect balance' between 'happy families' and 'happy (effective) work organisations' (Perrons, 2003). Conversely, popular and practitioner-focused publications tend to simplify or gloss over the tensions and conflicts inherent in this discourse. In this study we attempted to investigate the changing patterns of relationships following the introduction of homeworking. We found that organisational agents actively use the WLB discourse to assist in the achievement of their respective projects; but we also found that the appropriation of the WLB discourse is the prerogative of some agents at the expense of others. In this regard this empirical investigation of homeworking paints a more complex picture of the WLB discourse and its effects.

In the first instance, the selection of homeworkers was driven by the 'work' part of the WLB discourse. The criteria for selection was the 'task' of the employee, with high discretion tasks being perceived as being geographically flexible. This, in turn, narrowed selection to people in more senior and professional roles. Any claims to homeworking based on the area of 'life' of the WLB discourse were not considered as legitimate – in this regard the 'meaning of work' dominated early discussions and selection activity. This finding confirms what has been established by Felstead et al (2002a: 204) that the option to work from home is frequently 'another perk for those already occupying an advantaged position in the labour market' – for example highly educated, professional and managerial staff. Felstead et al base their argument on statistical analysis of labour market trends and differentiate between those whose jobs require them to work at home and those entitled to work at home if they wish. Similarly, our case setting points to the uneven application of the WLB discourse, in which this desired mode of working was facilitated for some people but not for others (Bryant, 2000). Those already in privileged positions were better able to appropriate the inherent meaning systems of the discourse to further their plans and projects. Thus, our findings reported here confirm the macro trends described by Felstead et al (2002a), but by focusing on a micro-setting we have highlighted the consequences of such inequality for work (and non-work) relationships.

Following its appropriation by management, the WLB discourse provided a clear frame for action, visible in selection decisions, monitoring systems and the use of IT for communication purposes. Managers thus drew on the discourse to discuss and improve the service quality and deliver increases in its effectiveness. Problems were framed as technical and to be resolved in a rational manner. It was left to team leaders and colleagues to pick up the 'emotional' fall-out arising from the pilot. They had to invest more effort to lubricate the social-relational aspects of the work environment. This study does not reveal major and drastic changes in the cultural environment of the departments, rather it shows a cementing of cultural difference along established oppositional lines ('us–them') and points to lingering feelings of injustice and resignation. In this regard the WLB discourse conserves and confirms existing patterns of social intercourse and standing, rather than being an instrument for change and challenge. Also, while it provided a frame for systematic action for the managers, it did not do so for the team leaders, whose efforts to soothe perceptions of injustice and divide remained more disparate and linked to their individual endeavour. For them, the WLB discourse proved problematic in its use, because it highlighted disparity and difference, fracturing the collective and its emotional bonds.

The group of homeworkers gained most out of the pilot. They framed their homeworking activities initially almost exclusively in terms of work: all their expectations materialised in terms of increased quantity and quality of their work. This was also related to feelings of immense satisfaction and professional pride. Furthermore, the increase in their personal well-being was astonishing – despite some of them only homeworking for a maximum of one day a fortnight (two homeworked as little as one day a fortnight; most homeworked a day per week). They had neither feared, nor experienced, negative consequences for their careers or feelings of isolation (Ammons and Markham, 2004; MacDermid et al, 2001; Rogier and Padgett, 2004). If anything, they had to learn to homework in terms of criss-crossing the cultural boundaries between 'home' and 'work' (Tietze and Musson, 2005 forthcoming) and become more astute managers of their professional and private selves (Felstead and Jewson, 2000; Moore and Crosbie, 2003; Musson and Tietze, 2004). Mainly, it was feelings of guilt and concomitant self-monitoring (Felstead and Jewson, 2000; Tietze and Musson, 2005, forthcoming), which affected their thinking and actions about work and life. Their actions were certainly not affected by closer monitoring through electronic means (cf. Sennett, 1998); rather the locus of control was developed through a stronger internal focus. Thus, homeworking took place in the context of existing high-trust relationships between professional staff and management (Felstead et al, 2002a) and assisted in the deepening of such trust relationships. We concur with Ammons and Markham (2004), who note that problems (isolation, distractions and temptation at home, workaholism) as experienced by skilled white collar workers may have been exaggerated in the past. Rather, in total we found a very sanguine experience of homeworking. Even in the private realms existing relationships were not radically affected, rather homeworkers became slightly more drawn into their respective households and some renegotiation of spatial and temporal boundaries took place[3] (Hardill and Green, 2003; Sullivan, 2003a). However, these renegotiations were neither conflict-ridden nor particularly strenuous to maintain.

Of all the stakeholder groups discussed in this chapter, the homeworkers were most able to appropriate the WLB discourse and achieve a degree of balance between its related meaning worlds. This finding is in line with other studies of professional homeworkers, who work in this mode 'sometimes' rather than permanently (Felstead et al, 2002a; Musson and Tietze, 2004). Similarly, the LA itself gained advantages in the form of improvements in its service delivery[4] and its effectiveness (Glass and Estes, 1997; Pillinger, 2002). The inclusion of other affected stakeholders, however, shows that not everyone was able to appropriate the discourse in such advantageous ways. In particular, team leaders and office-bound colleagues of clerical status were less well-positioned to draw on the discourse to further their own WLB. In this regard the WLB discourse does not 'deliver on all fronts'.

In sum, relationships between the different groups of stakeholders had indeed been changed in and through the introduction of homeworking. It would be an exaggeration to talk of drastic and radical changes in the network of social and organisational ties. However, the texture of relationships had been affected in that the nuances of emotional and cultural webs had been subtly altered. Some of the existing relationships had indeed become more complex, having to combine and consider multiple roles and responsibilities.

Conclusion

In this chapter we took a critical look at some of the assumptions of the WLB discourse, and we investigated its consequences when implemented in an organisational setting. Within the context of a UK LA, which tried hard to be a good employer and take an inclusive approach to introducing homeworking, we found that diverse organisational stakeholder groups are positioned differently when it comes to appropriating this discourse: the more powerful agents (managers, professionals) were better able to tap into its meaning systems and achieve personal or organisational objectives. The less powerful groups (team leaders; clerical staff, who remained office-bound) were still affected by the discourse, but less well-placed to actively draw on it and thereby to shape their organisational world.

The WLB discourse shows no sign of waning. While much has been said and established about its effectiveness (or lack thereof), its possible manifestations in flexibility schemes and how to manage them, it seems to us that the WLB discourse contains the potential for genuinely rethinking the relationship and importance of 'work' and 'life'. These possibilities, however, will become lost if the ideological work accomplished in over-optimistic and sweeping accounts of the all-round benefits of 'the WLB' is allowed to overshadow the tensions and contradictions in this discourse. Our case study has shown that the WLB discourse enables as much as it constrains, that it confirms as much as it challenges, that it contains technical and material aspects as well as cultural and emotional ones. It is not an unequivocal vehicle for progress and a better life. Future work could therefore productively focus on developing this 'stakeholder perspective', and the inclusion of internal and external customers might be of particular importance in this endeavour. Such work, in turn, might broaden the WLB debate from a vehicle with which to discuss organisational flexibility and family-friendly employment practices, to encompass ideas on the limitations of flexibility and choice, both organisational and societal, and the role of interest and power in the making of a balanced world and balanced lives.

Acknowledgment

The authors would like to acknowledge the support of the ESRC (Award: RES-000-22-0501) as the funding body for this programme of research.

Notes

1. We are mindful of the different terminologies used to express different modes of teleworking and homeworking (Sullivan 2003b). We decided to adopt the terminology used by the case organisation upon which this paper is based. Homeworking in this paper then refers to the practice of conducting paid work at home for a recurrent period, but not on a permanent basis.
2. The European Social Fund is designed to stimulate job creation, provide assistance for vocational training and retraining, targeted at unemployed young people, socially disadvantaged groups and women. European Structural funds alongside UK government and private sector resources cover 1.3 million people in South Yorkshire. As a research team, we have not been given access to the financial support given to the WLB programme.
3. Our study is not necessarily representative of gender patterns in homeworking (cf. Felstead et al, 2002a, 2002b; Sullivan, 2003a; Smithson et al, 2004). Being located in the Social Services Directorate, where the majority of staff is women, out of the 16 homeworkers we interviewed and visited, only three were male. The three male homeworkers did not display any different patterns of behaviour vis-à-vis the household as compared to the female homeworkers.
4. It is beyond the bounds of this study to explore which effects such reported increases in the quality and quantity of service delivery actually had on internal and external customers (i.e. service receivers). We have some anecdotal but otherwise unsystematic evidence that internal customers did not report any less effective service. With regard to the external customers and their potentially improved experience of the service, we have quite convincing examples provided by homeworkers, who described improvements in how they could reflect about and research possible consequences of policies and their implementation. This process – according to the homeworkers – could never occur in the noisy and busy environment of the office.

References

Ammons, S.K. and Markham, W.T. (2004) 'Working at home: Experiences of Skilled White Collar Workers', *Sociological Spectrum*, 24: 191–238.

Bailey, D.E. and Kurland, N.B. (2002) 'A Review of Telework Research: Findings, New Directions, and Lessons for the Study of Modern Work', *Journal of Organizational Behaviour*, 23: 383–400.

Brocklehurst, M. (2001) 'Power, Identity and New Technology Homework: Implications for New Forms of Organizing', *Organization Studies*, 22(3): 445–66.

Bryant, S. (2000) 'At Home on the Electronic Frontier: Work, Gender and the Information Highway', *New Technology, Work and Employment*, 15(1): 19–33.

Burr, V. (1995) *An Introduction to Social Constructionism*, London: Routledge.

Employment Act (2002) Part 4 Flexible Working, Section 47. www.dti.gov/uk/er/employ/index.htm.

Felstead, A. and Jewson, N. (2000) *In Work. At Home. Toward an Understanding of Homeworking*, London: Routledge.

Felstead, A., Jewson, N., Phizacklea, A. and Walters, S. (2002a) 'The Option to Work from Home: Another Privilege for the Favoured Few?' *New Technology, Work and Employment*, 17(3): 204–23.

Felstead, A., Jewson, N., Phizacklea, A. and Walters, S. (2002b) 'Opportunities to Work from Home in the Context of Work-Life Balance', *Human Resource Management Journal*, 12(1): 54–77.

Glass, J.L. and Estes, S.B. (1997) 'The Family Responsive Workplace', *Annual Review of Sociology*, 23: 289–313.

Hardill, I. (2003) 'Editorial: Teleworking', *New Technology, Work and Employment*, 18(3): 156–8.

Hardill, I. and Green, A. (2003) 'Remote Working – Altering the Spatial Contours of Work and the Home in the New Economy', *New Technology, Work and Employment*, 18(3): 212–22.

Mail on Sunday (2001) 'The Working Week is Starting to Shift', 11 February: 73.

MacDermid, S.M., Dean L.M. and Buck, M. (2001) 'Alternative Work Arrangements among Professionals and Managers', *Journal of Management Development*, 29(4): 305–17.

Moore, J. and Crosbie, T. (2003) *The Homeworking Experience. The Effect on Home and Family Life*, School of Social Sciences and Law, University of Teeside, UK.

Moraes de Renault, L.F., Ostrognay, G.M., Sparks, K., Wong, P. and Yu, S. (2004) 'A Cross-National Comparative Study of Work-Family Stressors, Working Hours and Well-Being: China and Latin America versus the Anglo World', *Personnel Psychology*, 57: 119–42.

Musson, G. and Tietze, S. (2004) 'Feelin' Groovy: Appropriating Time in Home-Based Telework', *Culture and Organization*, 10(3): 251–64.

Perrons, D. (2003) 'The New Economy and the Work-Life Balance: Conceptual Exploration and a Case Study of New Media', *Gender, Work and Organization*, 10(1): 65–93.

Personnel Management (2001) 'Flexible Working Policies Ring in Reward for BT', 27 September: 11.

Pillinger, J. (2002) 'The Politics of Time: Can Work-Life Balance Really Work?' *Equal Opportunities Review*, 107: 18–22.

Rogier, S.A. and Padgett, M.Y. (2004) 'The Impact of Utilising a Flexible Work Schedule on the Perceived Career Advancement Potential of Women', *Human Resource Development Quarterly*, 1(1): 89–106.

Sennett, R. (1998) *The Corrosion of Character. The Personal Consequences of Work in New Capitalism*, London: Norton and Company.

Shumate, M. and Fulk, J. (2004) 'Boundaries and Role Conflict when Work and Family are Co-located: a Communication Network and Symbolic Interaction Approach', *Human Relations*, 57(1): 55–74.

Smithson, J., Lewis, S., Cooper, C. and Dyer, J. (2004) 'Flexible Working and the Gender Pay Gap in the Accountancy Profession', *Work, Employment and Society*, 18(1): 115–35.

Steward, B. (2000) 'Changing Times. The Meaning, Measurement and Use of Time in Teleworking', *Time & Society*, 9(1): 57–74.

Sullivan, C. (2003a) 'Space and the Intersection of Work and Family in Homeworking Households', *Community, Work & Family*, 3(2): 185–204.

Sullivan, C. (2003b) 'What's in a Name? Definitions and Conceptualisations of Teleworking and Homeworking', *New Technology, Work and Employment*, 18(3): 158–65.

Sullivan, C. and Lewis, S. (2001) 'Home-Based Telework, Gender and the Synchronization of Work and Family: Perspectives of Teleworkers and their Co-Residents', *Gender, Work and Organization*, 8(2): 123–45.

Tietze, S., Cohen, L. and Musson, G. (2003) *Understanding Organizations through Language*, London: Sage.

Tietze, S. and Musson, G. (2005, forthcoming) 'Recasting the Home-Work Relationship: a Case of Mutual Adjustment?' *Organization Studies*.

12
Work Patterns and Work-Life Balance Challenges in Canadian Healthcare

Claudia Steinke

Introduction

There are aspects of the new economy that have increased work and personal life conflict, particularly longer working hours, more women in the paid workforce, increased competition, more rapid change, less job security, less predictability, and the need to capitalise on opportunities as they present (Reich, 2000). Work-life conflict has emerged as one of the most important concerns of employed men and women, yet despite this, employees in the industrialised world are working longer hours and taking on greater demands than ever before. This situation is all too familiar within healthcare. This chapter gives attention to particular issues in the Canadian healthcare system, which has been subject to extensive change since the early 1990s, driven particularly by a perceived need to control the escalation of costs within healthcare. Redesigning and restructuring activities have become a common way of life for healthcare providers and this presents various work-life related challenges. The purpose of this chapter is to explore the issues and provide a perspective on the work environment in healthcare and the impact this has on healthcare providers.

Following a review of the literature and current thinking within the fields of healthcare, human resource management, and industrial relations, consistent findings in the research that addresses the impact of hospital restructuring on healthcare providers shows decreases in job satisfaction, professional efficacy, ability to provide quality care, physical and emotional health; along with increases in turnover, overtime hours, disruptiveness to working and non-working relationships, and perceived levels of work-life conflict (Burke, 2003; Duxbury, Higgins and Johnson, 2004; Hertting, Nilsson, Theorell and Larsson, 2004; Lewis, Rapoport and Gambles, 2003; PHRSC, 2003; RNABC, 2001; Thorpe and Loo, 2003). The duration and scheduling of working patterns in healthcare, together with related levels of workload and work pressure raise important questions in the quest of providers to achieve meaningful work-life balance. The working patterns of different occupational groups in healthcare, such as physicians and nurses, create pressures for satisfactory work-life balance in general, as well as more specific concerns relating to performance, health, safety, and job satisfaction. The complexity and diversity of the healthcare environment, including its workforce and practice settings, means that there is no single work-life issue to be addressed but rather a constellation of issues each contributing in a different way to a series of work-life related challenges. The evidence indicates a pressing need to revise the demands placed on healthcare providers. The findings and implications from this research set the groundwork for a future empirical study that focuses on the role and design of organisational workplaces, structures and practices as contributors to longer-term work-life balance within healthcare.

Context

The changing nature of work

Based on the work of some of the prominent researchers in the work-life field, the author will provide a brief overview of the changing nature of work in Canada over the past decade. In a report for the Public Health Agency of Canada, Duxbury et al (2004) state that the 1990s were a decade of turbulence as companies downsized, rightsized, restructured and globalised. The recession of the early nineties was followed by the jobless recovery of the mid-nineties and job security was the issue that absorbed many working Canadians. Organisations were faced with a surplus of employees from which to choose and therefore paid little attention to 'good practice' in the area of human resource management (Armstrong and Armstrong, 2002; Fooks, Duvalko, Baranek, Lamothe and Rondeau, 2002). Much of the literature reports how technological change and the competition of the global market increased pressure on organisations and employees alike to keep up with the racing demands that presented. Time in employment in terms of hours worked increased for many, as did many forms of non-standard employment. Personal life demands also increased as family structures continued to change and the percentage of working Canadians with dual-income families, childcare and eldercare rose. Since that time, there has been a complete turnaround with respect to the issue of work-life balance due to the unmistakable trend towards jobs becoming more stressful, time consuming and less satisfying, particularly in hours worked and the amount of work having to be done. Despite the ideals of 'good practice', research shows that as the 24-hour, seven-day working week gains ascendancy, achieving satisfactory work-life balance is proving an elusive goal for more and more people; if anything, paid work has become increasingly invasive in people's lives (Duxbury et al, 2004; Lewis et al, 2003; Shamian and Griffin, 2003).

The issues associated with balancing work and family are of paramount importance to individuals, families, organisations, professional associations, governments, and the larger society. In the past much of the literature on work-life balance and conflict issues was viewed in terms of its considerable human costs, and the associated direct and indirect costs borne by organisations (Bailyn, 1993; Bailyn, Fletcher and Kolb, 1997; Burke, 2004; Duxbury et al, 2004; Fletcher and Bailyn, 1996; Fletcher and Rapoport, 1996; Lewis et al, 2003). However, work stress and work-life conflict are not only problems of individuals and their employing organisations, but are wider societal problems that are ultimately shared by all members of society (Duxbury et al, 2004; Cooper, Liukkonen, and Cartwight 1996; Needleman, Buerhaus, Mattke, Stewart and Zelevinsky 2002; White, Hill, McGovern, Mills and Smeaton, 2003). Work-life conflict is not only a moral issue – it is also a productivity, economic, workplace, and social issue as suggested by Duxbury et al (2004) who estimated that in 2001, the healthcare costs of high work-life conflict were approximately six billion dollars a year attributable to high overload and five billion dollars a year to caregiver strain. Role overload is the greatest culprit and if eliminated could reduce the number of physician visits per year by 25 per cent and emergency room visits by 23 per cent. Caregiver strain is also problematic, and aging demographics and the greater need to provide eldercare is overwhelming employees' ability to cope with both work and life demands.

The following sections address the main external factors and trends relevant to human resource planning within healthcare, illustrating some of the challenges experienced by healthcare providers in achieving work-life balance. While there are a multitude of workers within healthcare, the working lives of nurses and physicians will be the focus of investigation. The researcher brings to light the current situation surrounding healthcare providers from three levels of analysis – the societal, organisational, and individual levels.

The changing nature of healthcare in Canada

The societal context

This review of the environment of healthcare provides a better understanding of the external factors and trends in the demographic, social, fiscal, economic and technological arenas that affect providers' capacity to achieve work-life balance. The industry of public sector healthcare in Canada is a unique and highly complex industry, due to its structure, conditions of the external environment, and the fact that the labour market in healthcare is unlike any other; it defies standard human resource planning and management methods (Fooks et al, 2002). Prior to delving into some of the larger, societal issues affecting healthcare, it is important first to acquire an understanding of the general structure of Canada's healthcare system. In Canada, healthcare is provided under the umbrella of Health Canada, which is the federal department responsible for helping the people of Canada maintain and improve their health and well-being. In partnership with provincial and territorial governments, Health Canada provides national leadership to develop health policy, enforce health regulations, promote disease prevention and enhance healthy living for all Canadians. Through its administration of the Canada Health Act, Health Canada is committed to maintaining the country's health insurance system which is universally available to permanent residents, comprehensive in the services it covers, accessible without income barriers, portable within and outside the country and publicly administered. Each province and territory administers its own healthcare plan with respect to these five basic principles of the Canada Health Act. It is the responsibility of each individual province or territory to manage and deliver health services. Provincial and territorial governments are responsible for the delivery of Canada's healthcare and hospital services; and the federal government shares in the cost of these services through annual Canada health and social transfer allocations (Health Canada, 2004).

Cost is an enormous driver of healthcare. The Canadian healthcare system has undergone many changes and forms of restructuring over the past 15 years due to rising costs and healthcare expenditures as well as political pressures, shifting demographics, changing healthcare needs, and changing expectations (Montague, 2004; PHRSC, 2003; Thorpe and Loo, 2003). Healthcare reform is the goal and expenditure reduction is seen as the only key to balancing budgets. Koehoorn, Lowe, Rondeau, Schellenberg and Wagar (2002) report how political decisions to cut healthcare budgets in the 1990s are still reverberating through the healthcare system. In the ten-year period between 1987 and 1997, government spending on hospitals as a percentage of total healthcare expenditures declined from 46.0 per cent to 33.6 per cent. The system was restructured in the wake of such cuts including bed closures, regionalisation, workforce reductions, and work reorganisation. This restructuring typically had a bottom line focus that did not consider the longer-term consequences for the human resources of healthcare. Between 1997 and 2002, total health spending in Canada increased by almost $34 billion dollars, an unprecedented rate of increase in response to rising costs amid larger macro pressures. Total health spending is currently at an all-time high and although government spending on healthcare has increased significantly over the past several years, the number of supported services has dropped. It is estimated that between the years 2000 and 2020, total healthcare spending in Canada will grow by 56 per cent from $2,626 per person to over $4,100 annually, and total spending will rise from $81 billion to $147 billion during those years (Maxwell, Jackson and Legowski, 2002).

Four macro-pressures in particular operate and have collided in this decade, placing the healthcare system under considerable strain. These pressures are to: eliminate deficits, a supply and demand imbalance, an aging population, and changing expectations. Taken together, the synthesis of these factors creates considerable strain on the human resources of healthcare and their ability to provide quality care for both themselves and the consumers of healthcare services. The funding cuts and restructuring significantly disrupted any possible equilibrium between supply and demand in the healthcare labour market. A combination of lack of recruitment, reduced intake into training programs, and deteriorated working conditions fueled labour shortages. For example, the Canadian Nurses Association (2002) made projections with regard to nursing supply and demand for the next 10 to 15 years, concluding that there will be a shortage of 78,000 registered nurses in 2011 and 113,000 registered nurses by 2016, about 30 per cent of the current nursing labour force. A survey by the College of Family Physicians of Canada (2001) predicts a shortage of 6,000 family physicians by 2011. According to the Canadian Institute for Health Information (2002), physician supply in Canada has suffered a 5 per cent decline since 1993, bringing the ratio of physicians to population down to the level it was 15 years ago, one physician for every 1,063 people. A recent report by the Canadian Medical Association indicates that in 2003, 1.2 million Canadians were without a family physician. This number is significant considering the population of Canada (approximately 32 million) and the fact the healthcare sector in Canada is a large, resource intensive industry employing more than 1.5 million Canadians (see Commission on the Future of Health Care in Canada, 2002).

The aging population represents another trend responsible for some of the challenges confronting the healthcare system. According to recent projections by Statistics Canada and the Physician Human Resource Strategy (2003), the proportion of Canadians aged 65 years and older will be 14 per cent by the year 2010. A growing geriatric population means that Canadians are living longer with chronic illnesses and co-morbidities, their conditions are complex and multi-focal, which results in the increased need for healthcare services, hence greater demands placed on healthcare providers (OECD, 1998; Ontario College of Family Physicians, 2001). This trend is also responsible for Canadians living longer at home or at other private residences, which results in greater numbers of needed home and community-based care services. A related trend appears to be the growing number of retirees moving from urban centers to rural areas where provider supply is short (Hutten-Czapski, 1998). An important issue related to the aging population is the fact that while home-based and community-based healthcare needs are growing as the population ages and hospitals discharge earlier, the skill levels of some home/community care providers may be less due to community care contracts being awarded increasingly on the basis of cost. Demographic trends raise concerns for the workforce in healthcare as employers prepare for the imminent wave of retirements given that the average age of physicians (47.5 years), specialists (49 years), and nurses (44.5 years) in Canada is now well above the Canadian labour force average. There is concern not only about the potential demands placed on the health sector by an aging population but also with the capacity of the aging workforce in healthcare to keep up with those demands (CNA, 2002, 2003; Koehoorn et al, 2002; PHRSC, 2003).

Changing expectations and a sense of entitlement to health services on the part of the consumer have led to greater demands placed on healthcare providers. As technology increases, the demands for healthcare increase as consumers expect to gain access to the latest and often costly medical technology, in effect broadening the scope of diagnosis and treatable illness. The use of the internet has raised expectations further as consumers have access to the latest research and technologies in the advancement of health, they are more knowledgeable and informed, and expect to obtain these services for both themselves and their families (Armstrong and Armstrong, 2002; CFHCC, 2002). In a survey conducted by the CMA (2002), one physician made the comment of how changing expectations have 'more to do with what was presented during our provincial nightly news or the latest episode of ER than with any basis in reality' (526). The PHRSC (2003) suggests, 'The distinction between demand and need is blurring. Patients' increasingly sophisticated demands, coupled with emerging knowledge about the potential for interventions are raising the intensity of intervention with no corresponding drop off in other interventions' (28). The Organisation for Economic Co-operation and Development (OECD) estimates that the impact of technology on increasing healthcare costs is seven times higher than that of demographic changes (Kralj, 1999; OECD, 1998). It has been observed that new technologies produce better health outcomes; however they are often very expensive and add significantly to healthcare costs and the demands placed on healthcare providers.

The organisational context

It is important to first recognise the specificity of healthcare and the fact that healthcare is not a business like the rest and the people working in healthcare differ in some significant ways from those employed in other sectors. Many of the differences may seem obvious, such as the fact that the labour force in healthcare is highly organised, with 62 per cent belonging to a union and an additional number represented by professional associations. More than 30 occupations and professions are regulated under various pieces of provincial or federal legislation. Moreover, there is considerable diversity among jurisdictions in terms of rights of individual providers, unions, and employers, as well as considerable diversity in rules and practices linked to different work locations. But perhaps the most obvious difference is that in healthcare we are dealing solely with human lives and the risks and consequences cannot be assessed exclusively or even primarily in economic terms (Akyeampong, 2001; Armstrong and Armstrong, 2002; Fooks et al, 2002; Koehoorn et al, 2002). In saying that, extensive changes and ideologies within the system in regard to the roles and responsibilities of healthcare providers, government, and the public have been forced on the system due to the conditions of the economic climate and the perceived need to control the escalation of costs within healthcare. Much hope has been placed on the restructuring of the system to reduce costs and increase provider efficiencies, however, the literature suggests there is little consensus on whether new payment methods, new delivery models, and further integration/substitution of services actually achieves these objectives. Armstrong and Armstrong (2002) report that cases of hospital amalgamation mimic similar amalgamations in the corporate sector. Across Canada, more than 30 major teaching hospitals have been merged into giant organisations and many small community hospitals have been closed or completely transformed. Markham and Lomas (1995) argue there is no empirical evidence to demonstrate economic efficiency, quality or human resource gains with multi-hospitals, and some evidence to suggest that costs may actually increase, flexibility and responsiveness to individual needs decline, job demands increase, there is reduced control and perceived job insecurity, relationships with employers deteriorate, and the incidence of work-life conflicts increase (Hertting et al, 2004). Similarly, downsizing in healthcare organisations imitates a strategy used in other sectors, even though research on downsizing corporations indicates that a majority of those initiatives did not increase productivity, a significant number raised expenditures, and both morale and trust usually declined (Applebaum, Everard and Hung, 1999).

In an attempt to contain costs, governments have been trying to move centers of care away from the highest cost elements of the system – the hospitals, which has a large impact on healthcare providers. Some of the most visible impacts of reform in Canada thus far have been the complete closure of some hospitals and the severe reduction of beds in others; the move towards group practice, home/community-based practices, and integrated community health centers; and the substitution of tasks once performed by physicians and nurses to other healthcare occupations. The magnitude of the change that has taken place has been considerable and whilst the concept of 'reform' itself is touted with positive connotations, in fact, the results have been devastating to both the consumers and providers of healthcare services (Keddy, Gregor, Foster and Denney, 1999). The discourse around reform was phrased as though government, health professionals and the community would work together mutually for true reform, waste and inefficiencies would be reduced, and the system would become revitalised.

In fact, this has not been the case, rather there are disruptions in care, increased burdens on women as caregivers, disparities between urban and rural resources and services, and loss of jobs for healthcare providers. Scott (1995) states that some associations representing the healthcare professions have resisted the adoption of new models of care delivery and therefore become highly politicised largely in response to cutbacks and reforms that were perceived to be instituted without proper consultation. The initial reaction has been to protect existing positions and move away from compromise, which has led to a turbulent work environment within healthcare. As CFHCC (2002) states in a report entitled 'The Future of Health Care in Canada', the Canadian healthcare system is in a state of crisis, the problem as it stands is not so much about 'people' as it is about 'economics'.

As the cost of healthcare providers account for a significant proportion of healthcare dollars, funding cuts have had a serious impact on the supply, work environment, and overall satisfaction of healthcare providers (Shamian and Griffin, 2003). The consequences of these strategies are obvious in the high rates of illness and injury among healthcare providers. Health sector workers are 50 per cent more likely than other workers to miss work due to illness or injury (Armstrong and Armstrong, 2002). There are high burnout rates, feelings of job insecurity, and work-family conflicts. The intensity of the workload and the increase in patient acuity complicates the work setting further by placing greater demands on healthcare providers (CIHI, 2002; Thorpe and Loo, 2003). Numerous reports indicate a substantial cause for concern about the supply of healthcare providers in Canada as lower supply is associated with rising workloads and increased demands hence quality of care and quality of work-life is affected. As Grinspun (2003) reports, for nurses, the impact of the restructuring has been especially hard as it led to massive layoffs, escalation in the casualisation of the nursing workforce, a wage and compensation freeze, a decline in the number of senior nursing positions, combined with an increase in non-nursing duties, the introduction of unregulated healthcare providers, and an increase in client acuity and task-oriented client care. Keddy et al (1999) state that besides the bed shortage, the system is breaking down because there are too many casual nurses on the job and the full-time nurses who are more familiar with the facilities are being forced to take time off due to stress. Part-time and casual employment is much more common in nursing than in other sectors, and so is multiple job holding; however in many cases it is because of employer not employee preferences (Grinspun, 2003; Wortsman and Lockhead, 2002). Part-time levels in nursing rose from 38.7 per cent in 1991 to 47.6 per cent in 1998, whereas the percentage of the general workforce in Canada that worked part-time in 1999 was 18.5 per cent (CNA, 2001; Grinspun, 2003). There is little doubt that the economic restructuring and massive layoffs of the 1990s led to substantive involuntary employment patterns amongst the ranks.

The gender composition of the workforce in healthcare is another factor that adds complexity and has implications for work-life balance. The CIHI (2002) reports that out of the 1.5 million people that work in the paid health and social services fields, more than 80 per cent of them are women. The CNA reports that in 2003, out of a total of 241,342 registered nurses, 228,597 were female and 12,745 were male, an increase from 1999 when there were 10,598 male nurses in Canada. In 2000, women accounted for 49.6 per cent of all students graduating with medical degrees, a significant increase from 1980 when only 32 per cent of the medical graduates were women (Fooks et al, 2002). Although women are moving in increasing numbers into the healthcare labour force and also into traditionally male-dominated professions such as medicine, more men are moving into the female-dominated professions such as nursing. The data indicate changing demographics within the professions; however nursing and support occupations primarily remain 'women's work' and so does care in the home (Armstrong and Armstrong, 2002; Keddy et al, 1999; Majomi, Brown and Crawford, 2003). Morris (2001) notes that the female domination of this work has contributed to the invisibility of many skills involved in care, as well as to the invisibility of the paid and unpaid care work now being done by women to make up for the gaps left by healthcare reforms. Most role strain research assumes that women are the ones with multiple roles and are therefore most affected, juggling the demands of work and family. The stress from competing work and family obligations in healthcare is exacerbated by the similarity of the 'caring work' and 'emotional labour' involved in these roles – an interlocking complex of caring roles. After all, a nurse does do physical work, some of which can be compared to caring for a family member at home; nurses are also involved in relational work in the provision of emotional support; and involved in coordinating efforts of other healthcare workers as they do with their own family. These patterns have significant implications for pay, workforce distribution, and care location as well as for openness to change. Policies to promote change in support of work-life balance need to take both paid and unpaid care, as well as the gendered nature of the workforce and the specificity of healthcare work into account.

The aging of the workforce has implications for the current and future supply of healthcare providers and their ability to achieve work-life balance. Nurses make up the largest component of the healthcare workforce (35 per cent) while physicians account for 8 per cent, the remainder includes administrators and allied healthcare professionals (57 per cent). Similar to the Canadian population, the average age of physicians in the country is increasing and retirement is predicted to accelerate over the next 10 to 15 years (CIHI, 2002). Historically, physicians have tended to work beyond traditional retirement age, however an increasing number are opting for earlier retirement than a decade ago. Recent data from the

Ontario Physician Human Resource Data Centre points to an acceleration of physician retirements; where in 1995 a total of 60 Ontario physicians retired, five years later that number had increased to more than 400 retirees (OMA, 2002). Within the nursing profession, there is a decline in the number of nurses under 35 years of age and an increase in the number over 45 years of age (Fooks et al, 2002). In 2003, 17 per cent of nurses in Canada were between 25 and 34 years of age, whereas 52.3 per cent were of 45 years of age and older – indicative of an ongoing imbalance between those entering and those leaving the profession (CNA, 2002, 2003). Moreover, with the cutbacks throughout the past decade, there is an age gap in the labour force with very few people between the oldest and youngest groups. The age gap in healthcare has contributed to intensified working conditions in ways that have limited possibilities for sharing knowledge with new recruits.

While the shortage and aging of the current cohort has led to interest in improved working conditions, the complexities surrounding the environment of healthcare make it difficult to implement various policies and practices. The complexities of the environment facilitate the rigid structuring and restructuring of the workplace. There are more than 30 healthcare occupations and professions regulated under provincial and federal legislation in Canada. The degree of cooperation or conflict found in relations between healthcare employers and these unions and/or professional associations can either enable or disable any change initiative. Successful workplace improvement initiatives will require the cooperation of management with unions and professional associations; recognition of the diversity of care settings, populations needing care, and occupations in healthcare; acknowledgment that people in unregulated occupations or providing unpaid care for family, friends, and neighbours are vital to the system; gender-sensitive approaches that take explicit account of the competing demands placed on women in particular; initiatives to retain older healthcare providers and help them share their knowledge with the younger generations; and ongoing attention to shifts in the population requiring care. Their ability to effectively respond to employee problems, complaints, and grievances on a day-to-day basis will impact the overall quality of the healthcare working environment including any initiative designed to promote work-life balance.

The individual context

Changing demographics and changes in the organisation and delivery of healthcare services have had a direct impact on the individual practice of healthcare providers. For instance, head nurses and clinical nurse specialists have been eliminated or severely reduced in many jurisdictions. This change has reduced professional and clinical support for nurses while also transferring the responsibility of many non-nursing functions onto nurses such as administrative (the scheduling of staff and the ordering of supplies), dietary (preparing meals) and housekeeping (cleaning rooms) duties. This competes against their clinical responsibilities adding further stress to the workplace. Staffing levels are another area of concern. Studies by Aiken et al, (2001, 2002), claim that 45 per cent of Canadian nurses report deterioration in the quality of client care over the previous year along with a decrease in nurse-to-patient ratios (from 1:4 to 1:10). There are direct links between high patient-to-nurse ratios and mortality rates in hospitals along with higher emotional exhaustion, greater job dissatisfaction, and increased incidence of work-life conflict amongst nurses (Shamian and Griffin, 2003). Although higher levels of nurse staffing are associated with lower mortality rates in neonates and adults; lower re-admission rates; lower rates of urinary tract infections, upper gastrointestinal bleeding, hospital-acquired infections, shock, cardiac arrest, failure to rescue attempts; and higher rates of patient satisfaction – the effects of massive cuts in hospital budgets have resulted in staff cuts leading to increased workloads, poor working environments, job dissatisfaction, and unsafe patient care (Aiken et al, 2001; Needleman et al, 2002; Shamian and Griffin, 2003). The Registered Nurses Association of British Columbia (2001) reports that legislated nurse-to-patient ratios are a controversial approach to improving client care and reducing demands on nurses, although some jurisdictions in the United States have advocated for and achieved legislation to set minimum nurse-to-patient ratios. In Canada, there are currently no national staffing standards. Nurses in Canada cite work overload as the key reason for difficulty in meeting their standards for registered nursing practice. There is a relationship between stress and illness, and, according to the National Population Health Survey, nurses suffer the greatest stress of all healthcare workers (Sullivan, Kerr and Ibrahim, 1999). It comes as no surprise that the Health Canada Advisory Committee on Human Health Resources (Shannon and French, 2005) reports that in any given week more than 13,000 registered nurses (7.4 per cent of the Canadian nursing workforce) are absent because of injury, illness, burnout, or disability. The rate of absenteeism among registered nurses is 80 per cent higher than the Canadian average (8.1 per cent compared with an average of 4.5 per cent for 47 other occupations) and is the equivalent of 9,000 full-time nursing positions (Montague, 2004; Sullivan et al, 1999). To add to this, increasingly nurses are being faced with mandatory overtime; scheduled overtime; mandatory on-call; refusal of holidays or time-off for education or personal leave; and being placed to work in areas outside of their specialty area. Further, nurses in Canada work almost a quarter of a million hours of overtime per week, the equivalent of 7,000 full-time jobs per year. It is estimated that the cost of overtime, absentee wages, and replacement for registered nurse absentees is between $962 million and $1.5 billion annually (Fooks et al, 2002; Shamian et al, 2003). Nurses are leaving the profession due to stress, poor working conditions, and poor morale; many are choosing to retire early. Brooks and Anderson (2004) conducted a study of 1,500 registered nurses to explore how acute care nurses rate their quality of work life. The findings revealed that workload was too heavy and there was not enough time to do their job well, they had little energy left after work to socialise or do anything constructive at home, they were unable to 'balance' their professional and personal lives, and stated that overall, rotating shift work negatively affected their lives. Shift work, comprised of eight to 12-hour shifts and rotating days and nights, is associated with a number of potential psychosocial problems including high work and personal stress, fatigue, low sense of mastery and relationship problems (Shields, 2003). Recognition that clinician fatigue may promote ineffective care and lead to adverse patient outcomes provides a compelling rationale for the enforcement of duty-hour guidelines for both physicians and nurses.

Results from the CMA's annual survey (2002, 2003) show that many of the complaints received by physicians concern the unrelenting demands of medical life. Heavy workloads, high patient demands and expectations, lack of flexibility in working arrangements as well as training and career development issues all appear to impact the recruitment and retention of physicians to a greater degree than does remuneration. Many headlines in the literature point to medicine as the 'dispirited profession' (Sullivan and Buske, 1998). One of the most significant findings revealed that more than two-thirds of younger physicians aged 35–44 (68 per cent) and 70 per cent of those aged 45–54 said their workload is heavier than they would like and more than half (55 per cent) say their family and personal life has suffered because they chose medicine as a profession. The work can be physically and emotionally demanding, it allows limited rest, is associated with sleep deprivation, and allows limited involvement in activities outside of work. One rural physician made the following comment: 'I see 50 patients or more each day and have nothing to show for it except total and absolute exhaustion. I'm writing this at 2230 hours after seeing 48 patients, 3 emergency calls, surgery until 2200 hours, and now charting until midnight' (CMA, 2003: 525). The administrative and other professional activities associated with current medical practice has been a source of added stress and dissatisfaction for physicians. A number of physicians appear to want off the 'medical treadmill' (CMA, 2003) and in fact, many have resigned their hospital privileges and restricted certain practices not only to achieve higher levels of expertise but also to maintain 'office-only' obligations, avoiding the burden of providing more comprehensive on-call care and the frustration of receiving inadequate compensation for it.

Clinical work alters normal physiology and current guidelines and work practices do not mitigate significant fatigue along with the physical, mental and emotional stress entailed (Howard and Gaba, 2004; Parshuram,

Dhanani, Kirsh and Cox, 2004). 'Sleep deprivation, of the magnitude experienced by healthcare practitioners has been shown to impair performance, worsen mood and compromise patient and provider safety' (Brooks and Anderson, 2004: 975). Parshuram and colleagues (2004) report a study that reveals some new and important physiologic information in regard to physicians and on-call periods. The study revealed physiologic alteration such as dominance of the sympathetic nervous system along with urine specific gravity and ketone levels that indicated significant dehydration. The physiologic alterations may have been due to the inherent stress of being on call and the lack of sleep or to the increased activity of the subjects who walked an average of 6.3 kilometers during their shift. Their study suggests that a potential strategy to mitigate some of the effects of fatigue would be to add another physician to the call team, thus distributing the workload of physicians.

While clinical work alters normal physiology it also affects the lifestyle of the individual. There is debate in the research about whether younger physicians are changing the balance between work-life and family-life. An interesting finding in the research is that younger physicians (less than 45 years), on average, are providing less direct patient care in terms of working hours per week than physicians of the same age group in 1982, a 21 per cent decrease in patient care hours (CMA, 2004). The claim is that they are opting for fewer total hours of work and less hours after work; there are clear changes in the nature of their practice – largely in family medicine in the provision of less service after hours and in the trend to move towards group practices; they are choosing to specialise and subspecialise; opting for more predictable hours by reducing the number of on-calls, house calls, and emergency department shifts; and changing their geographic distribution opting to practice in urban rather than rural centers due to greater professional incentives and personal lifestyle preferences (Fooks et al, 2002; PHRSC, 2003).

Research by Hertting et al (2004) reveals that job strain has a negative impact on individuals and organisations. At the individual level personal relationships are strained along with a higher incidence of work-life conflict, sick time, stress-related illnesses, interpersonal conflict, and diminished job satisfaction. At the organisational level, stressful working conditions are associated with a higher incidence of absenteeism, job dissatisfaction, rapid turnover, and recruitment difficulties. If healthcare organisations are going to be able to effectively address the labour shortages and intensification of demands placed on healthcare providers, the working environment must be improved. A study by Lowe and Schellenberg (2001) found that high quality work environments contributes to strong employment relationships, which leads to improved quality of work-life and organisational performance. Trust is at the core of the psychological contract between workers and employers, and in healthcare many have lost their sense of trust in the workplace.

These researchers studied the four pillars of the employment relationship: trust, commitment, communication, and influence, and found that healthcare providers had the lowest scores of occupational groups on all four dimensions. Further, healthcare providers were the least likely of all occupational groups to describe their work environment as being 'healthy'. Koehoorn et al (2002) argue that the first step towards building a comprehensive healthy workplace change program must be to address the demands placed on healthcare providers. Although the problems somewhat vary for the different professions along with their levels of autonomy and control, the expectations placed on providers are similar (CFHCC, 2002). Despite the changing nature of the healthcare environment, the underlying assumptions and expectations have not changed and initiatives designed to promote healthy work-life practices have not been eagerly implemented. Noting that current practices have produced growing job dissatisfaction among healthcare providers, the Canadian Nursery Advisory Committee (2002) is blunt in the urgent need to address issues such as workload, overtime, absenteeism, illness, injury, and turnover. It concludes that the need is not to repair the professions, but rather to renew and repair the work environment of healthcare providers.

Discussion

The overall purpose of this chapter was to explore the issues and provide a perspective on the work environment in healthcare and the impact this has on healthcare providers. The findings suggest the imperative need to reduce the demands placed on healthcare providers with a focus on improving the work environment in support of work-life balance. The healthcare environment in Canada as it stands is taking its toll on providers affecting their work life, their personal life, and overall health and well-being, as well as having direct consequences for patient care and other outcomes – the larger society as a whole. The compelling consistencies with which similar findings emerge throughout the literature lend support to the call that there needs to be action to improve the working conditions within healthcare. Fiscal constraints and the constant debate over money have overshadowed the need to reorganise the system in ways that not only 'reduce duplication and waste' but also provide a quality work life for healthcare providers (CFHCC, 2002). While accessibility and the quality of health services are the larger issues on the part of the patients, the quality of the working environment and the ability to achieve a satisfactory work-life balance are larger issues on the part of the providers.

Research has shown that the work environment has physical and psychosocial dimensions that are influenced by human resource management practices (Houtman, 1995; Koehoorn et al, 2002). The most relevant issues for healthcare providers identified in the work environment literature include: physical hazards, workload and demands, work schedules, employment patterns, job control, role stressors, and job insecurity. A key research finding is how these factors influence employee health and well-being. Workload, workpace, and work scheduling, all potential stressors, are among the most important work environment issues facing healthcare providers. Job design, including the design of the workspace, and how it is integrated into organisational systems provides the foundation for a high quality, meaningful, satisfactory work environment. Lowe and Schellenberg (2001) found that high quality work environments contribute to strong employment relationships, and are in turn related to improved quality of work life, perceptions of work-life balance, and organisational performance. The first step in any comprehensive workplace change program must be addressing work intensification. The cumulative impact of funding cuts, changing demographics, advancements in technology, changing expectations, workforce reductions and current labour shortages have resulted in heavier workloads, longer work hours, less predictability, less control, and intensified demands placed on health providers. A starting point may be to improve upon the smaller, tangible qualities of the working environment such as the physical working environment and use small successes to build on incrementally throughout the system.

Studies conducted by Shamian et al (2003) report that improved benefits including the addition of personal/discretionary days, an on-site day care, improved staffing levels, and increased flexibility in scheduling, were claimed to be potential solutions to some of the current challenges facing healthcare providers (also see Dastmalchian and Blyton, 2001). Specific interventions such as improving upon the physical working environment to facilitate work flow and organisational and individual practices would also contribute in responding to these issues. For example, having adequate and functioning equipment and furnishings available for patient care and their families; providing quiet rooms where providers can relax; and fitness facilities or wellness programs where providers can actively participate to both reduce stress and maintain health and well-being – these are all examples of positive, tangible workplace changes that have not eagerly been implemented in the majority of healthcare organisations in Canada. These are examples of life-enhancing organisational design attributes that could positively impact the work environment within healthcare. It is interesting to note that while the desire to care for people, a family history of professional healthcare work, and security in career choice are documented reasons for entering the health professions, reasons for leaving include workload, poor work environments, overall dissatisfaction and harassment (O'Brien-Pallas and Baumann, 1992). Nurses and physicians in every province and territory express serious concerns about the deterioration in the quality of their working environments; they feel demoralised, undervalued, and disrespected as professionals and in some cases as human beings (Wortsman and Lockhead, 2002; Shamian and Griffin, 2003). It is clear from the literature that current policies, practices, and procedures are not congruent with what healthcare providers need to attain a satisfactory work-life balance. Therefore, perhaps more immediate and small-scale interventions should be implemented to measure and assess the effectiveness of system-wide change efforts and the impact they have on healthcare providers.

Conclusion

In healthcare, the complexity and diversity of the workforce and of practice settings mean that there is no single work-life issue to be addressed, but rather a constellation of issues each contributing in a different way to the problems that present. Perhaps the most obvious difference is that in healthcare we are dealing solely with human lives – in all stages and forms, which means that the risks and consequences cannot be assessed exclusively or even primarily in economic terms. We often hear of the term 'crisis in health care' but realistically, is the 'crisis' the result of the workplace itself, the practice of the professions, the health of the people, or the values of society? Despite the ongoing changes in the Canadian Health Care System and years of study, we appear to make little progress in the area of human resource development and striving to achieve work-life balance is still an issue. Seemingly ironic in an environment whose mission is to support those in need – we do everything we can to meet the needs of the people requiring care but seem unable to meet the needs of those providing care. Work-life conflicts create serious ethical dilemmas for both individuals and organisations and there are numerous negative consequences of ignoring the constraints. Further, there are many options to reduce the strain, each with its advantages and disadvantages, however such options are especially difficult to implement given the current state of the system. Recently, researchers have begun to recognise that the nature of jobs, the environment, and more generally the culture can have a significant impact on the ability of workers to achieve satisfactory work-life balance. Work-life balance is not just a matter of benefits and formal family-friendly policies, rather it depends on the characteristics of jobs, the environment of the working enterprise, the value placed on jobs, and the value placed on individuals and quality of life. This chapter offers no prescriptions for change about how to live and/or better integrate our work and personal lives. What it does offers is a critical picture of the situation as it stands in Canada; a starting point to think about the place of healthcare work in our lives given today's employment realities.

The implications of this research include priority issues within healthcare that relate to improvements in the quality of the workplace and work life for healthcare providers with a focus on the role and design of organisational workplaces, structures and practices as contributors to longer-term work-life balance. The review contributes to organisation development in the anticipation of future inquiry on the impact of the physical working environment on social behavior within healthcare. Future research could focus on the approaches of employers and professional associations in the design of the workplace and its effect on performance, productivity, satisfaction, and well-being. In addition, a focus on the design of the home environment and the measures in place that support work-life balance would be another interesting area of inquiry. Research focused on nurturing the younger generation of healthcare providers is also needed to encourage and support realistic expectations in regard to work-life balance.

References

Aiken, L., Clarke, S. and Sloan, D. (2001) Nurses' reports on hospital quality of care and working conditions in five countries, *Health Affairs*, 20(3): 43–53.

Aiken, L., Clarke, S., Sloane, D., Sochalski, J. and Silber, J. (2002) Hospital nurse staffing and patient mortality, nurse burnout, and job dissatisfaction, *Journal of the American Medical Association*, 288(16): 1987–93.

Akyeampong, E. (2001) Fact-sheet on unionization, *Perspectives on Labour and Income*, 13(3): 46–54.

Applebaum S., Everard, A. and Hung, L. (1999) Strategic downsizing: Critical success factors, *Management Decision*, 37(7): 535–52.

Armstrong, P. and Armstrong, H. (2002, October) *Planning for care: Approaches to health human resource policy and planning*, Commission on the Future of Health Care in Canada, Discussion Paper No. 28, Ottawa, ON.

Bailyn, L. (1993) *Breaking the Mold: Women, Men, and Time in the New Corporate World*, New York: Free Press.

Bailyn, L., Fletcher, J. and Kolb, D. (1997) Unexpected connections: Considering employees' personal lives can revitalize your business, *Sloan Management Review*, 38: 11–9.

Brooks, B. and Anderson, M. (2004) Nursing work life in acute care, *Journal of Nursing Care Quality*, 19(3): 269–75.

Burke, R. (2003) Nursing staff attitudes following restructuring: The role of perceived organizational support, restructuring processes and stressors, *International Journal of Sociology and Social Policy*, 23(8/9): 129–57.

Burke, R. (2004) Work and personal life integration, *International Journal of Stress Management*, 11(4): 299–304.

Canadian Institute for Health Information (CIHI) (2002) *Supply and distribution of registered nurses in Canada: 2001 report*, Ottawa, ON: Canadian Institute for Health Information.

Canadian Medical Association (2002, September) Results from the CMA's 2002 physician resource questionnaire, *Canadian Medical Association Journal*, 167(5): 521–2.

Canadian Medical Association (2003, March) Medicine, the unhappy profession? *Canadian Medical Association Journal*, 168(8): 75–2.

Canadian Medical Association (2004, April) Younger physicians providing less direct patient care, *Canadian Medical Association Journal*, 170(8).

Canadian Nursing Advisory Committee (CNAC) (2002) *Our health, Our Future: Creating Quality Workplaces for Canadian Nurses*, Ottawa, ON: Canadian Nursing Advisory Committee.

Canadian Nurses Association (CNA) (2001) Registered Nurses 1998 Statistical Highlights, *Canadian Nurse*, Ottawa, ON: Canadian Nurses Association.

Canadian Nurses Association (2002, June) Planning for the future: Nursing human resource projections, *Canadian Nurse*, Ottawa, ON: Canadian Nurses Association.

Canadian Nurses Association (2003) Highlight of 2003 nurses statistics, *Canadian Nurse*, Ottawa, ON: Canadian Nurses Association.

College of Family Physicians of Canada (2001) National family physician workforce survey, Mississauga, ON: College of Family Physicians.

Commission on the Future of Health Care in Canada (CFHCC) (2002, November) *Building on values: The future of health care in Canada – Final Report* (Romanow Report), Government of Canada, Ottawa, ON: National Library of Canada.

Cooper, C., Liukkonen, P. and Cartwight, S. (1996) *Stress prevention in the workplace. Assessing the costs and benefits to organizations*, Dublin, IR: European Foundation for the Improvement of Living and Working Conditions.

Dastmalchian, A. and Blyton, P. (2001) Workplace flexibility and the changing nature of work: An introduction, *Canadian Journal of Administrative Sciences*, 18(1): 1–4.

Duxbury, L., Higgins, C. and Johnson, K. (2004) Report 3: Exploring the link between work-life conflict and demands on Canada's Health Care System, *Public Health Agency of Canada*. Retrieved on March 19, 2005 from http://www.phac-aspc.gc.ca.

Fletcher, J. and Bailyn, L. (1996) Challenging the last boundary: Reconnecting work and family, in Arthur, M.B. and Rousseau, D.M. (eds), *Boundaryless Career*, Oxford, UK: Oxford University Press: 256–7.

Fletcher, J. and Rapoport, R. (1996) Work-family linkages as a catalyst for change, in Lewis, S. and Lewis, J. (eds), *Rethinking Employment: The Work-Family Challenge*, London, UK: Sage: 147–68.

Fooks, C., Duvalko, K., Baranek, P., Lamothe, L. and Rondeau, K. (2002, October) Health human resource planning in Canada: Physician and nursing work force issues, *Commission on the Future of Health Care in Canada*, Ottawa, ON: Canadian Policy Research Networks.

Grinspun, D. (2003) 'Casual and part-time work in nursing: Perils of health-care restructuring', *International Journal of Sociology and Social Policy*, 23(8/9): 54–70.

Health Canada (2004) About health Canada, *Health Canada Online*. Retrieved from http://www.hc-sc.gc.ca on March 17, 2005.

Hertting, A., Nilsson, K., Theorell, T. and Larsson, U. (2004) Downsizing and re-organization: Demands, challenges and ambiguity for registered nurses, *Nursing and Healthcare Management Policy*, 45(2), 145–54.

Houtman, I. (1995) Risk factors and occupational risk groups for work stress in the Netherlands, in Sauter, S.L. (ed.), *Organizational Risk Factors for Job Stress*, Washington, DC: American Psychological Association.

Howard, S. and Gaba, D. (2004) Trainee fatigue: Are new limits on work hours enough? *Canadian Medical Association Journal*, 170(6): 975.

Hutten-Czapski, P. (1998) Rural incentive programs: A failing report card, *Canadian Journal of Rural Medicine*, 3(4): 242–7.

Keddy, B., Gregor, F., Foster, S. and Denney, D. (1999) Theorizing about nurses' work lives: The personal and professional aftermath of living with healthcare reform, *Nursing Inquiry*, 6: 58–64.

Koehoorn, M., Lowe, G., Rondeau, K., Schellenberg, G. and Wagar, T. (2002) *Creating high quality health care workplaces: A background paper for Canadian Policy Research Networks' National Roundtable*, Ottawa, ON: Canadian Policy Research Networks.

Kralj, B. (1999, April) *Physician human resources on Ontario: a looming crisis*, Ontario Medical Review: 16–20.

Lewis, S., Rapoport, R. and Gambles, R. (2003) Reflections on the integration of paid work and the rest of life, *Journal of Managerial Psychology*, 18(8): 824–41.

Lowe, G. and Schellenberg, G. (2001) *What's a good job? The importance of employment relationships*, CPRN Study W-05, Ottawa, ON: Canadian Policy Research Networks.

Majomi, P., Brown, B. and Crawford, P. (2003) Sacrificing the personal to the professional: Community mental health nurses, *Journal of Advanced Nursing*, 42(5): 527–38.

Markham, B. and Lomas, J. (1995) A review of the multi-hospital arrangements in the literature: Benefits, disadvantages and lessons for implementation, *Health Care Management Forum*, 8(3): 24–35.

Maxwell, J., Jackson, K. and Legowski, B. (2002, June) *Report on citizen's dialogue on the future of health care in Canada*, Commission on the Future of Health Care in Canada, Ottawa, ON: Canadian Policy Research Networks.

Montague, T. (2004) *Patients First: Closing the Health Care Gap in Canada*, Wiley and Sons: Canada.

Morris, M. (2001) *Gender Sensitive Home and Community Care and Caregiving Research: A Synthesis Paper*, Final Report to the Women's Health Bureau, Ottawa, ON: Health Canada.

Needleman, J., Buerhaus, P., Mattke, S., Stewart, M. and Zelevinsky, J. (2002) Nurse-staffing levels and the quality of care in hospitals, *New England Journal of Medicine*, 346: 1715–22.

O'Brien-Pallas, L. and Baumann, A. (1992) Quality of nursing worklife issues: A unifying framework, *Canadian Journal of Nursing Administration*, 5(2): 12–6.

Ontario College of Family Physicians (2001) *Where have all the family doctors gone?* Response to the George Panel of Health Professional Human Resources Report, Mississauga, ON: Ontario College of Family Physicians.

Ontario Medical Association Human Resources Committee (OMA) (2002) *Position Paper on Physician Workforce Policy and Planning*, Ottawa, ON: Ontario Medical Association.

Organization for Economic Co-operation and Development (OECD) (1998) *Health policy brief: Aging and technology*. Retrieved from http://www.oecd.org on March 30, 2005.

Parshuram, C., Dhanani, S., Kirsh, J. and Cox, P. (2004) Fellowship training, workload, fatigue and physical stress: A prospective observational study, *Canadian Medical Association Journal*, 170(6): 965–70.

Physician Human Resource Strategy for Canada (PHRSC) (2003) *Physician workforce in Canada: Literature review and gap analysis*, Ottawa, ON: Physician Human Resource Strategy for Canada: Task Force Two.

Registered Nurses Association of British Columbia (RNABC) (2001) Legislated Nurse to Patient Ratios, *RNABC*, Vancouver, BC: Registered Nurses Association of British Columbia.

Reich, R. (2000) *The Future of Success*, New York: Knopf.

Scott, G. (1995) *Report of the fact finder on the issue of small/rural hospital emergency department physician service*, Toronto, ON: Ontario Medical Association.

Shamian, J. and Griffin, P. (2003) Translating research into health policy, *Canadian Journal of Nursing Research*, 35(3): 45–52.

Shamian, J., O'Brien-Pallas, L., Thomson, D., Alksnis, C. and Kerr, M. (2003) Nurse absenteeism, stress and workplace injury: What are the contributing factors and what can/should be done about it? *International Journal of Sociology and Social Policy*, 23(8/9): 81–103.

Shannon, V. and French, S. (2005) 'The impact of the re-engineered world of health-care in Canada on nursing and patient outcomes', *Nursing Inquiry*, 12(3): 231–41.

Shields, M. (2003) The health of Canada's shift workers, *Canadian Social Trends*, Ottawa, ON: Statistics Canada.

Sullivan, P. and Buske, L. (1998) Results from the CMA's huge 1998 physician survey point to a dispirited profession, *Canadian Medical Association Journal*, 159(5): 525–8.

Sullivan, T., Kerr, M. and Ibrahim, S. (1999) Job stress in health care workers: Highlights from the national population health survey, *Hospital Quarterly*, 2(4): 34–40.

Thorpe, K. and Loo, R. (2003) Balancing professional and personal satisfaction of nurse managers: Current and future perspectives in a changing health care system, *Journal of Nursing Management*, 11: 321–30.

White, M., Hill, S., McGovern, P., Mills, C. and Smeaton, D. (2003) High-performance management practices, working hours, and work-life balance, *British Journal of Industrial Relations*, 41(2): 175–95.

Wortsman, A. and Lockhead, C. (2002) *Full-time equivalents and financial costs associated with absenteeism, overtime, and involuntary part-time employment in the nursing profession*, Report commissioned by the Canadian Nursing Advisory Committee, Ottawa, ON: Canadian Labour and Business Centre.

13
Commitment, Community and Happiness: A Theoretical Framework for Understanding Lifestyle and Work

Carmel Goulding and Ken Reed

Introduction

This chapter examines the role of lifestyle choice in work-life imbalance, posing the question of why people make unsatisfying lifestyle choices. Drawing on rational choice theory, the argument is presented that time stress, resulting from the pressure to balance work and family responsibilities, is a socially constructed lifestyle choice which is largely influenced by an actor's subjective interpretation of their life situation. Taking radical lifestyle change, such as downshifting and voluntary simplification, as evidence of alternative lifestyle choice, the chapter argues that normative influences contribute to the construction and maintenance of time stress lifestyles.

By way of an explanatory framework, a reconstructed account of rational choice theory which incorporates the influence of commitment to group beliefs and norms on lifestyle choice is proposed. Based on the conceptions of post modern community life as proposed by Pahl and Spencer (2004), the chapter argues that lifestyle choice is mediated by an individual's commitment to the norms, values and beliefs embedded in their social networks. Accordingly, a lifestyle choice framework is developed which demonstrates the influences of social networks on an actor's subjective interpretation of their objective life situation. Firstly, the framework identifies the subjective nature of choice arguing that economic and social constraints and resources are largely perceptual and essentially bounded by a person's world view. Secondly, it proposes that the ultimate goal of individual action is the actualisation of personal well-being, and consequently considers happiness a universal and subjective value.

In the context of understanding the social factors that mediate lifestyle construction around long working hours and reduced personal time, alternative lifestyle choices bring to light a number of important considerations for the work-life research agenda. Firstly, understanding how and why people make unconventional choices in allocating time – such as radical life changes – offers the potential to provide new insights into time allocation decisions in general. Secondly, it focuses attention on the motivations which influence people's work-life balance choices. And thirdly, it offers a framework for understanding how social and personal values are translated into various types of lifestyle.

Work and lifestyle choice

The issue of balancing work and family has emerged as a major source of pressure for people in Australia and other OECD countries. For example, in the 1997 Australian Time Use Survey (the most recently available data) people were asked how often they felt rushed or pressed for time (Australian Bureau of Statistics, 1998). Of those responding that they always feel rushed or pressed for time, 54 per cent said the main reason for this time stress was trying to balance work and family responsibilities. Similarly, UK studies indicate that juggling work and home demands is a major source of stress for workers and long working hours are a primary cause of such time stress (see Hurst and Baker, 2005; Hurst and Richards, 2004; Jones, 2003).

However, for many workers the effect of time stress appears to be paradoxical. For example, according to Hurst and Richards in their annual study of work-life balance in the UK, the impact of long working hours on subjective well-being is two-fold. On the one hand, workers report negative experiences such as guilt and stress from missing out on family occasions due to working long hours and yet on the other, seem to enjoy working (2004). This paradox appears to be mirrored in Australia, with research indicating that while workers report the impact of long working hours as stress and guilt resulting from perceptions of neglecting family responsibilities (Hamilton, 2004), among the most satisfied of workers are fathers who work greater than 60 hours per week (Weston et al, 2004).

While the evidence suggests that the relationship between life satisfaction and time stress is complex, overwhelmingly the literature identifies long working hours as detrimental to personal, family, and community well-being. For example, negative impacts include reduced leisure and personal time, impaired personal relationships, poor health, stress and fatigue, as well as limited participation in community and voluntary activities. Given the negative effect of time stress on subjective well-being, the question arises as to what motivates people to construct and maintain lifestyles which may result in less than optimal life satisfaction? This question is particularly salient in the context of prosperous, liberal, modern societies where the range of lifestyle choices available to men and women has widened (see Hakim, 2000, 2002; Peichl, 2004).

By way of explanation of modern society's work-life paradox, Hamilton (2004) proposes that social and economic life is driven largely by 'deferred happiness syndrome' – the willingness to suffer now (for example, long working hours, a pressured job, a chaotic home life) in the expectation of future happiness. That this constitutes a lifestyle choice is evidenced by the fact that some people adopt lifestyles that involve a voluntary reduction in working time and income, in return for a slower pace of life and increased free time – the phenomenon popularly known as 'downshifting'.

Downshifting as alternative lifestyle choice

Alternative lifestyle choices and radical lifestyle changes which focus on shifting away from dominant ideologies and structures are not a new phenomenon. Over time, various alternative lifestyle movements have emerged – many of these driven by the opening up of new social opportunities and the removal of social and economic constraints. For example, during the 1960s and 1970s the number of alternative religious movements surged in the US and this is in part attributable to the climate of social and political change in which young people began to explore alternative lifestyles. Many of these alternative lifestyles were geared around communal and self-sufficiency living, and generally based on the ethos of 'dropping out' of mainstream society by way of developing new social systems. However, while empirical research on downshifting is not well developed, the evidence suggests that downshifting is a 21st century response to work-life imbalance rather than a cohesive movement aimed at radical social change.

The research on downshifting suggests that downshifters are not dropping out of society but want to make changes to balance life and reducing work hours is the most popular way of achieving this. In a study on Australian downshifters, Hamilton and Mail (2003) estimate that during the last 10 years, 23 per cent of adults aged 30–59 have made a voluntary, long-term change in their lifestyle, other than planned retirement, which resulted in them earning less money. Hamilton's study of downshifting in the UK shows similar results, with an estimated 25 per cent of British adults having downshifted over the last 10 years (2003a). According to the research, downshifting is not necessarily the domain of the affluent, with the Australian study indicating that blue-collar workers are just as likely to downshift as white-collar workers, with proportionally more downshifters on low incomes (less than $30,000) than high incomes (more than $60,000).

The research identifies several motives for the lifestyle change including giving more to the family in the form of time rather than money and leading a more fulfilling and balanced life. And for the majority of downshifters, the lifestyle transition is one generally aimed at creating and living a simpler life. According to Murphy (2002), the downshift process is often characterised by a geographic relocation, particularly from a metropolitan to a regional or coastal community. Other authors suggest that rather than simply being a point-in-time change such as a relocation of residence, the downshifter's lifestyle construction is a process of change which requires conscious modification and readjustment over time (Donahoo, 2005). This process of readjustment, according to the research, is aimed at sustaining lifestyle satisfaction and this in part is mediated by the social systems which emerge as part of the lifestyle change.

For some downshifters, the lifestyle change is made through both choosing the level of participation in paid work while at the same time, putting in place systems to support self-sufficiency. In this context, ideological considerations about the limitations of an overly-consumptive lifestyle may motivate the transition, though according to the Australian study, few downshifters actively acknowledge reasons of principles as the primary motive for the lifestyle change (Hamilton and Mail, 2003). For the majority of downshifters, the lifestyle transition is geared towards better balancing competing time use priorities and this is generally achieved through modification to paid working hours. Viewed in this light, downshifting is a radical response to work-life imbalance and while such a life choice is bounded by a person's social and economic roles that both impose constraints and resources – it is a *choice* – often taken after a long period of questioning.

The proposition that downshifting is a considered and complex choice is supported by recent Australian case study research which examined the transition process for 40 families and individuals who had downshifted to small, regional communities in central Victoria (Donahoo, 2005). According to Donahoo's study, downshifters make a conscious choice to enter the transitional labour markets, with none forced into a variable job market because of redundancy or the desire for career change. On the basis of the lifestyle change, Donahoo argues that downshifters actively contribute to the restructuring of rural economies by redefining and reintegrating the concepts of work and community. He also notes that engaging more actively in cooperative community activities and being connected to a community is part of the reason to downshift. Consequently, communal gardens, food cooperatives and numerous informal trade and barter arrangements form part of the downshifter's social system. Cooperative approaches to managing work-life issues such as cooperative childcare arrangements also form part of the redefined social system of support.

Overwhelmingly, the research on downshifting suggests that downshifters are happy with their lifestyle choice and that for many, personal fulfilment is the ultimate goal of the lifestyle change. However, reactions to downshifters may be hostile, with colleagues, friends and relatives often viewing the choice as selfish and neglectful of family responsibility (Breakspear and Hamilton, 2004). Yet even in the face of such normative constraints, downshifters actively make lifestyle changes which they believe will provide for a better life.

In the context of a lifestyle choice, several aspects of the downshifting process identify it as a conscious and deliberate transition. In the first instance, the evidence indicates that the lifestyle change is a voluntary transition aimed at reducing time stress, typically generated by competing work-life priorities. For downshifters, a reduction in paid working hours appears to be the dominant approach to achieve greater work-life balance, and for some, a corresponding increase in self-sufficiency characterises the lifestyle transition. The evidence further suggests that the focus of the downshift is increased personal, family and community well-being. Geographic relocation particularly to small, rural localities appears to be a feature of the downshift process, however, for some it is merely a redefinition of their present life situation with a greater focus on less money and more time. The stimulation of new social systems that foster community engagement also appear to be a feature of the downshift process.

Thus the evidence of downshifting as a lifestyle choice in modern economies indicates people can modify lifestyle to overcome work-life imbalance. Yet only a relatively small proportion of people choose to do so. In order to broaden the research agenda, this chapter considers two key questions. Firstly, it addresses whether behaviour which leads to less than optimal satisfaction, such as time stress lifestyle construction, is purposive action. And secondly, in the context of rational action, it considers why people make lifestyle choices that are less than optimal.

Lifestyle choice as rational action

If we assume people more or less act rationally in allocating time, then many of the basic components of explanation of why people construct time stressed lifestyles are provided by rational choice theory. In simple terms, rational choice theory proposes that people select courses of action that maximise utility (in economic terms) or actualise values (in sociological terms), given the constraints they face, the resources at their disposal and their beliefs about appropriate ways of doing things (norms).

Fundamental to rational choice theory is the contention that all social phenomena can be explained in terms of rationally calculated actions made by self-interested individuals. For example, Elster (1986, 1989) endorses a traditional instrumental (or *homo economicus*) conception of rationality, according to which actions are not valued or chosen for themselves, but represent an efficient means to a further end. Elster proposes that choices are essentially based on the filtering out of several alternatives, as illustrated in Figure 13.1 (Norkas, 2000). This simplified version shows that firstly, an actor assesses the restrictions or opportunity sets available to them so defining the set of logically possible actions. Secondly, the wants and expectations of the actor determine the best possible course of action – the principle of utility maximisation describes how this second filter functions.

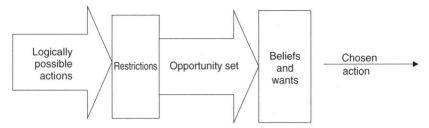

Figure 13.1   Elster's filter model of instrumental rational action (Norkas, 2000)

Thus, taking this simplified version of rational action and holding beliefs and values as constant, one explanation for a time stress lifestyle is that it is a rational response to an assessment of available resources and constraints within one's situation. For example, a sole provider may consider the financial cost of reducing working hours greater than the benefit of increased personal or family time. Conversely, in this formulation, down-shifting is a lifestyle optimisation answering the question 'do I need to work, given the resources available to me?' Or, the flip side, 'what else can I do but work long hours in a boring job, given low skills, two kids and a mortgage?'

Another explanation emphasises the influence of beliefs and wants. Under this formulation, lifestyle choice is driven largely by the wants and beliefs of the actor. Thus, lifestyle choice is a rational response based on the actor's beliefs and attitudes about work, wealth and consumption. For example, an actor's belief that wealth maximisation is the ultimate goal (ends) provides sufficient reason for the time stress lifestyle (means). Therefore, one explanation for lifestyle construction around long working hours and reduced personal time is that it is symptomatic of a materialist value orientation. On the other hand, this explanation for downshifting emphasises the role of a reprioritisation of values, reflected in shifting attitudes and, presumably, new lifestyles. This is the claim of the emergence of a 'postmaterialist' values orientation within affluent societies (e.g. Inglehart,[1] 1971, 1977). Inglehart's claim is that affluence, in a sense, solves pressing problems of material life and so new societal concerns increase in priority. These include concern with the environment, social justice, personal autonomy and identity. At the individual level, this can be understood as the declining marginal returns to material gain – the joy of having two cars is not twice as great as having one. People operate with competing values and preferences, and affluence leads to a lower prioritisation of material goals. In this context, downshifting is a rational response to a reprioritisation of values.

A further explanation emphasises the role of social and economic constraints as well as values on lifestyle choice. For example, Hakim's preference theory attributes a central role to lifestyle preferences and values as determinants of people's employment decisions in modern economies, especially labour market participation for women (2000; 2002).

The theory proposes that recent social and economic changes, such as the availability of contraception and equal employment opportunity policies, provide the historically significant context for women to make genuine and unconstrained choices. Hakim's survey of 3,650 British adults provides evidence of three distinct combinations of labour and family work, with the study estimating that for 17 per cent of women, family life and children are the main priorities; 69 per cent of women are adaptors who combine work and family or have unplanned careers; and 14 per cent are work-centered whereby the priority in life is employment or equivalent. Preferences for males are almost equally divided, with 48 per cent choosing adaptive lifestyles while the remaining 52 per cent are work-centered. In this context, the explanation of lifestyle choice is based on the priority and value attached to work and family life. However, as noted by McRae (2003) it is not only institutional constraints but people's subjective interpretation of the courses of action open to them relative to their goals, as well as ideologies about family and work life, which influence lifestyle choice.

Overall, there are limitations to these explanations of lifestyle choice as traditional rational action. The fundamental problem presented by these explanations is that they take the components of the choice situation as given and treat the actor as an atomised individual making choices in a social vacuum. This in part is attributable to the fact that rational choice theory to date says a lot about the way people make choices, given their values and belief, but says little about the actual values and beliefs held by the actor, and says nothing about the origin of those values and beliefs (Marini, 1992).

Limitations of rational choice

Traditional rational choice theory has been widely critiqued and the literature identifies several distinct problems (see for example, Boudon, 1989; Norkas, 2000; Scott, 2000; Zafirovski, 1999). Firstly, the utilitarian conceptionalisation of rationality reduces all action to a single class of economic variables such as utility, profit, or wealth maximisation, to the exclusion of all other non-economic variables. Zafirovski (1999), in arguing for a multidimensional model of rational choice, claims that the boundary between rational and non-rational action is fluid, with rationality oriented not only to utility, profit and other economic variables but also to power, prestige and related non-economic variables. Furthermore, according to other authors, traditional rational choice offers incomplete explanations of processes in social groups such as altruistic behaviours and other micro-social interactions and exchanges (Scott, 2000).

Traditional theories also propose that actors have a high level of knowledge and an ability to calculate and evaluate the consequences of alternative action. However, decision-makers often have limited information – that is, their rationality is bounded – and they are frequently unable to anticipate the effects of action. On this basis, actors do not seek the best alternative in the feasible set, but limit themselves to what seems to be good enough or satisfactory. Furthermore, objective information is often subjectively interpreted. For example, people's beliefs about their actual income (objective information) and subsequent ability to make ends meet (subjective interpretation) are often at odds. This is evidenced by recent research which suggests that some of the wealthiest households in Britain believe they spend all their income on the basic necessities of life (Hamilton, 2003b).

In recognition of the subjectivity and social context of choice, Boudon's (1989) conceptualisation of rationality proposes the principle of subjective rationality whereby 'X is reasonable, plausible, or not plausible because ego believes Y'. Thus for Boudon 'actions need not produce good outcomes to be subjectively rational, but need only be carried out for reasons seen as good by the actor' (173). From this point of view, action is subjectively rational because people behave purposefully when they behave in accordance with their internalised beliefs and values. Furthermore, Weber's (1968) influential typology of action recognises traditional action, emotional action and various forms of value-oriented action alongside purely rational action. As noted by Zafirovski (1999), Weber's formulation of instrumental rationality and value-rational action is shown by the typical behaviour of the Protestant entrepreneur engaged in utilitarian rational action (profit-making) only as a means of attaining non-utilitarian ends (religious grace). In this context, it is inattentive to treat such action as non-rational, as economic action may just be a means to a value-based goal.

Overall, the limitations of traditional rational choice bring into question its explanatory power as a general theory for all action. Firstly, people do act in ways which less than optimise their life situation. Secondly, information is often limited and interpreted in subjective ways. Thirdly, traditional theory is unable to adequately account for faith-based actions, in particular religious-oriented behaviours. Finally, traditional rational choice takes the components of the choice situation as given and treats the actor as an atomised individual making choices in a social vacuum. And as noted by Marini (1992), only through the proposition of rational action 'in conjunction with knowledge or well-reasoned hypotheses about what people value and the alternatives they perceive to be available can an intentional explanation be useful in explaining and predicting human behavior' (34). In response, we propose a more moderate conceptualisation of rational choice through incorporating the social and normative pressures which influence the subjective interpretation of the choice situation. Our framework identifies that economic and social constraints and resources are largely perceptual and essentially bounded by a person's world view.

The subjectivity of choice elements

Social and economic roles provide resources as well as impose constraints. For example, the capacity to access childcare is partly contingent on the income generated by employment; access to labour markets is contingent on skills and qualifications; and power relations and socio-economic status mediate access to important social goods including human capital (Putnam, 2000). Thus the social and economic roles played by an individual influence the feasible sets of action available to them. However, the extent to which constraints and opportunities influence decisions depends largely on the extent to which they are perceived as such. People will make calculations about optimal ways of achieving what they want on the basis of beliefs about what is and is not feasible. Normative and cultural pressures, such as moral and ethical obligations, act as a primary influence on perceptions of choice.

Normative and cultural pressures create incentives or disincentives for individuals to spend more or less time in work. For example, 'presenteeism' has emerged as the phenomenon by which individuals stay at work after standard working hours in order to be seen to be present and therefore, dedicated. Some research indicates that little is accomplished during this time but staying behind is largely symbolic (see for example, Perlow, 1999). Probert, Ewer and Whiting (2000) argue that workers feel compelled to work longer hours without claiming entitlements because norms of 'normal hours' have weakened.

Commitment to work and its positive moral value is also socially constructed. For example, Hochschild's study on why people work long hours when family-friendly policies are available to them, shows that people are compelled to work long hours as a show of work commitment (1997). According to Fevre's review of the Hochschild study, this commitment has strong moral undertones, with workers more likely to acknowledge the shame of not showing the necessary commitment to work, rather than 'admit that it might be shameful to fail to discharge their obligations to their families' (2004: 44). Fevre's review further suggests that such a level of commitment is indicative of action based on belief rather than knowledge, with workers demonstrating 'a commitment to their employer that was well beyond anything merited by sober consideration of expectations of return' (53).

Taking into account the social construction of choice, the relationship between subjective choice and normative and cultural pressures is shown in Figure 13.2. It illustrates that choice is not the objective course of action but the course of action as subjectively defined. However, it does not

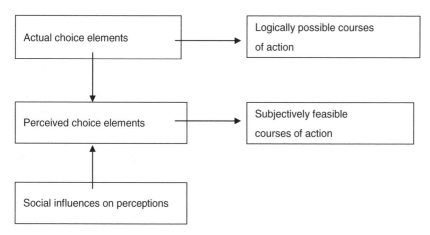

Figure 13.2 The subjectivity of choice elements

address the question of where these beliefs and norms come from. The next section emphasises the importance of social networks and personal communities in shaping people's interpretations of their life situation.

A model of lifestyle choice

Rational choice theory suggests that individuals make choices based on the knowledge and information available to them. More broadly, subjective rationality emphasises the role of beliefs and the subjectivity of information in the decision-making process. Regardless of emphasis, the question that is not adequately addressed by rational choice is what supports and sustains the decision filtering information and belief sets. More importantly, from where do they originate? In response, we argue that information and beliefs are mostly socially constructed through the complex sets of social networks that influence an individual's life, and that inputs to the decision-making choice (such as information, beliefs, judgements) originate and are supported within the personal communities that comprise one's social world. Accordingly, a framework is set out which shows the relationships between subjective rationality, commitment, personal communities and lifestyle choice. This framework emphasises the subjectivity of choice and the role of personal communities and social networks in bringing about recognition of shared norms and values, and subsequently mediating the lifestyle choice.

The role of commitment and personal communities

Commitment based on shared values and beliefs is a salient consideration in understanding individual action. Research into communal life offers an interesting insight into the role of commitment in fostering cooperative and altruistic behaviour. Moss Kanter's (1972) work on the role of commitment in shared communities shows that personal and social commitment is fostered by shared beliefs and thus play a significant role in the cohesiveness and longevity of collectivities. In a study of utopian communities in the 19th century, Moss Kanter theorised that commitment is the central process through which the personality system and social system become articulated (Hall, 1988). She identified three basic problems of commitment, namely: continuance (sustaining individual interests and participation); cohesion (building affective solidarity); and control (exercising authority without overall domination). According to the Moss Kanter thesis, social systems which address these problems should be more successful than those which do not; commitment building mechanisms, such as rituals and beliefs, play an important part in sustaining communal activity. Evidence from more recent studies on the impact of beliefs in fostering commitment in peer-shared households and utopian communes further supports the proposition that group ritual and shared beliefs are strong factors in mediating group commitment (see Heath, 2004; Sosis, 2000).

Berger's views on plausibility structures also show that an individual's continued acceptance of a belief system is largely dependent on their participation in networks of individuals who share that belief system (see Berger, 1967; 1970). According to Berger, any religious system remains plausible only as people articulate it through their social interactions, with beliefs becoming more believable through discussion with similar-minded individuals. The social interactions that maintain the religion form its plausibility structure. For many, religious institutions, family and friendship networks, and local communities serve as the plausibility structure for their religion and belief system. For example, Petersen and Donnenwerth's (1998) study on religion and declining support for traditional beliefs about gender roles and homosexual rights, shows that intra-group influences such as face-to-face interaction and communication are more significant in affirming and sustaining belief sets than extra-group influences such as exposure to the media.

Research from Pahl and Spencer (2004) on personal communities and the role of relationship choice in people's micro-social worlds also provides insight into the social context of people's life choice. In theorising the concept of community based on the 'social relationships of belonging' Pahl and Spencer argue that the dichotomy between family of fate (kin or given relationships) and family of choice (non-kin or chosen relationships) is more suffuse than previously conceived. According to the study, personal communities contain multiple social networks, many of which do not overlap, with people embedded in highly complex sets of relationships in which they invest different levels of commitment. They further note that both given and chosen relationships which involve high level commitment are increasingly important in people's life situation. Interpreted in another way, commitment takes precedence over the intrinsic nature of the relationship, that is, either familial or chosen.

Social networks exert a normative influence on people's action and this influence is determined by the level of individual commitment to the network's shared values and beliefs. Subsequently, if a person's high commitment relationships are formed around a shared understanding of work and the satisfaction and rewards attributable to such activity, this will influence them to remain in situations which are not of direct or immediate personal benefit. For example, within a person's high commitment social networks, beliefs about happiness and what provides for it are subjectively defined. So for a person whose high level commitment is based on the acceptance of 'deferred happiness' that is, suffer now in less than satisfying life circumstances for some future reward – then alternative life situations will not be seen as feasible. The fact that alternatives are available (objective information) is mediated by the beliefs and level of commitment within the actor's social network (subjective rationality). The question then becomes who among your friends, family and colleagues – your personal community – is not time stressed and trying to manage numerous conflicting priorities. Hence, in this context, time stress is essentially a normatively defined lifestyle choice.

On the other hand, the evidence shows that the redefinition and pursuit of happiness is a fundamental goal of radical lifestyle change such as downshifting. This pursuit of happiness is often at the cost of social sanctions such as hostility from relatives, friends and colleagues. In response, many downshifters redefine their social networks either by a geographic relocation or active engagement in submerged network communities (Cherrier and Murray, 2002). Importantly, however, the time stress and downshift lifestyler are similar in that their definition of happiness is subjectively defined.

Happiness as a subjective value

Understanding an individual's sense of happiness and what circumstances provides for it is a fundamental consideration in the growing body of literature on well-being and happiness (see for example, Emmons, 1999; Kahneman et al, 1999; Kashdan, 2004). The literature identifies that happiness is not about life state, income or personal circumstances. It is more broadly conceived as a universal value which people may pursue through various means such as the ability to maintain trusting and loving relationships, being free of social and cultural pressures to conform in ways that are inconsistent with inner standards and having a clear sense of personal direction and purpose in life. Importantly, this broad interpretation illustrates that happiness is a subjectively defined value. In the context of the subjectivity of choice, people are inclined to do things which they *believe* will make them happy. For example, work provides one means of achieving a sense of well-being and fulfilment. However, as evidenced by Hamilton's (2004) Australian findings on the tendency for people to endure life situations that are less than optimal, for many people work does not produce this happiness. Conversely, it may produce habitual stress and anxiety about neglecting family responsibilities and this is endured on the basis of a belief about the future expectation of happiness, such as in retirement. On the other hand, the evidence on downshifters suggests that the belief in happiness as a state of the present rather than the future, is a motivator of lifestyle choice. Thus happiness is an end goal where downshifting constitutes the means to achieve it. The same can also be said of people that sacrifice current happiness for some future return – the belief in and expectation of future happiness influences their current lifestyle choice. However, what influences the situation to change? Or alternatively, what influences the lifestyle choice to remain the same?

How personal communities mediate lifestyle choice

In order to address the fundamental question of what mediates lifestyle choice, the relationship between subjective choice, personal communities and happiness is presented in Figure 13.3. The model proposes that choice is bounded by the subjective nature of social and economic resources and constraints, and that norms about what is right and wrong mediate the choice process. These normative pressures are essentially grounded in the complex and multifaceted personal networks within which people are submerged. Personal communities form around shared beliefs and tend toward homogeneous world views, for example, you and your family are culturally very similar or you choose friends because you have compatible views and interests. Furthermore, people recognise shared values and beliefs through interactive communication and involvement with others. Personal communities are based on varying degrees of commitment and through the

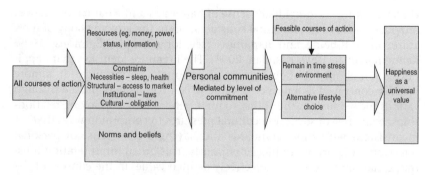

Figure 13.3   A model of lifestyle choice

process of communication and interaction, commitment is fostered to the norms, values and beliefs embedded in the social network. In this context, personal communities sustain work-life imbalance by mediating the choice process.

A research agenda

The traditional approach to rational choice treats values and beliefs as ordered utilities, which tend to remain constant during an actor's life course. This simplistic approach to value and belief formation however, ignores the role of significant social networks in mediating the values and beliefs that promote individual action. Correcting this problem requires an empirical understanding of what actors value and believe, as well as independent knowledge of the way in which values and beliefs conjoin with an individual's social context and subsequent world view.

As a way of broadening the research agenda, we propose a redefined formulation of rational choice in which the content and context of social values and beliefs are viewed as fundamental elements of the choice process. Importantly, our framework focuses on the subjectivity of choice arguing that the interpretation of one's situation is largely subjective (even allowing for objective factors such as financial resources and constraints). Furthermore, it shows that social networks and personal communities bring about recognition of shared norms and values and subsequently act as a strong mediating factor in people's work and life choices. Understanding choice in this way enables a broader and more encompassing assessment of lifestyle choice and this is particularly salient to the work-life agenda.

To date, the work-life research agenda has considered that imbalance is a consequence of increasing and competing time pressures and that this can be addressed through a range of policy responses including improved leave schemes, flexible working time patterns, phased retirement strategies and other time improvement mechanisms (Drago, Scutella and Varner, 2001; Stricker, 2005). However, it has ignored the essential question of why people construct lifestyles which are less than optimal.

In response, our framework proposes that on the one hand, time stress is a conscious and considered course of action based on the actor's beliefs about subjective well-being; in this formulation personal well-being is conceived as a future goal. On the other, downshifting is a conscious and considered course of action based on the decision-maker's beliefs about subjective well-being, with happiness conceived as an immediate goal rather than some future state. Beliefs about work and its value to personal well-being also influence the choice process. These beliefs are largely determined by the social networks which subjectively define and mediate a person's world view.

Importantly, this framework focuses attention on the role of work as a means of achieving happiness. The literature clearly identifies that time stress lifestyles have less than an optimum effect on personal, family and community well-being. However, the motivations and beliefs behind people's work-life choices are not well understood. For example, in modern economies are people working to live or living to work? In our view, addressing such fundamental issues and building an improved empirical understanding of lifestyle choice in modern economies, forms part of a broader work-life research agenda.

Conclusion

Radically redefining one's life to achieve greater work-life balance is both a challenge and a choice. It is more of a challenge in the face of social opposition and sanction. However, as a choice it reveals important aspects of the relationship between the individual and their perceptions of community and modern life. It points to a rejection of the normal 'way of living' in favour of a more unconventional lifestyle, with a greater focus on achieving personal well-being and fulfilment. In this way, alternative lifestyle choice brings into question commonly held perceptions about what constitutes fulfilment – work, family, material security, acquisition, leisure time and so on – and how this is achieved in modern economies. More importantly, it shows that in such societies, lifestyles which provide fulfilment are a choice.

Alternative lifestyle choice also brings attention to the relationship between the individual and community well-being and significant questions emerge in respect to the influence of downshifters on community integration. For example, downshifters have the time to participate more actively in voluntary and community-based activities and for many, this is an important motive for the lifestyle change. In contrast, time stressed people find it difficult to actively engage in voluntary and community-based activities. Consequently, is there a flow-on effect to overall community well-being? Or more specifically, are communities which foster the downshift lifestyle more integrated than other more traditional communities?

Downshifting also focuses attention on the importance of beliefs about work – the moral compulsion of work – and beliefs about family and community. For the downshifter, it appears that their beliefs about these fundamental aspects of life change but at what point and under what conditions? In the context of understanding the decision-making process leading to lifestyle change, a salient consideration is the relationship between the social construction and maintenance of beliefs and commitment to family, friends and colleagues.

It is clear that rational choice theory has limitations in providing a holistic account of all social action. In response, we propose a more moderate formulation of rational choice in which the content and context of social values and beliefs are viewed as fundamental elements of the choice process. This formulation is based on three propositions. Firstly, non-economic goals such as greater personal fulfilment, motivate purposive action. Secondly, choice is subjectively defined and action is rational if it is consistent with an actor's internalised beliefs. And finally, social networks mediate commitment to shared beliefs through the process of interaction and communication. In this way, lifestyle choice is a social construct which we can explain in part, by reference to the mediating role of social networks. This complex relationship between lifestyle choice and normative social influences is worthy of greater empirical attention.

Notes

1. The shift toward post materialism values was first postulated by Inglehart (1971, 1977), and is based on the thesis that advanced industrial societies have been undergoing a linear trend from a materialistic to post materialistic values orientation. The associated index, drawn from World Values Survey, has received widespread interest and critique (see for example, Hansen and Tol, 2003; Wilensky, 2003). The Ingelhart-index is derived from four items which have been used in the World Values Survey since the early 1980s. The survey asks respondents to identify the most important goal for their country. The four options are a) Maintaining the order of nation; b) giving the people more say in important government decisions; c) fighting rising prices or d) protecting freedom of speech. a) and c) reflect materialist values; b) and d) reflect post materialist value orientations. A mixed type is also considered and this is first a choice of a) and c) and second, a choice from b) and d).

References

Australian Bureau of Statistics (1998) *1997 Time Use Survey*, ABS, Canberra.

Berger, P.L. (1967) *The Sacred Canopy: Elements of a sociological theory of religion*, Garden City, New York: Doubleday.

Berger, P.L. (1970) *A Rumor of Angels: Modern society and the rediscovery of the supernatural*, Garden City, New York: Doubleday.

Breakspear, C. and Hamilton, C. (2004) *Getting a Life: Understanding the downshifting phenomenon in Australia,* Discussion Paper 62, Canberra: The Australia Institute.

Boudon, R. (1989) 'Subjective rationality and the explanation of social behaviour', *Rationality and Society*, 1(2): 173–96.

Cherrier, H. and Murray, J. (2002) 'Drifting Away from Excessive Consumption: a new social movement based on identity construction', *Advances in Consumer Research*, 29: 245–7.

Donahoo, D. (2005) 'More time, less money: Downshifting as a progressive transition solution for rural Australia and the future', *Transitions and Risk New Directions in Social Policy Conference Papers*, Centre for Public Policy, Melbourne: University of Melbourne.

Drago, R., Scutella, R. and Varner, A. (2001) *Work and family directions in the US and Australia: a policy research agenda*, Report for the Department of Family and Community Services, Melbourne Institute of Applied and Economic Research.

Elster, J. (1986) *Rational Choice: readings in social and political theory*, Oxford: Basil Blackwell.

Elster, J. (1989) *Nuts and Bolts for the Social Sciences*, Cambridge: Cambridge University Press.

Emmons, R.A. (1999) *The Psychology of Ultimate Concerns: motivation and spirituality in personality*, New York: The Guilford Press.

Fevre, R. (2004) *The New Sociology of Economic Behaviour*, London: Sage Publications.

Hakim, C. (2000) *Work-Lifestyle Choices in the 21st Century: Preference Theory*, Oxford: Oxford University Press.

Hakim, C. (2002) 'Lifestyle Preferences as Determinants of Women's Differentiated Labor Market Careers', *Work and Occupations*, 29(4): 428–59.

Hall, J.R. (1988) 'Social Organization and Pathways of Commitment: Types of communal groups, rational choice theory and the Kanter thesis', *American Sociological Review*, 53(5): 679–92.

Hamilton, C. (2003a) *Downshifting in Britain: A sea-change in the pursuit of happiness*, Discussion Paper No. 58, Canberra: The Australia Institute.

Hamilton, C. (2003b) *Over consumption in Britain: a culture of middle-class complaint?* Discussion Paper No. 57, September, Canberra: The Australia Institute.

Hamilton, C. (2004) *Carpe Diem? The Deferred Happiness Syndrome*, Web paper, May, Canberra: The Australia Institute.

Hamilton, C. and Mail, E. (2003) *Downshifting in Australia: A sea-change in the pursuit of happiness*, Discussion Paper No. 50, Canberra: The Australia Institute.

Hansen, O. and Tol, R.S.J. (2003) *A Refined Inglehart Index of Materialism and Post Materialism*, Working Paper FNU-35, Research Unit Sustainability and Global Change, Hamburg University.

Heath, S. (2004) 'Peer-shared Households, Quasi Communes and Neo Tribes', *Current Sociology*, 5(2): 161–79.

Hochschild, A. (1997) *The Time Bind: When work becomes home and home becomes work*, New York: Henry Holt.

Hurst, J. and Richards, W. (2004) *Twenty4–Seven Work Life Balance Survey*, Work Life Balance Centre, Keele University.

Hurst, J. and Baker, S. (2005) *Twenty4–Seven Work Life Balance Survey*, Work Life Balance Centre, Keele University.

Inglehart, R. (1971) 'The Silent Revolution in Europe. Intergenerational change in post industrial societies', *American Political Science Review*, 65(4): 991–1017.

Inglehart, R. (1977) *The Silent Revolution: changing values and political systems among Western publics*, Princeton: Princeton University Press.

Jones, A. (2003) *About Time for A Change*, The Work Foundation in association with Employers for Work-life Balance, United Kingdom.

Kahneman, D., Diener, E. and Schwarz, N. (1999) *Well-Being: The foundations of Hedonic Psychology*, Russell Sage Foundation.

Kashdan, T.B. (2004) 'The Assessment of Subjective Well-being: issues raised by the Oxford Happiness Questionnaire', *Personality and Individual Differences*, 36(5): 1225–33.

Marini, M.M. (1992) 'The Role of Models of Purposive Action in Sociology', in Coleman, J.S. and Fararo, T.J. (eds) *Rational Choice Theory Advocacy and Critique*, Sage Publications, 21–47.

McRae, S. (2003) 'Constraints and Choices in Employment Careers: a consideration of Hakim's Preference Theory', *British Journal of Sociology*, 54(3): 317–38.

Moss Kanter, R. (1972) *Community and Commitment: communes and utopias in sociological perspective*, Harvard University Press.

Murphy, P. (2002) 'Sea Change: Re-inventing rural and regional Australia', *Transformations*, 2: 1–10.

Norkas, A. (2000) 'Max Weber's Interpretative Sociology and Rational Choice Approach', *Rationality and Society*, 12(3): 259–82.

Pahl, R. and Spencer, L. (2004) 'Personal Communities: not simply families of "fate" or "choice"', *Current Sociology*, 52(2): 199–221.

Peichl, M. (2004) 'What Do United Consumers of Europe Think?' *GFK insite*, (2), Germany: GFK Lifestyle Research.

Perlow, L.A. (1999) 'The Time Famine: Toward a sociology of work time', *Administrative Science Quarterly* 44: 57–81.

Petersen, L.R. and Donnenwerth, G.V. (1998) 'Religion and Declining Support for Traditional Beliefs about Gender Roles and Homosexual Rights', *Sociology of Religion*, 59(4): 353–71.

Probert, B., Ewer, P. and Whiting, K. (2000) 'Work Versus Life: Union Strategies Reconsidered', *Labour and Industry* 11: 23–47.

Putnam, R. (2000) *Bowling Alone: The collapse and revival of American community*, New York: Simon and Schuster.

Scott, J. (2000) 'Rational Choice Theory', in *Understanding Contemporary Society: theories of the present*, Browning, G., Haleli, A. and Webster, F. (eds) London: Sage Publications: 126–38.

Sosis, R. (2000) 'Religion and Intra-group Cooperation: Preliminary results of a comparative analysis of utopian communities', *Cross-Cultural Research*, 34 (1): 70–88.

Stricker, P. (2005) *Time Management and Life Transitions*, in Transitions in Australian Labour Markets, CEDA Information Paper No. 82, Melbourne.

Weber, M. (1968) *Economy and Society: An Outline of Interpretative Sociology*, New York: Bedminster Press.

Weston, R., Gray, M., Qu, L. and Stanton, D. (2004) *Long Work Hours and the Well Being of Fathers and their Families*, Australian Institute of Family Studies, Research Paper 35, Commonwealth of Australia.

Wilensky, L.H. (2003) *Postindustrialism and Post Materialism, A critique, rich democracies, political economy, public policy and performance*, Berkeley: University of California.

Zafirovski, M. (1999) 'What is Really Rational Choice? Beyond the utilitarian concept of rationality', *Current Sociology*, 47(1): 47–113.

Author Index

Subject Index